ANGLO-SAXON
OXFORDSHIRE

For

Sarah

aureum illud nomisma quod de Cantia venerat

ANGLO-SAXON OXFORDSHIRE

John Blair

SUTTON PUBLISHING

First published in the United Kingdom in 1994 by
Alan Sutton Publishing Limited, an imprint of Sutton Publishing Limited
Phoenix Mill · Thrupp · Stroud · Gloucestershire · GL5 2BU

Oxfordshire Books
Oxfordshire County Council · Leisure and Arts
Central Library · Westgate · Oxford

This edition published in 1998 by Sutton Publishing Limited

British Library Cataloguing in Publication Data

A catalogue record for this book is available from the British Library.

ISBN 0 7509 1750 4

942·57

Cover illustration: A late ninth-century sword found in the Thames near Abingdon
(reproduced by courtesy of the Ashmolean Museum, Oxford).

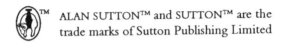 ALAN SUTTON™ and SUTTON™ are the
trade marks of Sutton Publishing Limited

Typeset in 10/12 Bembo.
Typesetting and origination by
Sutton Publishing Limited.
Printed in Great Britain by
WBC Limited, Bridgend, Mid-Glamorgan.

CONTENTS

LIST OF
ILLUSTRATIONS

PICTURE CREDITS

The author and publishers are very grateful to the following owners of copyright for allowing their illustrations to be used:

Ashmolean Museum, 10, 12, 15, 29, 49, 52, 58, 60, 64, 67, 83, 89; C.J. Bond, 26, 70, 76, 92; British Museum, 63, 90; Cambridge University Press, 74; G. Foard, 39; S.S. Frere, 9; E.M. Jope, 93; A.R. Hands, 25, 32; S.C. Hawkes, 8, 19; S.D. Keynes, 75; Museum of London, 71; D. Miles, 14; Oxford Archaeological Unit, 17, 18, 20, 21, 22, 23, 27, 56, 57, 66, 67, 68, 87, 88, 94, 95, 96; Oxfordshire County Council, 6; Paris, Archives Nationales, 75; Reading Museums and Art Gallery, 59; R.T. Rowley, 42; C.R. Salisbury, 72; B. Schumer, 2; C.J. Scull, 28; G. Speake, 37, 45; Victoria County History, 85; Trust for Wessex Archaeology, 73; E. Wilson, 97.

Thanks also to the Oxfordshire Architectural & Historical Society for many figures first reproduced in *Oxoniensia*.

Radiocarbon dating has now suggested that the supposed late Anglo-Saxon stone phase at Wood Eaton church (Fig. 81 on p. 136) is in fact a 12th-century aisle, added to the nave of *c.* 1100. The presence of a late Anglo-Saxon timber church has, however, been confirmed by further excavation.

PREFACE

This is a study of the society and institutions of Oxfordshire (as it existed until 1974) between the fifth and eleventh centuries AD. It is as well to admit at the outset that for most of that period 'Oxfordshire' did not exist. It is one of the most artificial of English counties, created during the last Anglo-Saxon century and shaped largely in relation to entities which already existed around it. A range of other terms (the Upper Thames, the Cotswolds, the Vale of Aylesbury, the Chilterns, Middle Anglia) describe much more neatly the various regions, geographical, social and political, which lie partly inside and partly outside Oxfordshire.

I have therefore allowed myself some flexibility from period to period in the geographical area covered. To discuss early Anglo-Saxon settlement to the north of the Upper Thames but not to its south would be meaningless: Chapter I, and to some extent Chapter II, consider the whole Upper Thames region. With the stabilisation of the Thames as the boundary between Wessex and Mercia during the ninth century, north Berkshire gradually fades out of the story: I have not, except in passing, described late Anglo-Saxon agriculture and land-holding in the Vale of the White Horse, nor the tenth- and eleventh-century topography of such places as Wallingford, Wantage or Faringdon. If this book has an undue emphasis on the Thames floodplain and gravels, it is because the bias of our sources and their users pushes inexorably in that direction. Crop-marks are most visible on the gravels, and gravel-digging has been the main stimulus for large-scale excavation; the archive-keeping monasteries were mostly by the Thames; and generations of Oxford scholars have lavished attention on places within an afternoon's cycle-ride. In fact the emphasis may not be so very wrong: that pagan-period cemeteries concentrated along the Thames, or that some of the most important early monasteries of southern England stood beside it, are not figments of distorted evidence. None the less, there is a strong case now for some more detailed work on other areas. As my research proceeded I became uneasily aware how much less systematic thought has been given to the early centres of the Cherwell Valley (Kings Sutton, Adderbury, Bloxham, Cropredy and so on) than to those of the Thames.

Flowing through all the themes of the book is the Thames itself, as frontier, highway and resource. Certainly its presence has been the greatest single influence on the political and economic development of Oxfordshire and Berkshire, and several parts of the book are framed around the 'Upper Thames Region'. It must be stressed, though, that this is a construct of variable relevance, not an unchanging reality. Since the Neolithic period the Upper Thames basin has sometimes been a border zone between different peoples or cultures, sometimes a heartland in its own right; the artery which united the late sixth-century Gewisse was the boundary between Wessex and Mercia in the ninth century, and between Berkshire and Oxfordshire in the eleventh.

The chronological balance of this book may surprise some readers, since it is for its pagan-period archaeology that the region is most familiar to Anglo-Saxonists. My principle has been to concentrate on less familiar themes, which happen to be the ones about which I know most. The rich cemetery evidence is exceptionally well covered already, both in a fundamental (though sadly unpublished) thesis by Tania M. Dickinson completed in 1976, and in a long and detailed paper by Sonia Chadwick Hawkes published in 1986. The last ten years have seen many new discoveries. Assessment of the cemeteries at Berinsfield and Lechlade, and of the settlements at Radley, Eynsham and Yarnton, is still in progress, while Helena Hamerow is working on a wider study of early Anglo-Saxon settlement in the Eynsham region. The weight of specialist argument and re-interpretation which the fifth- and sixth-century material bears is now very great, and the space available here is inadequate to do it justice. In these circumstances it would be foolish for someone whose interests lie mainly in the Christian Anglo-Saxon period, and who claims no expertise in the highly specialised field of grave-good studies, to attempt a comprehensive reassessment. The first chapter is therefore a quick scamper across some very well-trodden terrain.

To a very large extent, England as we know it was formed during the Anglo-Saxon centuries. The growing awareness of this fact during the last two decades has still made little headway against traditional perceptions, even among teachers of history. In the early 1990s schools have adopted a National Curriculum for secondary schools in which children pass straight from Roman Britain to the Norman Conquest. They therefore learn nothing about the making of the towns and villages in which we live, the names by which we call them, the roads which we use, the countryside which surrounds us and the language which we speak. It may be through local studies that the centuries in which the roots of local life are embedded can be made most accessible to people today. An important aim of this book is to convince some of the modern inhabitants of Oxfordshire that their Anglo-Saxon predecessors are worth studying.

ACKNOWLEDGEMENTS

This has been both an easy and a difficult book to write: easy because the archaeology and history of the Upper Thames have been so well-served by generations of scholars, difficult because of the volume of excavation reports, field surveys, local studies and regional syntheses which it has been necessary to assimilate. And the archaeological and local-historical community which has grown up in Oxford since the 1920s is the repository of far more knowledge than can currently be found in print. Oxford contains England's foremost university archaeological society, one of its most successful excavating units, an excellent Sites and Monuments Record and Victoria County History, and several of the leading historians of Anglo-Saxon England. Knowing the local scene is a prerequisite for a book such as this, and I could not have attempted it but for the contacts and friendships made during my twenty years in Oxford.

First I should like to thank the Oxford University Archaeological Society, and my friends from my undergraduate days in it: they had as great an influence on my development as any more formal academic training. At a time when the amateur tradition in British archaeology seems somewhat threatened, it is a pleasure to record that the most recent discovery reported in this book results from an O.U.A.S. excavation during May and June 1993 (see Fig. 81). No tribute to amateur archaeology in Oxfordshire would be complete without mentioning Roger Ainslie, tireless supporter of everyone's excavations including many of my own.

Nearly all the major excavations of the last twenty years have been the work of the Oxford Archaeological Unit. This book would have been quite impossible without the support and encouragement which I have received over the years from Tom Hassall and David Miles, its successive directors, and from Brian Durham, who has devoted so much of his career to the early development of Oxford. The last of these has shared his unrivalled knowledge with me over the years, and has generously provided me with draft sections from his forthcoming monograph *Oxford Before the University*. The Unit has excavated an exceptional number of major Anglo-Saxon sites during the last few years, and it is a great privilege to be allowed to use so many hitherto unpublished plans and photographs. I am indebted to other members of the O.A.U.'s staff for help of various kinds, especially Tim Allen (Abingdon), Angela Boyle (Didcot and Lechlade), Anne Dodd (Berinsfield), Gill Hey (Yarnton), Graham Keevill (Eynsham) and George Lambrick (prehistoric and environmental problems).

A predeliction for west Oxfordshire examples reflects many enjoyable days of fieldwork. My research project at Bampton would have been impossible without the support of many friends there, above all the Wearne family. The West Oxfordshire

Charter-Boundary Group, hosted by Rosamond Faith, has tramped along many miles of hedges and ditches on the boundaries of Witney and neighbouring estates.

The number of individual scholars whose work on relevant topics is currently in progress is a measure of the vitality of Anglo-Saxon studies. For access to unpublished texts and for answers to many questions I am deeply grateful to Steven Bassett (West Midland hundreds), Barbara Crawford (Danes under Cnut), Tania Dickinson (grave goods), Rosamond Faith (peasantry), Susan Kelly (Abingdon Abbey charters), Christopher Loveluck (post-Roman British influences), Michael Metcalf (sceattas), Maureen Mellor (pottery) and Christopher Scull (early Anglo-Saxon society). I hope that I have represented their views fairly.

Paul Smith (the County Archaeologist) and Ival Hornbrook have facilitated my use of the Oxfordshire Sites and Monuments Record, the strengths of which owe so much to the patient labours of Elizabeth Leggatt. Preparing the illustrations would have been much more arduous without the photographic skills of Bob Wilkins and Jenny Lowe. For help and advice of other kinds I would like to thank Marion M. Archibald (British Museum), Leslie Cram (Reading Museum), Malcolm Graham (Centre for Oxfordshire Studies), Bronac Holden, Simon Keynes, Arthur MacGregor (Ashmolean Museum), Mark Robinson, John Steane and Patrick Wormald. I apologise to any others whom I have inadvertently failed to mention. My colleagues at The Queen's College, Oxford, have been most considerate in helping me to find time for research and writing. Many owners of copyright, listed individually on p. ix, have kindly allowed their illustrations to be reproduced.

Drafts of various parts of the book have been read and criticised by Richard Bryant, Tania Dickinson, Brian Durham, Rosamond Faith, Helena Hamerow, David Miles, Christopher Scull and Barbara Yorke. My debt to all of them is great, especially to those who provided lengthy comments on Chapter One at very short notice.

Sarah Blair has been a great support and encouragement throughout, has accompanied me to many sites of Anglo-Saxon interest, and tolerated an increasingly frantic work regime as the book neared completion. She has also read every word, and has improved many.

INTRODUCTION

As artificial geographically as it is politically, the historic county of Oxfordshire lies slant-wise across many geological strata.[1] 'The formations', writes W. J. Arkell, 'run through this part of England in a SW–NE direction and are arranged like tiles on a roof, the lowest (and oldest) in the NW, the highest (and youngest) in the SE. They consist of alternating clays and limestones, with subordinate layers of sand. . . . In a broad view Oxfordshire comprises four ranges of limestone hills and three clay vales.'[2] From north-west to south-east, the hills are the ironstones in the extreme north around Banbury, called the Redlands after their rust-coloured stone and ploughsoil; the broad belt of Cotswold oolitic limestones which crosses the northern half of the county; the more modest hills of the Oxford Heights, running south-eastwards from Oxford through Headington, Elsfield, Shotover and Wheatley; and the south-western end of the Chilterns, where the tip of Oxfordshire rises abruptly over the chalk escarpment capped by clay with flints. Westwards beyond the Goring Gap, in an area which although south of the Thames will sometimes interest us, the Chilterns continue as the Berkshire Downs. The vales are the lias clay lowlands (only patches of which lie within Oxfordshire); the Kimmeridge and gault clays of the Oxford Vale and the Vale of the White Horse, spanning central Oxfordshire from the head-waters of the Thames to the marshy bowl of Otmoor[3]; and the gault clay vale, running north-eastwards from the Thames near Dorchester to join the Vale of Aylesbury.

Amidst this variety, the Oxfordshire and north Berkshire region has an overriding unity as the drainage basin of the Upper Thames.[4] From the time when glacial melt-water forced its way through the Goring Gap to join what is now the Lower Thames, the river and its tributaries have been alternately accreting terraces of limestone gravel and cutting down through them into the underlying strata. These broad, flat expanses of gravel, successively cut away and redeposited at a lower level, have determined human settlement in the Upper Thames basin. The first (Floodplain) and second (Summertown-Radley) terraces, respectively some 2.5 metres and 8.5 metres above modern water level, will often be mentioned in this book.

Some 10,000 years ago, the network of small, rapidly shifting water-courses snaking through the gravel terraces evolved into a simpler pattern of multiple incised channels which has remained relatively stable ever since. The character of the floodplain has, however, been transformed by alluvial deposition of fine sediments and by changes in the water level. The work of Mark Robinson and George Lambrick, based mainly on the Oxford Archaeological Unit's excavations, has yielded important evidence for the

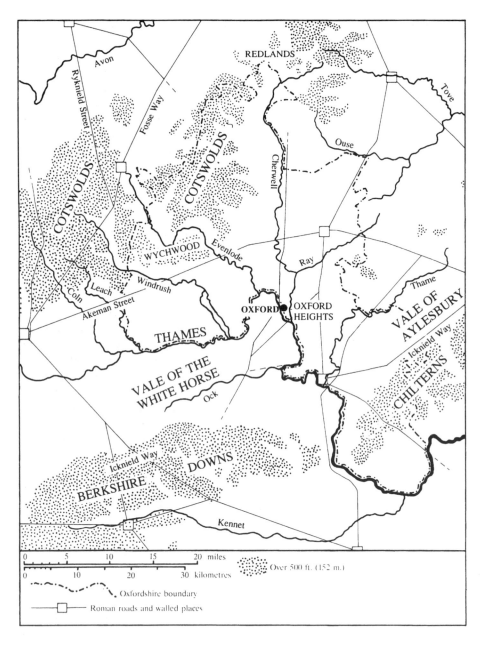

1 Oxfordshire and around: regions, rivers and Roman roads.

effect of alluviation on human activity – and of human activity on alluviation – during the last three millenia.[5]

Thus the river has shaped the solid geology to create a landscape of ridges and vales tied together by the drainage system and the floodplain. The only really high-quality farming land is on the Redlands around Banbury, on the Cotswolds, and along the Icknield belt in the vale below the Chiltern scarp,[6] and it was indeed here that population and farming were densest at the end of the Anglo-Saxon period (Fig. 74). At all times, however, the gravel terraces where the higher ground meets the floodplain have been favoured settlement sites, especially the well-drained second terrace with its fertile soil cover. The river itself, of course, has always been a major resource, and the expanses of regularly flooded grassland have been crucial for livestock husbandry since at least the early Iron Age.

The viability of the Upper Thames as a corridor for trade and transport is a question often raised, but never properly answered. In historic times the combined (or contrary) effects of canalisation, embankment, locks and mill-weirs have so changed the configuration of the river that the state of the main channels before the eleventh century is extremely hard to reconstruct.[7] For instance, the recent discovery that alluviation increased rapidly after the ninth century means that channels blocked with silt when first mentioned in documents could have been much clearer in, say, 700. The likelihood is that man has been capable of mastering the river whenever the incentive to do so has been strong enough; here it is taken as axiomatic that at least the down-river transport of goods in shallow craft from west Oxfordshire to the Thames estuary was practicable throughout the Iron Age, Roman and Anglo-Saxon periods.[8]

In the Upper Thames as everywhere else, the earliest structures are those of the Neolithic and Bronze Age. The region has its impressive monuments such as the Rollright Stones, the Devil's Quoits, Wayland's Smithy and the Drayton Cursus, as well as the ring-ditches of Bronze Age barrows which cropmarks reveal in their hundreds on the gravel terraces. But the Upper Thames was a fringe area in relation to, for instance, the Neolithic Wessex culture south-westwards and the Bronze Age round-barrow culture of eastern England.[9] Settlement and agriculture were light, and important monuments probably stood in clearings in an original forest cover which was gradually evolving into open grassland.[10] In the late Bronze Age and early Iron Age, however, agriculture spread from the light soils to the clays and the wetter soils at the floodplain edge. This coincided with a rise in the permanent water-table[11] which meant that much of the first terrace made excellent pasture but was hard to use as arable without artificial drainage, a situation which lasted to the Anglo-Saxon period and beyond.

By the late Bronze Age the river was a corridor for a long-distance trade in fine metalwork, in which the Lower Thames dominated the Upper.[12] The collapse of this economic system around 800 BC initiated an early Iron Age culture in which the Upper Thames region is notable for the intensity and variety of its settlements and farming practice. The heavier and more upland soils were regularly cultivated as well as the second and third terraces, while in the valley-bottom drainage was combined with some settlement on the first terrace.[13] Livestock still remained important; loom-weights and sheep bones show that woollen cloth was already a major product of the Cotswolds and Upper Thames, as it was to be in the Anglo-Saxon centuries and after.[14] Several hill-forts were built, perhaps the centres of emergent chiefdoms.

The late Iron Age (*c.* 100–0 BC) was a time of great social and political change. Agriculture continued to intensify, and towards the end of this century the run-off from heavy ploughsoils started to deposit large amounts of alluvial silt in the river-system.[15] The hill-forts were largely abandoned, but a series of great defended enclosures were laid out at river-confluences along the Thames:[16] Cassington Mill,[17] Abingdon,[18] and Dyke Hills at Dorchester (Fig. 8).[19] These valley-forts (or, more optimistically, *oppida*) are signs of the greater political integration also revealed by coins and Roman narrative sources. The Upper Thames was a borderland between three groups: the Dobunni westwards, the Atrebates southwards and the Catuvellauni eastwards.[20] Coin distributions suggest that the northern Dobunni were separated from the Catuvellauni by the Cherwell and from the 'sub-Dobunni' by the uppermost Thames, giving them a territory resembling that to be occupied later by the Anglo-Saxon Hwicce (below, p. 42).[21]

The development of long-distance trading patterns centred on the Thames catchment area foreshadows themes in this book. There is no clear evidence that goods were traded up-river, but the late Iron Age saw the kind of symbiotic relationship between a productive Upper Thames region and an economically advanced Thames estuary which we will meet again in the Anglo-Saxon period. The valley-forts acquired a role as markets and entrepôts, illustrated by the wide range of imported pottery and other material found at Abingdon.[22] David Miles writes:

> The most dramatic changes in late Iron Age society took place in the south-east. Large territorial *oppida* with urban characteristics, such as Verulamium and Camulodunum, developed at nodal points from *c.* 100 BC. Dyke Hills, Dorchester, may have risen to prominence as a gateway settlement, promoting contact between separate social and economic groupings; hence the impressive number of Iron Age coins from the area around Dorchester.[23]

With the Roman conquest[24] the region lost this gateway character, and was once again a peripheral area between the major towns of Cirencester, Silchester and St. Albans. Roads were laid out across it (Fig. 1), notably the main Cirencester–St.Albans road later called Akeman Street. Small towns were built at Alchester and Dorchester – the former destined to vanish after AD 400 , but the latter to be the main focus of early Anglo-Saxon activity in the region. Grain was probably shipped down-river to London and even overseas, and pottery from the huge Cowley works was reaching London in the third and fourth centuries.[25] Much of this Roman-period activity grew from Iron Age roots: Dorchester (Fig. 8) was the humble successor of Dyke Hills just as Cirencester replaced the great *oppidum* at Bagendon (Glos.), and the dense pattern of settlement and agriculture was a direct continuation of growth during the first century BC. Even the villas which sprinkled north Oxfordshire, the Cotswolds and the clay vale may often have been direct successors of native farms, with Mediterranean sophistication confined to the main buildings. For example, the concentration of villas in the Wychwood area north-west of Oxford (Fig. 2) may have grown directly out of a late Iron Age territorial entity bounded by the earthwork of Grim's Ditch.[26]

Intensive Romano-British management, and its subsequent collapse, are most clearly seen in the Thames floodplain. During the Roman period alluvial deposition

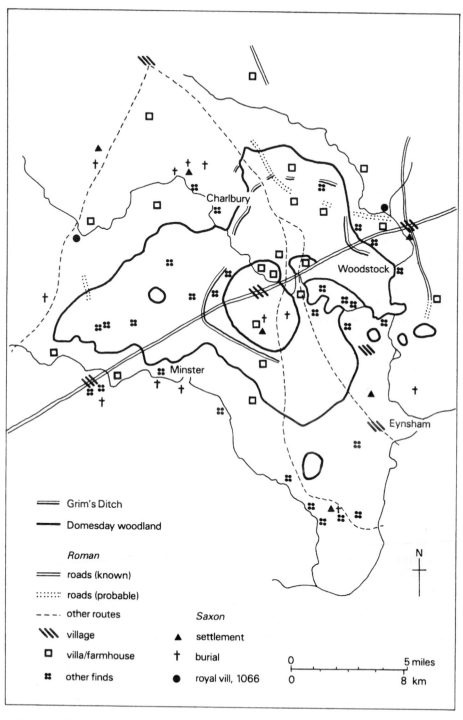

2 Wychwood Forest, showing the extent of Romano-British settlement in the area of the eleventh-century woodland. (Schumer 1984, map 3)

3 Chiltern landscapes (i): '*innan sigerdene*'. Here the tenth-century boundary of the woodland attached to Pyrton (S.104) runs up a typical Chiltern *denu*, the 'victory-valley'. Its name must recall some forgotten battle, possibly between English settlers and the Britons of the Chilterns.

continued to increase, the first terrace and alluvium were drained and managed on a large scale, and evidence for the mowing of hay-meadow occurs for the first time.[27] The breakdown of the Roman economic system after AD 400 had an immediate and drastic effect on the floodplain, where all sites so far excavated show a similar pattern: drainage channels were abandoned, and settlement and agriculture retreated from the first terrace to higher ground. Given the links already demonstrated between agriculture and alluviation, the drastic drop in alluvial deposition during the fifth to eighth centuries can only mean that cultivation of lands draining into the Thames was very much reduced.[28] As we shall see, the Anglo-Saxon settlers did not come into an abandoned wilderness. None the less, several centuries of steady economic growth were abruptly put into reverse, and the outward signs of Roman civilisation vanished fast. That there was suddenly more room to spare rather than less, and that a primitive regime replaced an organised and intensive one, are notable oddities of the fifth-century situation.[29]

The post-Roman colonisers of the Upper Thames region were at the mercy of nature moulded by man. Their survival depended on knowledge and mastery of soil, relief, drainage and the natural world, and they viewed them with a keen, discriminating eye. The greatest recent achievement of place-name scholars has been to show how names once dismissed patronisingly as bearing 'a very trivial character',

4 Chiltern landscapes (ii): '*þærut on þæne feld*'. From the valley shown in Fig. 3 the boundary rises up the Chiltern dip-slope to the plateau, where it leaves the woodland and runs 'thereout into the *feld*', the flat, open terrain in the foreground, before plunging down the scarp. In the far distance, beyond the Thames, are the Berkshire Downs.

or carrying 'a strong smack of the farmyard', are our most precious non-physical record from the first two Anglo-Saxon centuries. 'They are never "trivial"', writes Margaret Gelling; 'the wolves of Woolley, the geese of Goosey and the swine of Swinford were matters of life and death to the Anglo-Saxons, and the choice of word to describe the settlement-site is as serious as any statement which our forefathers have bequeathed to us.'[30] Their topographical vocabulary was astonishingly rich and sensitive: the modern usages of 'hill', 'valley', 'stream' or 'wood' are blunt instruments compared with the range of lost terms which are preserved in place-names, enabling us to decode the landscape as the Anglo-Saxons saw it.

Words for valleys and hills best illustrate this richness.[31] In the Chilterns, Ann Cole has demonstrated the contrast between the short, steep-sided *cumb* valleys (Swyncombe, Huntercombe etc.) of the scarp slope, and the long, narrow, gently sloping *denu* valleys (Checkendon, Dean Farm, etc.) of the dip slope (Fig. 3).[32] The commonest hill name is *dūn*, which in east Oxfordshire and Buckinghamshire often refers to low, flat-topped hills suitable for settlement. Toot Baldon ('Bealda's *dūn*') and Garsington ('grassy *dūn*') are examples of such hills in the countryside south-east of Oxford, 'a constellation of old English settlements perched on the outer edges of

5 Thames landscapes (i): The clay 'island' of Chimney ('Ceomma's *ēg*') stands high and dry above the alluvial *mōr* in the foreground. This was the nucleus of the estate given by King Eadwig to 'the holy man at Bampton and the community' in the 950s, and is also the site of a large late Anglo-Saxon cemetery (see pp. 73, 113).

slopes where the sands and limestones above give way to the clays below'.[33] Another characteristic Chiltern term is *ōra*, 'hill-slope' (Chinnor, Lewknor, Stonor, etc.), though it also occurs in the Cotswold zone at Hook Norton, the '*ōra* of Hocca's people'.[34]

The Anglo-Saxons arrived in a landscape from which most original woodland had long been cleared. Apart from the Chiltern plateau, the largest wooded area in England after the Weald,[35] the countryside had been mainly open during the Roman period, and current work suggests that regeneration of tree-cover after AD 400 may not have been as extensive as was once thought.[36] For the English as for their predecessors, woodland was not a useless wasteland but a vital resource to be carefully exploited. Pastoral husbandry depended on a balance of wooded and open pasture: *wudu* and *weald* on the one hand, *feld* and *hæþ* on the other. *Weald* seems to denote early woodland, only later developing the sense of modern *wold*, 'open high ground'; the Cotswolds were probably so called because wood-pasture partly covered them in the early Anglo-Saxon period.[37] Weald, on the clay near Bampton, was probably complimentary to the adjoining Clanfield (*clæne feld*, 'clean pasture' free from weeds or scrub) on the first gravel terrace.[38] There is a similar antithesis in Chiltern names, where *feld* (Rotherfield, Nuffield, etc.) denotes the open pasture of the plateau in contrast to its woods (Fig. 4).[39] *Hæþ* already had the sense of modern heath, widely and continuously used in Oxfordshire for rough pasture above the floodplain level; a

6 Thames landscapes (ii): This photograph taken near Caversham in about 1880 illustrates the flat, open landscape of the floodplain and some of its activities. On the side-channel to the right are Victorian versions of the eel-traps shown in Figs. 72–3. (Centre for Oxfordshire Studies, photograph OCC 8861)

hæþ feld (such as Eynsham Heath in 1005)[40] was presumably, unlike a *clæne feld*, overgrown with heather and scrub.

Although the collapse of the late Iron Age and Roman economy had been most dramatic in the floodplain, large areas there were probably still maintained as grazed grassland.[41] For such terrain the ubiquitous word was *mōr* ('moor'), both along the Thames and in the self-contained marshy zone of Otmoor (Fig. 76). Standing up from the riverine *mōr* are many islands and promontories of the gravel terraces and the underlying clay (Fig. 5). The importance to the English settlers of these sites, accessible from the floodplain but raised above it, is emphasised by the multiplicity of names ending in the term -*ēg*, 'island', 'dry ground surrounded by marsh', along the Upper Thames and its tributaries (Chimney, Witney, Binsey, Oseney, etc.).[42] These are of early formation, and Gelling sees them as 'names bestowed by the first English farmers who tackled the area'.[43]

A conspicuous human legacy in the landscape was its stock of ancient, abandoned monuments. Every society erodes the remains left by its predecessors: there were fewer Neolithic long-barrows in the Iron Age than in the Bronze Age, fewer still at the end of the Roman period. Knowing precisely what was left for Germanic settlers to find in the fifth and sixth centuries is not at all easy: an archaeologist can identify the ploughed-out remains of, say, Bronze Age round-barrows from aerial photographs, but rarely knows how many of them were flattened by medieval rather than Iron Age or Roman ploughing. For example, we know that the late Iron Age valley-fort at Dorchester was visible to Anglo-Saxon people because it is still there today, whereas any conclusion on those at Abingdon and Cassington Mill, or on the ring-ditch at Bampton (Fig. 31), must depend on topographical deductions and the circumstantial evidence of relationships between prehistoric and post-Roman features.

It is at least certain that ancient monuments were very much more evident to the Anglo-Saxons of Oxfordshire than they have been to its late medieval and modern inhabitants. Place-names which mention them show the same kind of lively perception as those describing natural features. Many of the local occurrences of the element *stān*, 'stone', record otherwise forgotten archaeological features, though we still have the cromlech which gave its name to Enstone (Fig. 7), and remnants of the henge (the 'Devil's Quoits') which stood between Standlake, *stān-lacu*, and Stanton Harcourt, *stān-tūn*.[44] *Beorg*, 'barrow', is common in field-names and often refers to groups of (presumably Bronze Age) barrows, such as the *trembergh* in Rollright and the *fifburghe* in Hook Norton.[45] Walking around the boundaries of Ardley in 995, one

7 'Enna's stone'. This Neolithic chambered tomb, which gave its name to the settlement and parish of Enstone, illustrates the prominence in the Anglo-Saxon landscape of monuments inherited from the past.

went from the 'earthwork' (*eorðbyrg*) to 'Cwichelm's barrow', and thence to the Roman 'port-street'; in 969 the landmarks of Witney (Fig. 77) included 'Hawk's barrow', 'Cycga's stone' and the 'little earthwork'.[46] The Roman walls of Alchester and Dorchester were still visible enough for the first English to recognise them as 'chesters', while the roads slicing straight through the countryside would have been as obvious, relatively speaking, as railways are today. Even a 'variegated floor' (*fāg-flōr*), in other words a Roman mosaic pavement, might still lie exposed in the countryside: one was a landmark at Water Eaton in 904 (*to fagan floran*), and another gave its name to Fawler.[47]

Here we run into an awkward word, 'continuity'. The proposition that Anglo-Saxon use of ancient structures indicates continuous use through the dark intervening period, and social contact between the new and the old occupants, has consumed gallons of ink. Sometimes it may be true, but probably not often. If a good, solid structure was there to be used, people would use it: it is much more likely that Widford church overlies a Roman villa because its eleventh- or twelfth-century builders found a convenient *fāg-flōr* than because some fourth-century owner began a continuous Christian tradition.[48] And sometimes we may have to deal with *created* continuity: the deliberate adoption of antiquities by invaders eager to legitimise their rule by giving it a spurious antiquity.[49]

Having acknowledged this, we can still be astonished how far the early development of English society in the Upper Thames was moulded by the hard infrastructure of former societies. The primary core area of fifth- and sixth-century settlement would probably not have developed where it did but for the two late Iron Age valley-forts of Abingdon and Dyke Hills and the Roman town of Dorchester; the secondary core area focussed, it now seems, on a Bronze Age enclosure at Eynsham. The correlation between the important prehistoric sites of the region and the important Anglo-Saxon ones is uncanny. Even allowing for the purely coincidental re-use of many prime sites on the second gravel terrace where the older monuments had been ploughed flat, it is clear that some of the key events of English settlement in the Upper Thames took place within and around prehistoric banks and Roman walls.

These adopted monuments were so important because neither invaders nor invaded were capable of building new ones. The British, whatever their pretensions to *Romanitas*, had reverted to a level of material culture lower than that of their ancestors in the first century BC. The settlers were eventually to found one of the most developed and organised societies of early medieval Europe, but they themselves were few, politically fragmented and un-Romanised, with no tradition of building anything larger than timber houses. Like children stumbling across a demolition site and picking up fragments of debris, British and English took the structures left by Iron Age and Roman communities and used them in their own more primitive ways, just as they exploited at a reduced level the much-managed landscape which they had inherited.

CHAPTER ONE

THE FORMATION OF ENGLISH COMMUNITIES

The Anglo-Saxon settlements were a small and relatively simple component in the vast, complex movements of European peoples between the fourth and seventh centuries AD. The main political effect of these movements was of course the break-up of the Roman Empire into successor states, based to a greater or lesser extent on Roman systems. Britain was rather exceptional in two ways: the success (in the short and medium terms) with which the central and western British resisted conquest, and the absence of Roman cultural influence on the 'barbarian' settlers. In assessing how far English society was moulded by what was here already, we must make a very clear distinction between British and *Romano*-British: the Britain which the invaders colonised had already ceased to be Roman.[1]

THE DORCHESTER PROBLEM: FROM ROMAN MERCENARIES TO SAXON RIVER-PIRATES?

The only available historical narrative of the settlements is that of the sixth-century British writer Gildas, which runs as follows: After the withdrawal of the Roman administration and army (datable to around AD 410) the former province was ruled by British 'tyrants'. Threatened by barbarian attacks, they invited groups of 'Saxons' to settle as a counter-force, an event which later writers placed in the 440s. The supposed protectors then rebelled against their hosts, and initiated a phase of concerted invasion and settlement.

There is nothing particularly implausible about this story, but historians have built on it more ambitious hypotheses about political continuity from invaded to invaders. In particular, supposed archaeological evidence for Germanic mercenaries (*foederati*) in late Roman Britain has been linked to Gildas's story of an invitation. Did the first

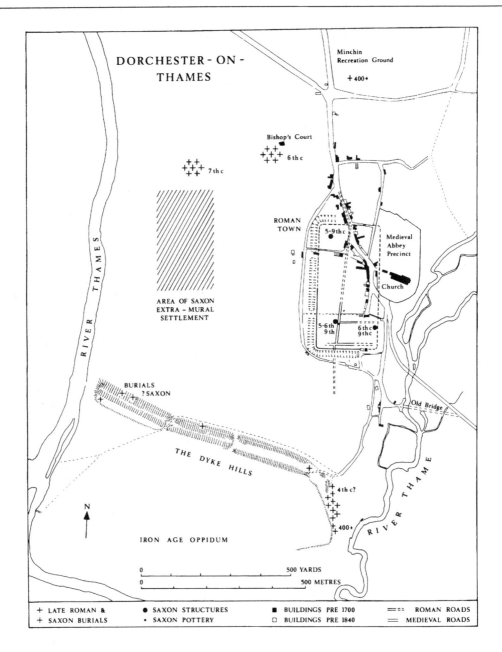

8 Dorchester-on-Thames: the late Iron Age valley-fort (*oppidum*), the Roman town, and evidence of English activity from the fifth to ninth centuries. (Sonia Chadwick Hawkes)

post-Roman British leaders employ 'Saxon' troops who had already served in the Roman army? And if so, did these inherit traditions of military and political organisation to pass on to sons who would soon assume the purple mantles of Romanising British 'tyrants'? This theory must be examined carefully here, for a key part of it concerns the small Roman town of Dorchester-on-Thames (Fig. 8).[2]

Let us start by clearing the ground a little. The most obvious fact of the early fifth century is that towns and villas became irrelevances, so that to look for 'continuity' in the modes of life which they served is to chase a will-o'-the-wisp.[3] Complex government, bureaucracy, coinage and long-distance trade simply could not survive the secession of Britain from the Empire. 'Civilisation', manifested in urbanism, specialised industry, plumbing, central heating, mosaics and all that was distinctively Roman, depended on these things, though occasional Roman structures succumbed to the inevitable oblivion slightly later than others. Here the Upper Thames region is no exception. In Dorchester a new stone building overlay a worn coin of 394–5 (Fig. 9, building I,1); at Barton Court Farm villa another hoard seems to have been hidden, perhaps as late as *c.* 430, in the roof of a surviving fourth-century building; at Shakenoak the villa decayed gradually to one room, where coins may still have been dropped into the 420s; at Ditchley the sequence probably resembled Shakenoak.[4] It does seem possible that the Oxfordshire villa-owners were unusually resilient, but to view such (anyway exceptional) survivals as links into the Anglo-Saxon future is topsy-turvy: they mark the last stages of a quick and total collapse.

If high-status Britons survived in the Upper Thames – as they almost certainly did – they belonged to the world of Gildas's 'tyrants': a sub-Iron Age lifestyle mixed oddly with half-forgotten *Romanitas*. Their late fourth-century ancestors had probably been pagan;[5] during the fifth century they might have become Christian (as the western British did comprehensively), or might not. They would have remembered that Dorchester had been a town, but as buildings started to collapse they would probably have stopped living there. All the analogies, above all from western Britain, point to a move into some convenient Iron Age earthwork: the adjacent Dyke Hills valley-fort, Wittenham hill-fort facing it across the Thames, or the valley-fort up-river at Abingdon.[6] No evidence has been found in any of these places – which may be because it has never been looked for.

The clearest signs of a coherent British community do in fact come from Dorchester, though they are of an entirely ritual character and are somewhat equivocal. First, it has been suggested that the rather odd location of the later Abbey church (Fig. 8), outside the east wall of the town in an area containing Roman cremations, implies a continuing cult based on a martyr's grave in an extramural cemetery[7] – which is a possibility but no more. Secondly, many groups of unfurnished, orientated burials have been found within the walled area, cutting through the latest Roman levels.[8] More work is needed on these neglected finds, but clearly at some time a substantial group of people was inhuming in the former town by a non-Germanic rite. Thirdly, the large late Roman cemetery at Queenford Farm, north-north-east of the town, has yielded a most perplexing group of radiocarbon dates, with a calibrated mean of AD 530–550 at 62 per cent confidence or AD 430–630 at 93 per cent confidence.[9] These results come from conventional graves in a cemetery of standard fourth-century type, and the proposition that such funeral arrangements could have continued not merely through the fifth century but well into the sixth is a large one to accept. More radiocarbon work on the

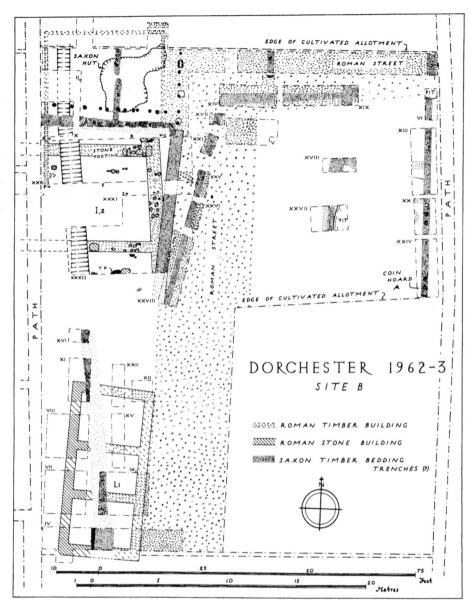

9 Dorchester: Roman to Anglo-Saxon occupation in the south-west corner of the town. The stone building I.1 dates from the very last years of Roman occupation. At the top of the plan is a sixth-century sunken hut, overlain by large and elaborate timber buildings which probably post-date the gift of the town to St. Birinus. (Frere 1984, Fig. 16)

10 The much-debated fifth-century belt worn by the man buried at Dyke Hills, Dorchester. Just under one-third actual size. (Ashmolean Museum)

Queenford bones is urgently needed; if it vindicates the first results, it will be most impressive evidence that the local British retained their identity through many generations of co-residence with Anglo-Saxons.

Also from the periphery of Dorchester are other graves which, though visually unimpressive, have probably been more argued over than any other English Germanic burials except Sutton Hoo. Among late Roman graves in the Iron Age rampart of Dyke Hills were two (perhaps, but not necessarily, associated with each other) of a woman and a man: the former with part of a Germanic brooch of *c.* 400, the latter wearing a late Roman official belt (Fig. 10) and accompanied by weapons.[10] Normal Roman burials do not include grave-goods of this type. So was this an original Englishman from within the Roman-British system: both a Roman soldier and an Anglo-Saxon immigrant? This attractive possibility has come under heavier and heavier attack, and two equally inconclusive views of the male burial now seem possible, depending on how the belt is dated. Placing it around 400–10 might identify the man as an alien serving in the Roman army, but not necessarily an Anglo-Saxon.[11] It has recently been asserted, however, that the belt is of a type worn in Gaul *c.* 430–60.[12] In that case its wearer, whether an Anglo-Saxon or a Frank, was active at least twenty years after the Roman army left Britain, and there is no particular reason to suppose that he had acquired it there 'officially'. Other belt fragments have been found at Shakenoak villa, but these are not necessarily military at all and could have belonged to the ordinary late Roman inhabitants.[13] The idea that some British tyrant in Dorchester retained federate

Germanic troops to control the Upper Thames region cannot be disproved, but the foundation on which this elaborate hypothesis was built has become very shaky.

That said, the evidence from Dorchester for co-existence between the first Anglo-Saxon generations and the first post-Roman British ones is quite impressive. Several burials containing Saxon jewellery of the early to mid-fifth century have been found, and these people must surely have had some contact with the inhabitants who were still burying their dead by the late Roman rite.[14] Indeed, quantities of very early Anglo-Saxon pottery have been found in the south-western corner of the former town, though unfortunately without any clear archaeological context.[15] Dorchester has produced more evidence for a combined British and English presence during the fifth century than most Romano-British towns, and whoever was in charge, there must have been a degree of mutual acceptance. As we shall see, there are good grounds for inferring contact and influence between British and Saxon communities elsewhere in the Upper Thames region. This is very different from the proposition that a group of Germanic *foederati* were poised to seize power which British authorities had inherited from Roman predecessors, and avoids the dubious assumption that the fifth-century immigrants had enough social and organisational cohesion to do anything of the kind. The problem has been well stated by Esmonde Cleary:

> The archaeological evidence from cemeteries and settlements is that the social hierarchy of the Anglo-Saxons in the fifth century was relatively flat and undeveloped. It was only in the late sixth century that we see the kingdoms developing out of simpler, more localised, earlier structures. This must lead us to ask whether there was in the first half of the fifth century any Anglo-Saxon power structure which could have meshed with something of the order of the late Roman state or municipalities? The underdeveloped nature of the early Anglo-Saxon social hierarchy and power structures strongly suggests not.

This discussion of Dorchester has already referred several times to 'Anglo-Saxons', without defining them. Some attempt must now be made to identify these alien people who took to burying their dead around the former Roman town.

SAXONS, ANGLES, FRANKS AND BRITONS

Those who came over were of three of the more powerful peoples of Germany: the Saxons, the Angles and the Jutes. From the Jutes are descended the men of Kent, the *Victuarii* (that is to say the people who inhabit the Isle of Wight) and that people who are today called the Jutes and are located in the kingdom of the West Saxons, opposite the Isle of Wight. From the Saxons (that is to say from that area which is now called Old Saxony) came the East Saxons, the South Saxons and the West Saxons. Next, from the Angles (that is to say from the country which is called *Angulus* and which is said to have remained deserted from that time to the present, between the lands of the Jutes and those of the Saxons) are descended the East Angles, the Middle Angles, the Mercians, all the race of the Northumbrians (that is to say of those peoples who live to the north of the river Humber), and the other Anglian peoples.[16]

So wrote the venerable Bede in the early eighth century, and his analysis remains a good one despite all the accumulated knowledge of modern history and archaeology. It would be quite anachronistic to envisage separate races with separate cultures who labelled themselves 'Saxons', 'Angles' and 'Jutes', or to imagine them colonising England in large, politically coherent groups which kept their identity in isolation from others. None the less, a strong correlation between specific areas of the homelands and specific areas of the settled territories is repeatedly confirmed by the artefacts. Here our concern is with the people whom in this passage Bede calls the 'West Saxons', but who elsewhere in his history are identified as the 'Gewisse'. To understand them further we must abandon all trust in written sources and turn to the archaeology.

By the second half of the fifth century, immigrants were settling the Upper Thames in some numbers. That this statement can be made at all is largely due to the highly distinctive funeral rites that they brought with them. It is ironic that the early Anglo-Saxons, more mysterious to us in life than any other inhabitants of England since the Bronze Age, are so conspicuous in death. They practised both cremation, the ashes being buried in decorated pottery vessels (Fig. 11), and a burial rite in which the dead went to the grave with their life-time attributes and adornments: weapons for free men, brooches and other jewellery for women. This material has been recognised since the eighteenth century, and although all too few of the cemeteries were excavated to modern standards there are large collections of the objects in museums. The analysis of grave-goods, and the recognition of parallel objects in the Germanic homelands, has become a highly technical and specialised study. The Upper Thames has been exceptionally well-served by the detailed research of Tania Dickinson and Sonia Chadwick Hawkes,[17] to which readers are referred for the evidence on which much of this chapter is based.

The grave-goods fully support Bede's view of the origins of the 'West Saxons': they show that fifth-century settlers in the Oxfordshire region did indeed come from the

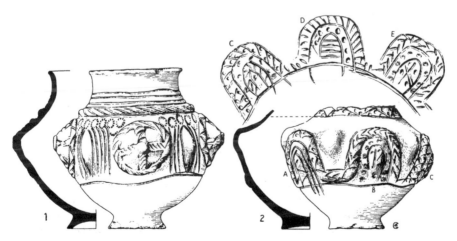

11 Decorated fifth-century pots from Harwell (left) and Oseney (right). These small vessels are representative of the kinds of urns used for burying cremated ashes, though the Harwell pot stood by the shoulder in an inhumation grave. Scale 1:4. (Kirk & Marshall 1956, Fig. 11)

coastal plain of northernmost Germany around the mouth of the Weser (the western part of later Saxony, in fact), not from the south end of the Danish peninsula where still today is a district called Angeln. The affinities of the jewellery are almost wholly with the Saxon homelands and with the other areas of Saxon settlement in England. Most characteristic are the pairs of round concave shoulder-fastening brooches known as 'saucer-brooches' (Fig. 12), imported into the region during the fifth century but thereafter made there in some quantity.[18] The view (propounded above all by E.T. Leeds) that the settlers came in along the Icknield Way from the Wash area was demolished by Dickinson, who proved that the affinities of the characteristic objects in fifth-century Upper Thames cemeteries are with Surrey, Essex, west Kent and Sussex. 'These items', she writes, 'imply that the Thames was a major line of communication for the Upper Thames region with other Saxon communities', though it looks as if objects also passed southwards overland to the areas that were to become Hampshire and Wiltshire.[19] Presumably it was also up the Thames that Saxons had originally penetrated to the Oxfordshire region.

12 Sixth-century brooches: *Above*: A pair of saucer-brooches from Brighthampton grave 23; the most distinctively Saxon of the adornments made and worn in the Upper Thames. *Below*: A pair of small square-headed brooches from Abingdon I grave 117, illustrating higher-status female fashion in the region but made under strong Kentish influence. Actual size. (Ashmolean Museum)

Links with the Anglian areas to the east and north were much weaker, and although there must have been a certain amount of intermixture and contact it is hard to pin down. There are few imports from those directions, and few instances of Anglian fashions. The place-names of the region, too, are basically Saxon rather than Anglian.[20] By the sixth century a very clear line can be drawn between the Saxon and Anglian cultural zones, running westwards from the Suffolk Stour to the Cherwell south of Banbury, and westwards again to join the lower Avon and Severn,[21] though this is less clear-cut in the fifth-century material.

One group whom Bede ignores are the Franks, yet some archaeologists believe that they were prominent in the settlement of southern England. The debate hinges on the undoubtedly Frankish objects in some fifth-century graves: were their owners also Frankish, or were they high-status Angles and Saxons with access to prestige goods? In the Upper Thames such objects are rare and are restricted to very few cemeteries, notably Abingdon and Long Wittenham.[22] At Abingdon, two graves with fifth-century swords made in the Namur region formed part of a group set apart: 'their occupants, overwhelmingly male, look like an intrusive warrior/military group, which remained distinct for at most two generations'.[23] Most remarkably, a child's grave at Long Wittenham contained both a cauldron from the Meuse valley and a stoup decorated with New Testament scenes made in northern Gaul.[24] The distinct character of these graves makes the idea of a small warrior élite from Gaul not implausible (in which case one wonders if one of them could have been the owner of the Dorchester belt). In any case the objects suggest a marked growth in the prosperity of the local settlers towards 500, as well as Frankish contacts which would be renewed to greater effect a century later.

As evidence for the extent of settlement by the late fifth century we have only the earliest cemeteries (Fig. 13), which stand out as a sufficiently small and distinct group to suggest that their distribution has some validity.[25] The first impression is of a tight core area in the Thames basin between the Ock and Thame confluences: Frilford, Abingdon, Long Wittenham, Harwell, Blewburton, Dorchester, Wallingford.[26] But the dispersal of peripheral sites is remarkable: up the Clay Vale to Dinton and Bishopstone (Bucks.), up the Cherwell to Souldern, along the Thames and Windrush to Cassington, Brighthampton and Minster Lovell, even pushing into the Cotswolds to Fairford, Lechlade and Hampnett (Glos.). The image of intrepid bands of pioneers, planted deep into enemy territory by a military commander at Dorchester, has proved attractive, but it suggests a greater degree of organisation than we might now ascribe to the fifth-century English. Two alternatives may be considered: that these communities co-existed peacefully with their British neighbours, and that some of them were not Saxons at all but Britons who had adopted Saxon culture.

'We can't see them but they must be there' is the highly unsatisfactory but undoubtedly true verdict of recent scholarship on the post-Roman British. The Welsh who self-evidently went on living further west did not engage in the activities (such as making pots) which would have revealed them to archaeologists; there are therefore no grounds for doubting their presence, likely on all common-sense grounds, in the South Midlands.[27] But we do not have the least idea how many of them may have lived in, say, the Upper Thames region in 500. Despite current revisionism a population collapse remains hard to doubt: the local environmental evidence is equivocal, but suggests a massive decline both in management of the floodplain and in cultivation near it (above,

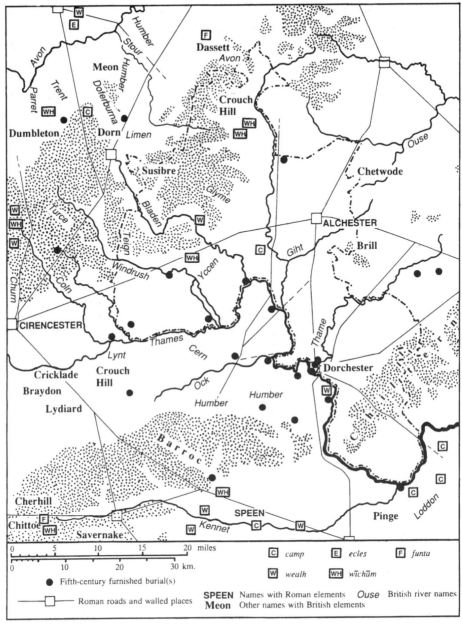

13 The British and the first English settlers: fifth-century cemeteries, plotted in relation to place-names of pre-English origin or reflecting contact with indigenous people. (Cemeteries after Dickinson 1976, Fig. 51, with minor additions, and omitting uncertain and undated sites; names mainly after Gelling.)

p. xx). It is likely that political authority was fragmented, and that competition for territory was not intense. These people could well have quarrelled with immigrant Saxons, but it is not a foregone conclusion that all of them would have quarrelled all of the time, and the evidence from Dorchester reviewed above suggests something rather different.

Nor do we know how many Saxons lived in the Upper Thames by 500. The current general debate swings wildly between the traditional model of mass migrations, and the conquest of millions of Britons by a tiny military elite. In the latter direction it has swung too far: we simply cannot estimate population levels from the (perhaps tiny) sample of known cemeteries, and a basic fact remains that today we speak English, not Welsh. All the same, it is unlikely that the Saxons either perpetuated themselves in ethnic isolation or maintained a monopoly of their material goods. Late fifth- and sixth-century 'Germanic' cemeteries probably contain people of mixed blood, not to mention Britons who had taken to Saxon dress fashions. Cultural distinctions remain useful, ethnic ones less and less so.

Fifth-century Saxons settled in the villa ruins at Shakenoak in west Oxfordshire and at Barton Court Farm near Abingdon (Fig. 14),[28] though in neither case is there real evidence that they had any connection with the former occupants. A much larger question is whether there was any contact or continuity between British and English at the basic level of farming, land-division or estate management. The large tracts of surviving pre-Roman field-systems which have been recognised in other areas[29] cannot yet be matched in Oxfordshire, and there is certainly less survival of pre-English place-names than can be recognised further west.[30] An area north of Witney, where a series of lanes run parallel to Akeman Street, may have possibilities (Fig. 77). Here, where the street passes through a linear Roman settlement near Wilcote, a charter of 969 mentions something called *wīchām*. As Margaret Gelling has shown, names of this kind belong to a very early stratum, and mostly lie on Roman roads and near Roman settlements:[31] they imply a perception of such places, conceivably because they remained in use as roadside markets through the fifth century. In the Wilcote case, it is a remarkable circumstance that *wīchām* lies exactly where the approach-road to Shakenoak villa leaves Akeman Street. Westwards, one might note the curious dead-straight track, called *suga rode* in the same charter, which intersects with the street and with Grims Ditch at one nodal point. This enigmatic topography may be telling us something about the transition from Roman to Anglo-Saxon land-use.

The apparently simultaneous practice of Roman and Germanic burial rites at Dorchester has parallels in two other cemeteries, where Roman and possibly post-Roman graves are associated with very early Saxon ones.[32] The large Frilford cemetery may have continued unbroken during the fourth to sixth centuries through a transition from a late Roman rite to one using Germanic grave-goods, though the excavation records are woefully inadequate.[33] The small fifth- and sixth-century cemetery at Cassington Mill adjoined five Roman-style but very strange burials: one grave, in which a fire had been lit before deposition of the body, contained fourth- or fifth-century bone plaques, while in another a young man lay face-down with an iron shears near his left hand and a Roman pot upside-down on his buttocks.[34] This bizarre case highlights the problem of recognising more orthodox post-Roman burials: there may be a great many more of them than we think.[35]

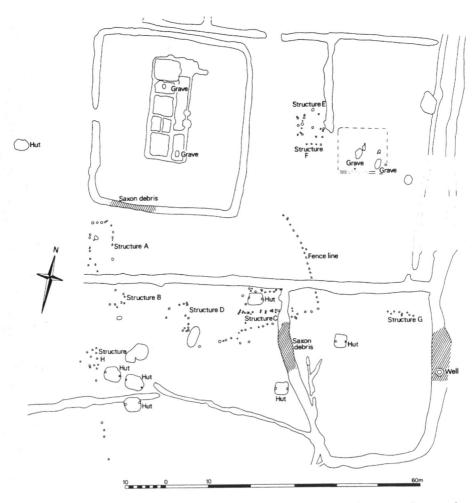

14 The after-life of a late Roman farm: Barton Court, showing fifth-century settlement spreading over the enclosure ditches, and later sixth-century graves inserted into the rooms of the villa building. (Miles (ed.) 1986, Fig. 13)

As Tania Dickinson showed, dress fashions and objects in some fifth-century graves reflect continuing late Roman styles and tastes. Multiple bracelets, a specifically late Roman fashion, sometimes occur in Saxon-style cemeteries, mainly in childrens' graves; a woman at Dorchester who wore seven rings and three late Roman bracelets, but also saucer-brooches, is a clear case of cultural influence in one direction or the other.[36] Disc-brooches, flat roundels with ring-and-dot ornament arguably derived from the late and post-Roman 'Quoit Brooch Style', are extremely common in the Upper Thames.[37] This style also occurs on the tin-plated sheath and sling of the Brighthampton knife (Fig. 15): a remarkable piece which may have been made by a British craftsman working to a Frankish pattern for a Saxon patron.[38] Current work by

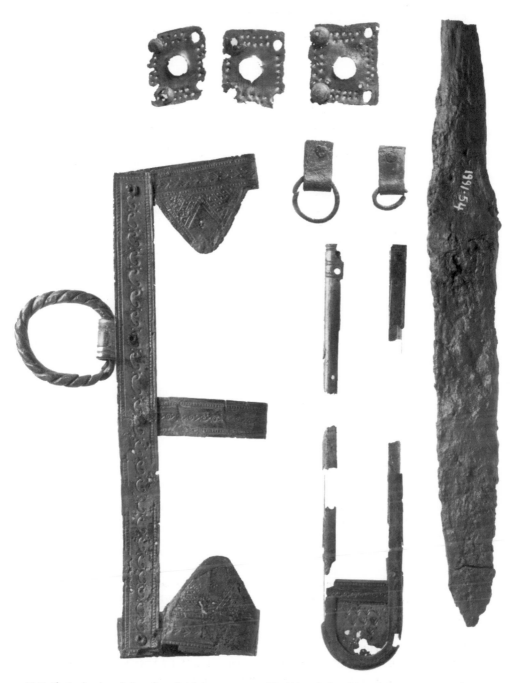

15 Knife, in sheath and sling, from Brighthampton grave 22. Although found in a sixth-century grave, its technique and decoration compare closely with late and sub-Roman objects. Probably made by a British craftsman, this could have been an heirloom of one of the Germanic families settled at the Thames-Windrush confluence. Actual size. (Ashmolean Museum)

Christopher Loveluck is suggesting the possibility that some raw materials, and imported items such as gold coins and Frankish glass beakers, may have entered the region overland from the British south-west as well as up-river from the English south-east.[39]

In the last analysis, however, links with the English and Frankish world were more important than links with the British world. Dickinson's view that the Thames was already a highway connecting the South Midlands with Kent is, if valid, of the greatest importance for the later history of the region. This view has its critics, who note the absence of early sites on the Middle, as distinct from the Upper and Lower, Thames.[40] An answer to this might be to point out that some totally different distribution maps (for example of seventh- and eighth-century minster churches, of sceatta coin finds, of tenth- and eleventh-century Shelly Wares or of late Anglo-Saxon mints) show concentrations and blanks on the same stretches of the river. It may be that from the late Iron Age onwards the Thames was always a corridor linking two important zones of production and consumption, one above Dorchester and the other below Staines.[41] A Thames highway remains the best explanation for the region's dominant cultural links.

THE EXPANSION OF ENGLISH SETTLEMENT

By 500 the immigrants had put down very strong roots in the region. The next century was to be one of consolidation and expansion, as communities grew in size, settled peripheral areas and probably appropriated larger tracts of land. In 450 the Upper Thames was British territory with pockets of Germanic settlers; in 600 it was English territory which may still have contained pockets of independent British. Certainly this period sees the disappearance of the local British as a visibly distinct group, presumably through assimilation into English culture.

Once again, our main evidence for expansion comes from the cemeteries (Fig. 16).[42] The distribution pattern may be distorted by accidents of retrieval, but it remains true that there are almost twice as many sixth-century cemeteries as fifth-century ones, and that as well as consolidating the core regions they spread into areas which lack fifth-century sites. Thus there was notable growth around existing peripheral cemeteries at the Thames–Kennet confluence,[43] on the Berkshire Downs, in the Clay Vale around the upper reaches of the Thame, and in the Cherwell Valley. Cemeteries appear for the first time in the Vale of the White Horse and on the scarp of the Downs.[44] None the less, the most striking expansion as measured in the cemetery record was in the primary settlement zones on the Thames itself, especially at the confluences of the Ock, Thame and Evenlode.

In the late sixth century the region probably still had two British frontiers. One was in the Middle Thames and along the Chiltern scarp, facing what may still have been an independent British polity in the Chiltern uplands and beyond to the east.[45] The other, more important, was north-westwards towards the Welsh of the Cotswolds and Severn Valley. The communities around the Leach–Thames confluence (represented by cemeteries at Fairford, Lechlade and Kempsford) were now pushing westwards into the Cirencester region, which seems to have been in English hands some decades

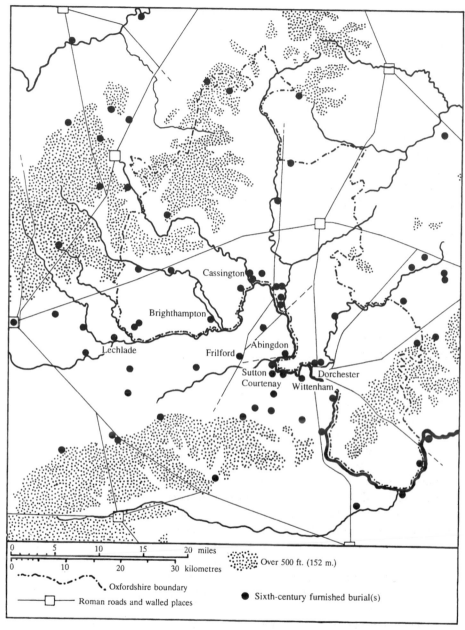

16 Sixth-century cemeteries. (Cemeteries after Dickinson 1976, Fig. 52, with minor additions, and omitting uncertain and undated sites.)

before the traditional date of '577' (below, p. 38).[46] By this time the Ouse and Nene valleys, and the Warwickshire Avon, contained Germanic communities with mixed cultural attributes including, in contrast to the Upper Thames people, strong Anglian elements.[47] By the later sixth century they were colonising the Vale of Evesham, the northern Cotswolds and the Severn Valley, where they would have encountered the much smaller numbers of Saxons who were moving into the Cotswolds from the Lechlade–Cirencester area.[48] Hence the hybrid communities of the seventh-century kingdom of the Hwicce (now Worcestershire, Gloucestershire and Warwickshire): Avon Valley Angles and Thames Valley Saxons inter-breeding with what was doubtless a British majority.

The direction of social and commercial contacts is suggested by analysis of brooch types.[49] During c. 500–50, cast saucer-brooches probably made in the Upper Thames region were disseminated southwards across the Downs to the developing Saxon communities in Hampshire and Wiltshire. Direct links with east Kent continued, and some of the material also reached the Angles of the Avon Valley.[50] Links with the East Midlands along the Icknield Way route, hitherto slight, were starting to develop. There is evidence here of developing exchange systems between regions, probably a mark of increased coherence within communities and contacts between them.

The sixth century, when English society in the region was established but still 'prehistoric' in documentary terms, is a good point at which to pause and take stock of some of its long-term features. One is that this culture was a warlike one, in which the warrior ethic always remained very important. The average Anglo-Saxon male

17 A late fifth- or sixth-century bucket from Berinsfield grave 29. (Oxford Archaeological Unit)

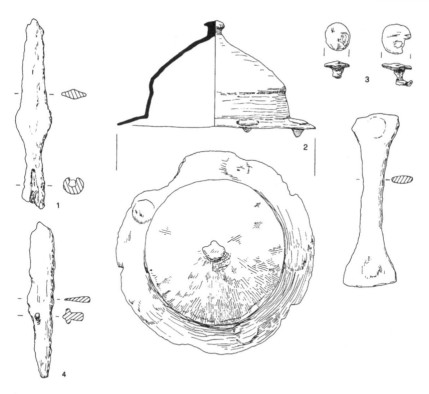

18 The equipment of a typical sixth-century male burial (Berinsfield grave 53): spear (1), shield (2), studs (3) and knife (4). One-third actual size. (Oxford Archaeological Unit)

knew how to handle spear and shield, not pen and parchment, though our sources are so dominated by bookish writers (and their use by bookish historians) that we often forget it. A few place-names are relevant here, even though they are impossible to date at all precisely. Bicester (*Bernecestre*) was the 'chester' of the warriors (*beornas*), and the first element in the name of *Fethanleag* near Stoke Lyne (traditionally the site of a battle in 584) is *fēþa*, a poetic and archaic word meaning 'foot-soldier'.[51] Another poetic term, *geseldas* or 'comrades', occurs in the name of *Sildenebrugg* at Warborough.[52] Some uncertainty surrounds the two cases (in Shirburn and Shifford) of Knightsbridge, 'bridge of the *cnihtas*'.[53] The basic meaning of this term, the root of later medieval 'knight', should be 'boys' or 'servants', but by extension it could have a sense similar to 'the lads' in modern colloquial English.[54] Thus the unique phrase *ðær ða cnihtas licgað*, a landmark on the boundary of Witney recorded in 1044,[55] might be translated as something like 'where the gang lies'. Remarkably, this apparently describes a known cemetery: the spot was near Shakenoak Roman villa, where excavations have revealed a group of thirteen orientated graves (Figs. 32, 77).[56] These were no ordinary burials: all but one were male, and four bore marks of weapon-blows on their limbs and head. Were these 'the lads', buried in their own cemetery and still recalled in folk-memory four centuries later?[57] It may be that *beornas*, *geseldas* and *cnihtas* were semi-wild troops of trainee warriors, a form of 'violent life on the margin of ordered society';[58] or they could have been established professional fighters at the service of any successful and generous lord. As complex polities developed during the late sixth and seventh centuries, such men may have determined which chiefdoms survived and which went under.

The pre-Christian religion of the region has left only the slightest traces. Occasional place-names probably indicate late-surviving cult sites (*weoh*, 'shrine', in Weedon, Northants. and the name of the god Tew in Tysoe, Warwicks.), but there are very few within the later boundaries of Oxfordshire.[59] Taston in Spelsbury and Tusmore may possibly mean 'Thunor's (i.e. Thor's) stone' and 'Thunor's pool'.[60] The lost name *Harowdonehull* in Wood Eaton probably includes *hearg*, 'shrine', in which case it might refer to the stone Romano-Celtic temple which stood on the main hill in the parish: a notable case of such a structure being re-used by Anglo Saxon pagans.[61] In a primitive, rural culture, nature-spirits and folk-magic would have been prominent. The term *elfen*, 'elf', 'fairy', occurs in two place-names and *pūca*, 'goblin' in six, normally describing pits and streams.[62] In Steeple Barton, goblins and demons haunted a barrow (*Succhelaue*) and a road (*Demnesweye*).[63] Fritwell probably had an 'augury (*freht*) well'.[64] Occasional grave-goods, notably the bags of salvaged Romano-British oddments found in some female burials, are best interpreted as amulets.[65] The Lechlade cemetery has produced the largest known collection of cowrie shells, a common charm of probably sexual significance. By the knees of one seventh-century woman there was a box containing a metal 'thread-box' (sometimes a Christian object, Fig. 49), a beaver-tooth and cowrie shell.[66]

Most people, of course, spent most of their time exploiting the land and producing basic necessities. The study of settlement and the economy is much younger than the study of jewellery and weapons, and has tended to lack chronological precision. This is now changing, and in ten years' time a great deal more will be known about the rich Upper Thames material. None the less, we are already starting to understand these sites much better, and to make sense of them in the light of recent general work on early Anglo-Saxon settlement patterns.[67]

Since the pioneer work by E.T. Leeds at Sutton Courtenay in the 1920s, many fifth- to seventh-century settlements have been excavated on the second gravel terrace. Two typical sites, New Wintles near Eynsham and Barrow Hills near Radley (Figs. 19, 21),[68] illustrate the general pattern. Characteristically a scatter of sunken-featured buildings (*Grubenhaüser*) are interspersed with a smaller number of rectilinear structures made of vertical earth-fast posts. Once considered the ubiquitous Anglo-Saxon house-type, *Grubenhaüser* are now mainly regarded as workshops and stores. Normally they contain a pair of large post-holes for the gables (Fig. 22), and many were floored over; lines of weights from weaving-looms are occasionally found in them. The post-built dwellings (Figs. 20, 23) are small and simple versions of the 'halls' that appear on high-status sites after 600. Plot-boundaries are rarely apparent, though Barton Court Farm and New Wintles had fences and pens for livestock.

The hallmark of these settlements, which distinguishes them sharply from later medieval villages, is their formless, haphazard layout and their tendency to sprawl over large tracts of the second gravel terrace. This is well illustrated by the sites excavated (mainly in advance of quarrying) around the Thames–Evenlode confluence near Eynsham and Cassington (Fig. 24), where a sometimes almost continuous scatter of

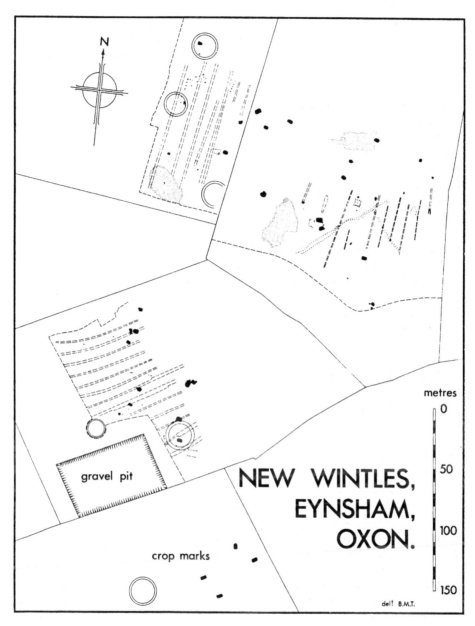

19 New Wintles, Eynsham: clusters of sunken-featured buildings interspersed with a few post-built structures. As so often, the Anglo-Saxon features overlie Bronze Age ring-ditches. (Clayton 1973, Fig. 2, after S. C. Hawkes)

20 Worton Rectory Farm, Yarnton: reconstruction of the main building in the late sixth- or early seventh-century settlement complex. Note (left) the square end annexe which was to become characteristic of large seventh-century timber halls. (Oxford Archaeological Unit)

settlements and cemeteries hugs the terrace-edge around the fringe of the alluvial floodplain. It has become clear, in fact, that no normal excavation can hope to recover an entire settlement complex: a total view needs a trench a mile wide! The extent of these complexes might suggest a huge population, but recent work, above all by Helena Hamerow at Mucking (Essex), points to a different solution: settlements were always on the move.[69] A small community – a hamlet or even a single farm – might wander around within its environs, shifting at intervals of a generation or more as buildings decayed and adjacent arable plots were worked out. A striking (if unusually long-drawn-out) case is Worton Rectory Farm, Yarnton, where the settlement seems to have crept slowly eastwards along the edge of the gravel terrace between the late Iron Age and the late Anglo-Saxon period.[70] Unlike medieval villagers constrained by their own economic systems, these people had nothing to tie them down.

Stock-breeding and its products are very conspicuous, both in the bone assemblages and in the quantities of weaving equipment. Except at Purwell Farm, Cassington, which seems to have specialised in cattle and pigs, sheep normally predominate; this is especially marked in the seventh-century material from the boundary ditch of Shakenoak Roman villa, where over half the animals were sheep (though the same assemblage contained cow-bells), and in the earlier settlement at Barton Court Farm.[71]

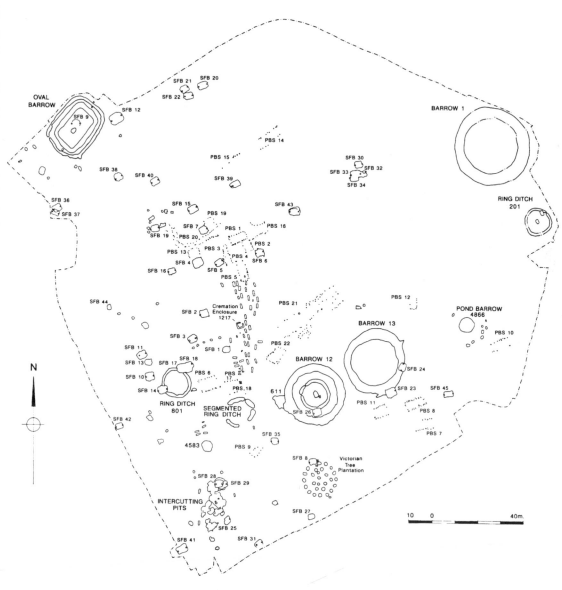

21 Barrow Hills, Radley: another large rural settlement, with forty-five sunken-featured buildings (SFBs) and thirteen post-built structures (PBSs). The Bronze Age barrows had mostly been flattened by the Anglo-Saxon period, though their ring-ditches are conspicuous on this plan. In the middle of the site is a Roman cemetery. (Oxford Archaeological Unit)

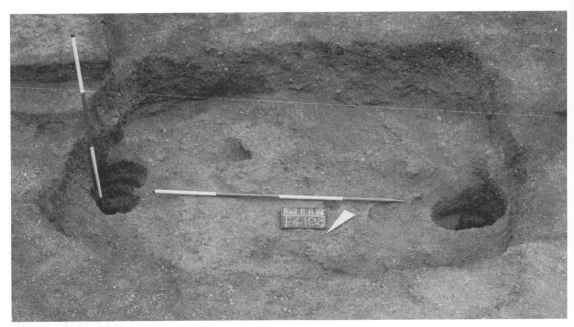

22 Barrow Hills, Radley: a sunken-featured building, showing the two holes for the large posts in the gable-ends. (Oxford Archaeological Unit)

That the sheep were kept for their wool, and that this was at least partly processed on site, is clear from the numerous finds of weaving-combs (Fig. 25), pin-beaters and loom-weights.[72] In harmony with the bone evidence, such material was sparse at Purwell Farm, plentiful at New Wintles and notably abundant at Shakenoak. The weaving equipment in high-status seventh-century female graves (for instance at Lechlade)[73] underlines the social importance of the industry in these communities. So perhaps the wool and cloth which were to be the main products of the medieval South Midlands were already being traded from the region before 600. The import of exotic luxury goods will be mentioned shortly; here, perhaps, are the bulk exports which made that possible.

People cannot only have lived in the river-valleys: our current impression of early Anglo-Saxon settlements suffers from a serious distortion. The Thames gravel terraces reveal crop-marks much better than any other local geology, and quarrying stimulates rescue archaeology. Thus gravel sites are more likely to have been known about in the first place, and also more likely to be excavated: arguably Fig. 24 is more a map of modern quarrying than of Anglo-Saxon settlement. This is a weighty objection, but it can be pushed too far. The concentration of known cemeteries on the second gravel terrace is just as strong, and although this too is to some extent a reflex of mineral extraction, the distinctive grave-goods have been recognised in a wide variety of circumstances over the past two centuries. The first terrace has been much quarried also, but has not yielded Anglo-Saxon sites. It is in fact quite plausible that the light, well-drained soils of the second terrace did have the biggest and most numerous

23 Barrow Hills, Radley: the post-holes of two post-built structures. In the right background is the ring-ditch of a Bronze Age barrow. (Oxford Archaeological Unit)

settlements, and the very strong concentration of -ēg ('island') place-names along the Upper Thames (above, p. xxiii) supports a predeliction for gravel sites raised above the floodplain edge. So the sites revealed by archaeology probably can be regarded as core settlements, even if they are thrown into too sharp relief by non-recognition of the peripheral settlement patterns that must also have existed.[74]

The communities at any one time were probably small. As with the cemeteries (where hundreds of bodies can represent only a few families burying in one place over several generations), first impressions produce inflated estimates. Even a large site like Barrow Hills, rebuilt periodically over a century or two, may never have contained more than five to ten households. In 600 the population level must still have been much lower than that of the fourth century. Unlike late Iron Age and Roman settlements, those of the early Anglo-Saxon period cluster on the second gravel terrace but conspicuously avoid the first terrace and floodplain alluvium. They represent a retreat to the higher, dryer ground where Neolithic and Bronze Age settlement had developed, just as agrarian practice and the use of resources had reverted to pre-Iron Age levels.[75] A waterlogged deposit at Barton Court Farm suggests that after 400 the surrounding landscape had remained open, with flax and some cereals still grown, but this evidence is hard to quantify or to extrapolate more widely;[76] the continued slow

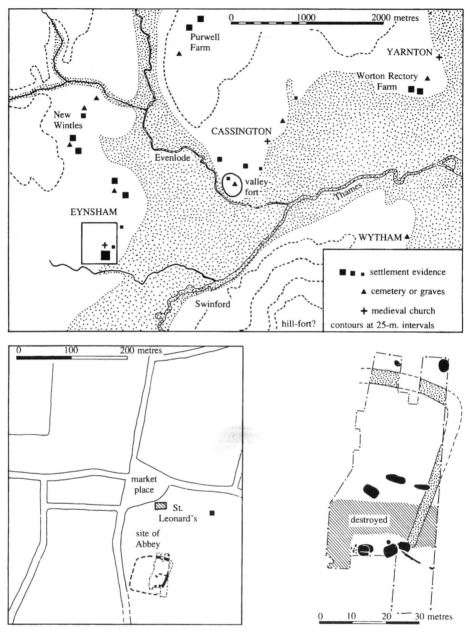

24 Early Anglo-Saxon settlement at the Thames–Evenlode confluence. *Above*: Fifth- to seventh-century settlements and cemeteries around Eynsham, Cassington and Yarnton (Oxfordshire Sites and Monuments Record and Oxford Archaeological Unit). *Bottom left*: Eynsham: the town centre, showing the Bronze Age enclosure (projected extent conjectural) which was the focus of Anglo-Saxon settlement, in relation to the later abbey and the market-place which developed at its gates. *Bottom right*: Eynsham: the Bronze Age enclosure (stippled), in relation to the overlying sunken-featured buildings (black) of the sixth- to seventh-century settlement (Oxford Archaeological Unit).

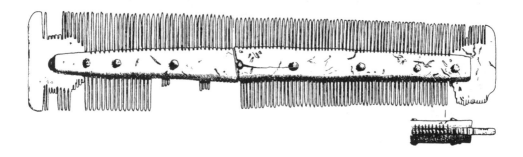

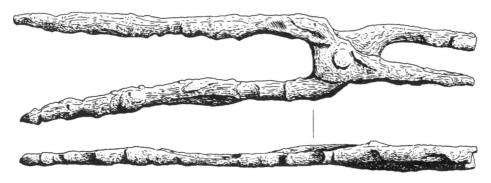

25 Industry at Shakenoak: a weaving-comb and a pair of blacksmith's tongs, from the seventh-century material filling the boundary ditch of the Roman villa. Two-thirds actual size. (Brodribb et al. 1972, Figs. 42 and 56)

rate of alluvial deposition[77] suggests that agriculture had not made any recovery from its post-Roman collapse. So in contrast to later centuries, when the life of so many communities was shaped by their great open fields, arable may have been a minor, shifting element in a primarily pastoral landscape which was closer to that of the Bronze Age than of the Roman or high medieval periods.

Woodland and waste for pigs and cattle, scrub and open pasture for sheep, were the essential resources of this society, but they are hard to recognise or quantify precisely because they existed in such abundance. It may have been only when they required clear demarcation between competing interests that they were named and defined: thus the prolific *lēah* names, which probably denote wood-pastures, seem to date from the eighth to tenth centuries rather than earlier.[78] An older layer (because well represented in pre-730 sources) may be the *feld* names common in the Chilterns (above, pp. xxii–xxiii). Transhumant grazing patterns are suggested by later territorial links: the Thames and Cherwell Valleys with Wychwood and the Cotswolds, or the Clay Vale with the Chilterns.[79] A major lost element is the whole category of herdsmens' dwellings, doubtless often seasonal, for pasturing the livestock whose meat and wool ended up on sites such as New Wintles and Shakenoak. There may be a trace of these forgotten communities in the names *fildena weg* and *fildena wuduweg*

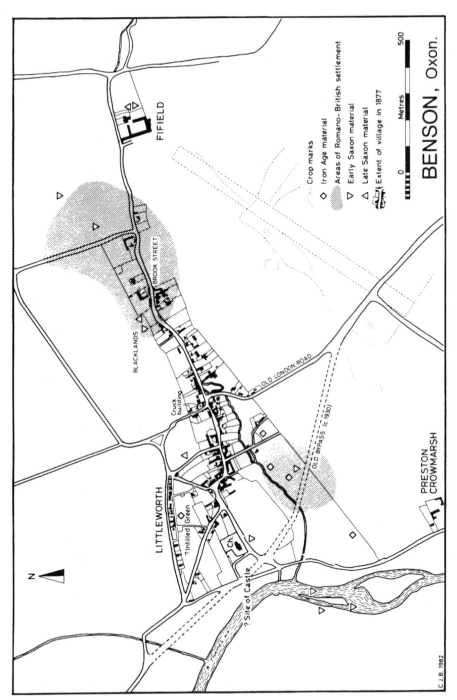

26 The royal vill of Benson: Anglo-Saxon finds and later topography. The distribution of early Anglo-Saxon material suggests two settlement foci, which might have resembled the better-recorded sites at Eynsham and Yarnton. As at Bampton (Fig. 44), the importance and complexity of the early settlement may be reflected in the linear topography of the medieval village. (Bond 1985, Fig. 9.3)

recorded in late Anglo-Saxon charters along the edge of the Chiltern scarp. They apparently mean 'way (or wood-way) of the *feld*-people',[80] and evoke an image of herdsmen moving their livestock from the Chiltern woodland and *feld* to the Icknield Way. Thus the patterns of exploitation which were later to produce linear estates crossing varied geographical zones (below, pp. 125, 133) may have had their origins in the early Anglo-Saxon period.[81]

The basic features of the fifth- to seventh-century rural economy were thus a lack of stability or structure and a strong pastoral emphasis. Moves towards something more organised and intensive are hard to pin down: the evolution of the 'early' settlements on the gravels can be traced until at least around 700, and more work on the local pottery is needed before we can understand developments during the eighth and ninth centuries.[82] The pattern may in fact have persisted until 900 or later, when basic changes started to give birth to stable communities with stable villages and fields.

If settlement was fluid, it was probably not anarchic. For the Mucking complex Hamerow suggests that 'this shifting occurred not at random, but within a territorial unit, and possibly within the framework of a regional administration';[83] the same might be said of the Upper Thames clusters. By the seventh century, as we shall see, large territorial units were organised around stable central places. One of the earliest traditions of the Chilterns and Upper Thames (below, p. 38), preserved in an annal ascribed (probably fictitiously) to '571', mentions four examples of the sort of place that was becoming important: Limbury, Aylesbury, Benson and Eynsham. A prime factor was the presence of a re-usable earthwork: Limbury and Aylesbury include the term *burh*, 'fortress', and at Aylesbury this has been identified as an Iron Age hill-fort enclosing the later minster church and town.[84] At Eynsham, recent excavations have shown that the nucleus of the Anglo-Saxon minster, medieval abbey and modern town was a rectilinear Bronze Age enclosure, chosen in the sixth or early seventh century for a group of sunken-featured buildings (Fig. 24).[85] No earthwork is known at Benson, but topography and fieldwork reveal a complex plan with settlement debris throughout the Anglo-Saxon period underlying the modern village (Fig. 26).[86] The annalist might well have named some other places, most obviously Dorchester and Abingdon.

What makes these sites special is their centrality and their long-term stability. With all the problems of imperfect data, it does look as though sixth- and seventh-century Thames-side settlement concentrated around three foci: Eynsham/Cassington (Fig. 24), Abingdon, and Dorchester.[87] The centres themselves we will meet many times in this book as the growth-points of later Anglo-Saxon (and indeed post-Conquest) development. Doubtless some failed (for instance the Cassington Mill valley-fort site: was it overtaken by Eynsham?), but in general these places show a new permanence which may tell us something about the consolidation of English society.

Social organisation at a more local level remains very obscure. One reasonable inference is that the 'clan' or 'extended family', the real or imagined descendants of a founder-ancestor and their dependants, was fundamental: the earliest known land-units were defined in terms of kinship (below, p. 35), and kinship remained legally and socially crucial through the whole Anglo-Saxon period.[88] In a world in which settlement and agriculture constantly shifted, and land-tenure in the later sense of the term was probably unknown, the clan would have been the main source of individual

27 A rich sixth-century woman buried at Lechlade. On her left shoulder was a great square-headed brooch, and festoons of beads hung on her breast from two saucer-brooches. By her head (top-right) were a bronze-mounted wooden bowl and a comb. The objects hanging from her waist (bottom-right) included 'girdle-hangers', probably symbolic keys denoting her control over the household; the 'key-carrying' (*locbore*) woman had a special status in the early Kentish laws. (Oxford Archaeological Unit)

identity and status. But society was not egalitarian, and grave-goods suggest that new hierarchies were developing. Whereas the exceptional fifth-century graves had been those of sword-bearing men, presumably military leaders, the mid- to late sixth century is notable for occasional opulently dressed women. Like their contemporaries in Kent (who were certainly influencing Upper Thames fashions), they wore great square-headed brooches, long festoons of beads, chatelaines and purses as well as the more usual saucer-brooches.[89] One such grave at Lechlade (Fig. 27) is among the richest known from sixth-century England.[90]

Clearly these ladies had status, but what kind of status is less straightforward.[91] The temptation to see a hereditary aristocracy established by the mid-sixth century should probably on the whole be resisted. A stratified society with a permanent upper class would be hard to reconcile with the apparent lack of differentiation within settlements. Unlike the 'special' seventh-century burials which will be considered later, these are not radically different in kind from ordinary graves but merely richer and more varied. The fathers or husbands of these women may have enjoyed the kind of rank that can be acquired within primitive, traditional societies today, most obviously as village head-men or military leaders. (Indeed, such wealth in such societies is often expressed in the adornment of womenfolk.) On the other hand, graves of infants with rich objects such as bronze cauldrons (as again at Lechlade[92]) show that status was shared at least by infants within the family group. These displays of rank are pointers towards a near future in which aristocracies certainly did exist. Like the emergence of territorial centres and the growth of trade and inter-regional contact, they set the scene for an era of rapid change which we must now consider.

TOWARDS KINGSHIP AND CHRISTIANITY

Even the rich lady of Lechlade seems primitive compared with English society of a century later, with its over-kings, taxation records, charters and churches. Assessing this transformation is made harder rather than easier by the sudden hiatus in the historian's materials, as cemetery evidence fades away and written evidence starts: do a sixth-century burial and a seventh-century charter show us different societies, or different aspects of basically similar societies? Before tackling the earliest narrative sources we need to look at four developments within the archaeological record itself, which would have suggested change even if no documents had survived: Kentish and Frankish dominance of luxury imports; 'princely' burials; monumental timber buildings; and the systematic re-use of prehistoric and Roman structures. Together these phenomena signal a more organised society, capable of creating larger and more stable polities and more receptive to civilising influences from abroad.

A new element in grave-goods of the period c. 580-630 is a range of exotic items imported from or through Kent: jewellery, elaborate glass-ware, copper-alloy cauldrons from Francia, even metal bowls from the eastern Mediterranean.[93] The Milton II cemetery near Sutton Courtenay contained two female graves with opulent gold-and-garnet composite brooches made in Kent in about 620-40.[94] The Upper Thames becomes, in fact, the edge of a distribution pattern running overland from Byzantium to northern Gaul and thence to Kent. The concentration of some items

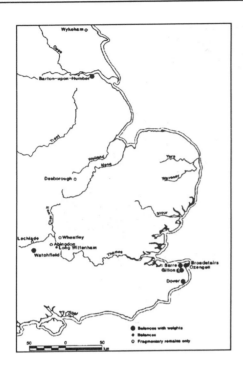

28 Finds of scales and weights in late sixth- and early seventh-century graves (Scull 1990, Fig. 9). One among several classes of artefact which show the close links between Kent and the Upper Thames.

(notably the cauldrons, which show clusters in the Fairford–Lechlade area and around Long Wittenham)[95] suggests that local groups or leaders had supply sources of a fairly specific kind. Christopher Scull's survey of scales and weights from Anglo-Saxon graves notes striking concentrations of finds in Kent and the Upper Thames (Fig. 28), and argues that they were used for weighing gold coins minted to Byzantine or Frankish standards (or bullion to the same standards).[96] The purse containing the scale-set from Watchfield grave 67 is inscribed in runes with the enigmatic message *hariboki wusa*: the oldest piece of written English from the region. Its meaning is controversial, but if the first word is equivalent to later Old English *hereboc*, 'book (i.e. accounts) of the army', it suggests a striking degree of social and fiscal organisation.[97] Some of the gold coins produced in Francia and south-eastern England in the early seventh century did in fact percolate to the Upper Thames, and it is even possible that one rare type bearing the runic legend *Benutigo* was minted there.[98] The context of the Franco-Kentish links is one of dominance, perhaps political overlordship, over Kent by the northern Frankish kings. To argue by extension that the Upper Thames was under Kentish dominance goes well beyond the evidence, but it is clear that Kent had a powerful influence on the region and a near-monopoly of its top-quality imports.[99] This growth of the Thames as an economic and cultural corridor, leading to Frankish-influenced Kent and to Europe beyond, was to be of crucial importance over the next two centuries.

Only rich people have access to opulent goods. Another new feature of the years immediately after 600 is the deposition of burials of previously unknown magnificence, usually under large barrows.[100] In the Upper Thames one burial in

29 Blue glass bowl, probably of Kentish manufacture, from the Cuddesdon burial. Luxury glassware such as this is characteristic of 'princely' graves around the year 600. Just below actual size. (Ashmolean Museum)

particular, excavated at Cuddesdon in 1847, has a claim to be associated with the political power that was emerging in the region around 600.[101] The known finds from it comprised two swords, two Kentish blue glass bowls (Fig. 29), an eastern Mediterranean bronze bucket and a garnet-studded fragment of bronze. Set out radially around the presumed barrow were several skeletons, laid face-down with their legs crossed and their heads pointing outwards. It seems highly probable, especially in view of recent comparable finds at Sutton Hoo, Suffolk, that these were victims whose sacrifice attended the funeral of some exceptionally important man. Such 'princely' graves show the English marking status in a wholly new way, mirroring the funerary practice of Continental royalty and high nobility.

Earlier Anglo-Saxon settlements in the region show little sign of social differentiation, but leaders of the status of the man buried at Cuddesdon may have been housed on a grander scale. Two crop-mark sites, one near Sutton Courtenay and Drayton (Fig. 30) and the other near Long Wittenham, contain impressive groups of large rectangular timber buildings, in both cases set out in L-shaped linear formation.[102] Neither has been excavated, but the apparent use of the post-in-trench technique makes a date before 600 unlikely. We have some idea of the scale of an early seventh-century royal palace thanks to the excavation of Yeavering in Northumbria, which Bede describes as such, and Drayton at least 'seems not much inferior in the scale of its accommodation to Yeavering itself'.[103] It cannot be proved that the owners

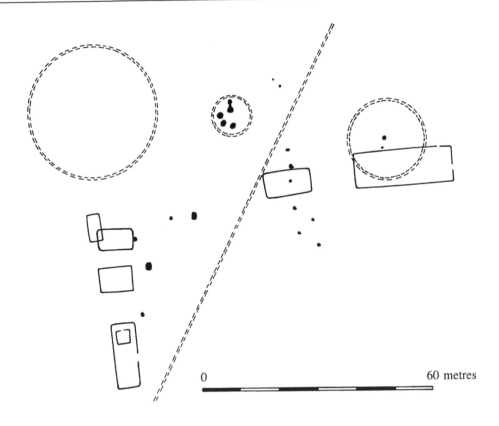

30 The Drayton 'palace': crop-marks of an L-shaped group of large rectangular timber buildings, associated with a scatter of sunken huts. The underlying prehistoric features (one ditch of the Neolithic cursus and three Bronze Age barrows) are shown in broken line. (After Benson & Miles 1974b)

of these places called themselves kings, but their proximity to the cemeteries which have produced coin-balances, copper-alloy cauldrons and Kentish composite brooches is striking.

The fourth straw in the wind is a new approach to ancient monuments. From the later sixth century Roman sites started to be used again, and even the adoption of prehistoric earthworks, which as we have seen came naturally to the earlier Anglo-Saxons, became more directed and systematic. The insertion of groups of graves into Bronze Age barrows, for instance, seems to be a characteristically (though not exclusively) post-600 phenomenon[104], foreshadowing the occasional later Anglo-Saxon use of such monuments as Christian cult sites (Fig. 31). Archaeologists' obsession with 'continuity' at Roman villas has obscured a more genuine pattern, their re-use during the seventh and eighth centuries. At Shakenoak the mass of domestic debris in the boundary ditch of the villa testifies to a post-600 settlement, so far unlocated, of considerable density, its last stages dated by early eighth-century coins.[105] More commonly, the ruined walls became a formal setting for graves. At Barton Court two mid- to late sixth-century burials were fitted neatly inside the rooms of the

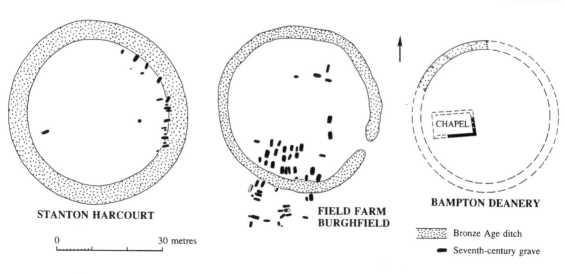

STANTON HARCOURT

FIELD FARM BURGHFIELD

BAMPTON DEANERY

0   30 metres

▨▨▨▨ Bronze Age ditch

● Seventh-century grave

CHAPEL

31 Three large Bronze Age barrow-ditches appropriated in the post-Roman period. The circles at Stanton Harcourt and Burghfield became the foci of seventh-century cemeteries; that at Bampton encloses the late eleventh-century episcopal chapel which lies immediately west of the main church (cf. Fig. 44). (After Harden & Treweeks 1945, Fig. 7; Butterworth & Lobb 1992, Fig. 6; *SMA* xxii (1992), 57)

main villa building,[106] while at Shakenoak the graves of the *cnihtas* take their careful, regular alignment from the axis of the villa (Figs. 14, 32). Conceptually similar are the isolated seventh-century graves at Great Tew (overlying demolition debris in one of the villa rooms) and Frilford (exactly half-way between the two Romano-Celtic temples), both marked by cairns.[107] This use of Roman remains for their architectural possibilities, not just as rubble, points towards practices that would become familiar in a religious context a generation later.

All these changes suggest a higher organisational capacity, both institutionally and physically. The occupants of 'princely' tombs must be, in degree if not in kind, a new élite controlling new resources and aware of new horizons, acquiring their attributes of status through Europe-wide exchange systems. Like many other new élites, they sought to legitimise their rule both by annexing ancient monuments and by building new ones.[108] In many cultures the appearance of planned, organised and regular structures has marked a key stage in social development; around 600 the English reached that stage. Graves orientated in neat rows or set radially around Bronze Age barrows, Roman buildings re-used for the sake of their grid-plans and defining walls, reflect the same impulse towards formality and order as the monumental complexes of timber buildings at Yeavering or Drayton.

This élite group was still pagan (no Christian, however vague his theology, would have had human sacrifices at his funeral), but Christian culture must have impinged on it. After the 590s the most visible source was the Kentish court, but a powerful hidden influence may have been the western British. Contrary to normal assumptions, the integrated and cosmopolitan English aristocracy of around 600 may have been more receptive to British-derived marks of status and sophistication than were the fifth-century settlers. The Gloucestershire folk were, as we have seen, of mixed British and

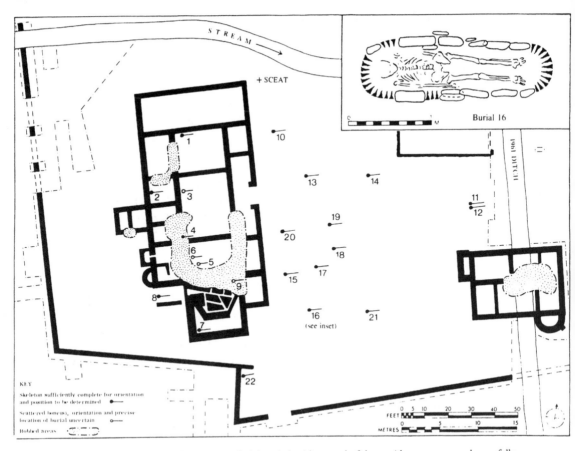

32 The *cnihtas* of Shakenoak? A group of adult male burials, several of them with weapon wounds, carefully aligned on the ruins of the Roman villa. (Brodribb et al. 1973, Figs. 16–17)

English stock; further north and west, 'we must consider the British population . . . not as "surviving" (which implies a struggle against adverse circumstances or superior numbers), but as continuing to be there and as forming the main stock of the population'.[109] English communities in those regions were almost certainly converted by a continuing British Church,[110] and the British may well have been the source of some English cultural innovations around 600, notably the practice of unaccompanied west–east burial[111] and the plans of rectangular timber buildings.[112] Cerdic and Ceawlin, the founder and the leading member of the dynasty soon to dominate the Upper Thames Saxons, had British names.[113]

The conversion of England during the seventh century happened from above downwards: the Upper Thames Saxons could become 'officially' Christian in the 630s because by that time they had a powerful king. That makes us face a problem which so far we have avoided: what were Anglo-Saxon kingdoms, and how did they start?

THE MAKING OF THE GEWISSE

Many answers have been given to this question, and probably more than one of them are right.[114] The Anglo-Saxons must have brought with them at least military and kin-group cohesion, but the territorial organisation of their society may have been powerfully moulded by what they found in Britain. There is a strong body of opinion that the first English land-units were often of Iron Age or Roman origin,[115] and one such land-unit might be the territory occupied by the fifth-century Britons who were burying their dead at Dorchester. Whatever the truth of this, settlement by a community or family characteristically reached a stage where it assumed territorial definition. Hence the large and important class of English district names incorporating the suffix -ingas: the Hæstingas ('kin of Hæsta') at Hastings, the Godhelmingas ('kin of Godhelm') at Godalming, and so on. Once regarded as evidence for the first English settlements, these names are now ascribed to a rather later phase marked by consolidation and demarcation. Arguably the ingas-type territories can be considered the first English kingdoms, though we very rarely know anything of their kings.

In recent years scholars have made great strides in reconstructing these early land-units, some with ingas-type names and others named from geographical or archaeological features (Fig. 39).[116] Oxfordshire sources do not lend themselves well to these techniques, but place-names take us some way (Fig. 33). The shadowy 'Færpingas' were probably based around Charlbury (below, p. 59); Goring in south Oxfordshire may preserve the name of a 'Gāringas' tribe, neighbours of the 'Rēadingas' and better-recorded 'Sunningas' of the Reading and Sonning areas.[117] Two other place-names suggest outlying settlements or pasture zones of tribes based around the fringes of Oxfordshire: Watlington (Wæclinctune in 887), separated by the Cilternsæte ('Chiltern-dwellers') from the 'Wæclingas' of the St. Albans area; and Horninga mære ('the Hornings' boundary') near Curbridge, recorded in a charter of 969, separated by the Thames from the 'Horningas' of Hormer hundred around Cumnor and Abingdon.[118] These are the scattered linguistic traces of tribal proto-kingdoms, otherwise forgotten, which may well underlie the administrative divisions and land-units discussed later in this book. When labourers in Victorian Oxfordshire spoke of 'Banburyshire',[119] they could have been recalling an entity well over a millennium old.

There was also a smaller unit which is of special importance to us, since we will meet it as the basic measure of land through the rest of Anglo-Saxon history. The 'hide', classically defined by Bede as the 'land of one family', seems in origin to have been exactly that: the share allocated by a kin-group to each of its adult male members.[120] When we encounter it in the first English documents it had already become a measure of obligations rather than of agrarian capacity, the unit on which kings and over-kings assessed taxes (below, pp. 77–8). Thus the ingas-type territory and the hide both suffered a transformation which speaks of evolution from a tribal society to a political one: from a world in which decisions were taken within the hierarchy of a family or settlement group to one in which resources, military and otherwise, were exacted by kings. The text called the 'Tribal Hidage', which may incorporate a late seventh-century tribute list for the south-east Midlands, lists a number of folk-groups, large and small, with the hidage assessments allocated to them.[121] Such groups of hides

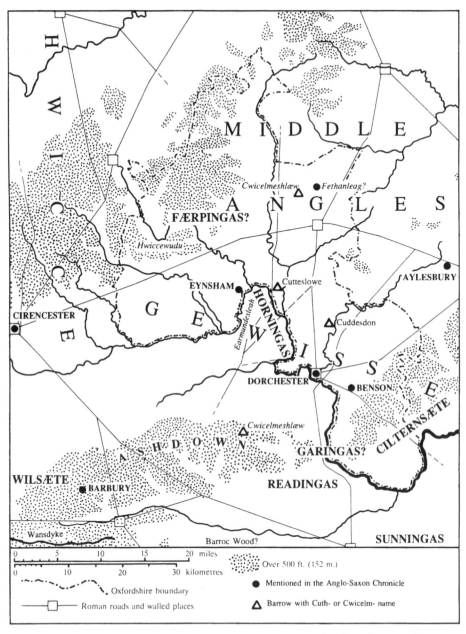

33 The Gewisse and their neighbours: folk-groups and places mentioned in the earliest narrative sources. Also shown are the names of the larger political confederations that were to emerge during the seventh century.

combined to form the larger kingdoms, familiar from the pages of Bede, of seventh- and eighth-century England.

The impulse behind kingdom-building seems to have been competition and dominance in a world of 'complex chiefdoms'.[122] Writing the political history of a non-literate culture can rarely be much more than futile, but it does look as though some decisive change happened around 570–600. This conclusion rests partly on the very clear impression that *ingas*-type units were fast amalgamating and fading from view during the seventh and eighth centuries, partly on the archaeological evidence which we have already considered. The men who obtained Frankish vessels and jewellery, who lived in halls such as Drayton and were buried in barrows such as Cuddesdon, evidently had new methods and resources to consolidate and extend their military gains and fiscal assets. Surely we can sensibly call them kings.

This plunges us straight into the texts which first claim, however deceptively, to record the history of the Upper Thames: the ninth-century Anglo-Saxon Chronicle and West Saxon Genealogical Regnal List, backed up (all too seldom) by Bede's far more reliable *Ecclesiastical History* finished in the 730s. Long gone are the days when the sixth-century annals in the Chronicle could be read as reliable history, and historians still argue about whether they contain any useful information whatsoever. Certainly before using them we must acknowledge three basic problems. First, the precise, factual format of the annals as we have them belies the nature of their lost sources, which seem to have been anything but precise and which may have lacked any real chronological framework. Secondly, the main purpose of the Chronicle was to glorify the late ninth-century kings of Wessex and their ancestors, the kin of Cerdic: convenient genealogical links may have been invented with gay abandon. Thirdly, the compilers grafted together the stories of different groups, active in different regions, to create a single history of King Alfred's supposed ancestors expanding triumphantly from their Hampshire base.

It is only very recently that historians have felt sufficiently emancipated from the 'official' narrative to grasp the clear message of the sixth-century annals: the main scene of action is not Hampshire but the Upper Thames region, and it is there that the first triumphs of the house of Cerdic must have been located in the underlying source-material. Thus the narrative evidence is more consistent with the archaeological evidence than has usually been thought, for both emphasise the Upper Thames, not Wiltshire or Hampshire, as the core region of settlement and consolidation. Once this crucial point is accepted, we can start to piece together a story of political amalgamation under a dominant military group. This brief account, which draws on recent fuller ones, will dwell on the little that may be true rather than the much that is probably fiction.[123]

One fairly safe fact about the Upper Thames leaders is that they called themselves the 'Gewisse'. Bede thus describes them from the first reference in his narrative (in about 620) until 686, when he switches to the familiar name 'West Saxons'. The meaning of 'Gewisse' has been much debated, but the latest view derives it from the adjective *gewis*, 'sure', 'reliable'.[124] This might mean that their neighbours trusted them, but it looks more like a self-conferred nickname ('the Trusties'?) which takes us back to the world of *geseldas* and *cnihtas*. It would be consistent with a less edifying origin than the one which King Alfred and his circle had in mind: a strong-arm gang controlling weaker neighbours by brute force.

The supposed history of these people is described in Chronicle annals concerned with the doings of leaders whose names all begin with 'C'. The more important passages are as follows:[125]

> *556*: 'Cynric and Ceawlin fought against the Britons at Barbury [Wilts.]'.
>
> *560*: 'Ceawlin succeeded to the kingdom in Wessex'.
>
> *568*: 'Ceawlin and Cutha fought against Æthelberht and drove him in flight into Kent'.
>
> *571*: 'Cuthwulf fought against the Britons at *Biedcanford*, and captured four vills (*tūnas*), Limbury, Aylesbury, Benson and Eynsham; and in the same year he died'.
>
> *577*: 'Cuthwine and Ceawlin fought against the Britons and killed three kings, Conmail, Condidan and Farinmail, at the place which is called Dyrham [Glos.]; and they captured three of their cities (*ceastra*), Gloucester, Cirencester and Bath'.
>
> *584*: 'Ceawlin and Cutha fought against the Britons at the place which is called *Fethanleag* [at Stoke Lyne in north Oxfordshire], and Cutha was killed there; and Ceawlin captured many vills and countless spoils, and went away in anger to his own land'.
>
> *592*: 'There occurred a great slaughter at 'Woden's Barrow' [at Alton Priors, Wilts.], and Ceawlin was driven out'.
>
> *593*: 'Ceawlin, Cwichelm and Crida perished'.
>
> *614*: 'Cynegils and Cwichelm fought at *Beandun*, and killed 2,045 Britons'.

The most sceptical judgement on these annals is that they were invented to suit later needs, probably in the eighth or ninth century.[126] A more charitable view, which we can reasonably take, is that they draw on oral tradition or poetry ('Ceawlin captured many vills and countless spoils, and went away in anger'), maybe an epic *Deeds of Ceawlin* in the manner of *Beowulf*. We have already seen, and will see again, the importance of Aylesbury, Benson and Eynsham. And Ceawlin certainly was a real and powerful king, whom Bede names in his list of English overlords immediately before Æthelberht of Kent. David Dumville, collating the Chronicle dates with the Regnal List, identifies distortions in the former and reconstructs a perceived sequence of reigns: Cerdic (538-54), Cynric (554-81), Ceawlin (581-8), Ceol (588-94), Ceolwulf (594-611), Cynegils (611-42).[127]

Even so, the received framework of events is likely to be highly misleading, both genealogically and politically. Given the strong motives for forging links we really cannot be sure how, if at all, these people were related: the one compelling argument is the unvaried C-alliteration of their names. Despite the impression of tidy lineal succession which the sources seek to convey, they are full of contradictions; it seems, for instance, that several princes called Cynegils have been rolled into one (or perhaps that different branches of the kin claimed descent from one Cynegils),[128] and Cwichelm, whom Bede names as king, is omitted from the Regnal List. It looks as though rulership was segmented between various rival branches which belonged (or were later held to have belonged) to the kin of Cerdic, and which may have had their own distinct territories.[129] A related point is that although the Chronicle lists several battles, we cannot necessarily believe the blanket identification of the enemies as 'the Britons'. Certainly the impression of a united English advance in the late sixth century is hard to reconcile with cemetery evidence, and it seems more likely that memories of battles of English against English were given an invented context which the age of Alfred found acceptable. The narrative can in fact be broken down and re-fashioned into a form more consistent with the archaeologists' and topographers' models: a competition for land and power between rival military groups, moving in fitful stages towards a more stable federation under Ceawlin and his kin.

Archaeologists have been quick to notice that several place-names in the Upper Thames region – most strikingly Cuddesdon with its princely grave – combine terms for 'hill' and 'barrow' (*dūn, hlæw*) with the personal names Cuth- and Cwichelm (Fig. 33).[130] To identify these as the tombs of the house of Cerdic is tempting indeed; the problem is that there are too many of them. Faced with two cases of 'Cutha's *dūn*', two of 'Cutha's *hlæw*' and two of 'Cwichelm's *hlæw*', we must surely conclude that folk-wisdom tended to assume a connection between prominent mounds and these founding fathers. (More recent analogies, such as 'Oliver Cromwell's House', suggest themselves.) While the occupant of the barrow excavated at Cuddesdon may indeed have belonged to the C-dynasty, Cutteslowe near Oxford seems to have been a Neolithic chambered tomb.[131]

After Ceawlin the Gewissian federation was clearly large and important, extending through Oxfordshire and north Berkshire into Wiltshire and the future West Saxon heartland. Bede presents them as a force to be reckoned with in the 620s, defeating the East Saxons in battle and plotting to murder the Northumbrian over-king Eadwine.[132] Written and archaeological evidence both point to two juxtaposed places as the centre of their kingdom: Benson, one of the *tūnas* in the '571' annal and later the biggest royal vill in Oxfordshire, and Dorchester only three miles away up the Roman road. Notwithstanding Dorchester's evident significance the case for a royal residence there has been exaggerated, and is in any case confused by the fact that the town was episcopal after the 630s. The early Anglo-Saxon material in the south-west corner of the Roman town was overlain by massive timber buildings (Fig. 9), but the (admittedly very unsatisfactory) evidence suggests that these were post-Conversion.[133] Nor can much be made of the settlement overlying late or sub-Roman enclosures outside the town to the north-west;[134] it yielded one remarkable find (Fig. 34), a lock in the form of a double bearded head, but there seems no more reason to associate this with the house of Cerdic than with the first bishops. The same might be said of the three gold coins (of various dates but probably an early seventh-century deposit) from Dorchester.[135] The gold-and-garnet pyramid (Fig. 34) found there in the eighteenth century[136] was a secular and top-status object, but it may derive from a burial rather than a settlement. Everything that we know about the general context of royal life would suggest an open-ground palace at nearby Benson as a more likely residence for the kings. We cannot even assume that Dorchester was hereditary property of Cerdic's kin. The essential point is that it was a place of visible ancient importance at a time when such things were starting to matter again: a dominant military group with aspirations to royal dignity would naturally take control of it.

By the reign of Cynegils one step was becoming increasingly obvious, and in the late 630s[137] he took it. Bede, writing nearly a century later, relates how the Italian bishop Birinus had come to Britain on a missionary expedition and intended to travel further inland,

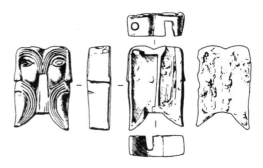

34 High-status objects from Dorchester-on-Thames. *Left*: Gold and garnet pyramid stop (after Dickinson 1974): this precious early seventh-century object, now lost, may have been made in the same workshop as the regalia in the East Anglian ship-burial at Sutton Hoo. *Right*: Bronze 'Janus-head' lock found at Bishop's Court (May 1977, Fig. 11): a unique object, but a high-status seventh-century context is on the whole most likely. Actual size.

but reaching first the people of the Gewisse and finding them all completely pagan, he decided that it would be more useful to preach the Word there than to continue in search of those to whom he was meant to preach. So he evangelised in that province, and having instructed the king [Cynegils] he washed him in the baptismal font with his people. At that time Oswald, the most holy and victorious king of the Northumbrians, happened to be present, and raised him up as he came from the font. Thus, by an alliance most lovely and acceptable to God, [Oswald] took as son the man, dedicated to God in a second birth, whose daughter he was about to take as wife. Then the two kings gave to that bishop the city (*civitas*) called *Dorcic* [Dorchester] to establish his episcopal seat in it. There, having built and dedicated churches and called many people to the Lord by his faithful labour, he passed to the Lord and was buried in the same city.[138]

For Bede the conversion of the Gewisse through the agency of his saint-hero Oswald was an act of God's providence; we may see in it a more secular sort of inevitability. Kentish influence on the region has already been emphasised in this chapter, and Birinus's Italian origins identify him with the Italo-Gallic Christianity of Kent. Travelling inland through the Gewissian territories, he had probably come up the Thames by the same route as the garnet jewellery and the bronze cauldrons. By the late 630s another great Christian power, the Northumbrians under Oswald, had achieved dominance in northern and central England, though in unstable counterpoise with the Angles of the Midlands who were also becoming an imminent threat to Cynegils and his people. An alliance of mutual interest between Northumbrians and Gewisse must have made excellent sense, and it is clear from Bede's narrative that Oswald was the dominant partner: receiving Cynegils as his godson, sealing the alliance by marriage, and confirming the gift of Dorchester in his role of overlord.

Thus the Upper Thames region became Christian under Northumbrian political dominance, reinforced by cultural influences percolating in from Kent and perhaps East Anglia.[139] But in one way or another conversion had to come: the political and cultural map was changing, and it was time for the Gewisse to join the Europe-wide club of civilised Christian peoples. The outward and visible sign of membership was *Romanitas* restored: a Roman town returned to its fourth-century role of ecclesiastical city, the seat of a bishop ruling its territory as imperial officials had done before him. Hence the grand word, *civitas*, which Bede applies to the really rather insignificant little ex-town of Dorchester. The growing English habit of re-using ancient monuments was reinforced by established Christian practice in the cities of Italy and Gaul, with which Birinus would certainly have been familiar.[140] English 'barbarian' society was starting to be re-integrated with the continuing post-Classical world of Rome and Byzantium. From this melting-pot some new and exotic products would come during the seventh and eighth centuries.

CHAPTER TWO

A MERCIAN FRONTIER PROVINCE

Cynegils may have seen himself in the mould of victorious Christian kings, but the days of the political order which his family had built in the Upper Thames were already numbered. Change came from the north, from the Angles whom we have so far met only as scattered communities in the Avon Valley. By about 600 the immigrant groups who had spread across central England were starting to coalesce into a federation under a powerful kin, the Iclingas, whose homeland was the Middle Trent Valley.[1] Just as Ceawlin's Gewisse had welded together the Upper Thames peoples, so in the next generation the 'Mercians', the Anglian communities of the Midlands, were welded together by the mighty Penda (?626-56).[2]

MERCIAN CONQUESTS AND THE RETREAT OF THE GEWISSE

The *Blitzkrieg* on several fronts which was to be a standard Mercian technique began abruptly around 630, with rapid impact on the British, the Northumbrians and the Gewisse. 'Mercians' (*Mierce*) means 'frontier people', and the frontier in question was almost certainly with the British to their north and west. A feature of Penda's reign is co-operation with the British, and with emergent western English states, against the larger kingdoms which had developed to the south and east during the previous generation. Bede's horrified description of an invasion of Northumbria by Penda and the north Welsh ruler Cadwallon in 633/4[3] suggests the character of Penda's simultaneous activities further south.

Early in the seventh century the mixed British, Saxon and Anglian peoples of the Severn Valley and Cotswolds (above, p. 16) coalesced as a kingdom, the Hwicce, under English rulers.[4] Whether Penda dominated them or merely formed an alliance of mutual interest, they seem to have provided a base for his early attacks on the Gewisse. In 628, according to the Anglo-Saxon Chronicle, 'Cynegils and Cwichelm fought against Penda at Cirencester and afterwards came to terms'.[5] This event probably explains why the head-waters of the Thames around Cirencester and Lechlade, though originally colonised by Saxons (above, pp. 14-16), are now in Gloucestershire rather than Oxfordshire. Penda's victory would have added them to the Hwiccian lands and, more importantly, given the Mercian confederation access to the lower Severn.

In 634/5, King Oswald of Northumbria defeated the Welsh–Mercian alliance. Penda's

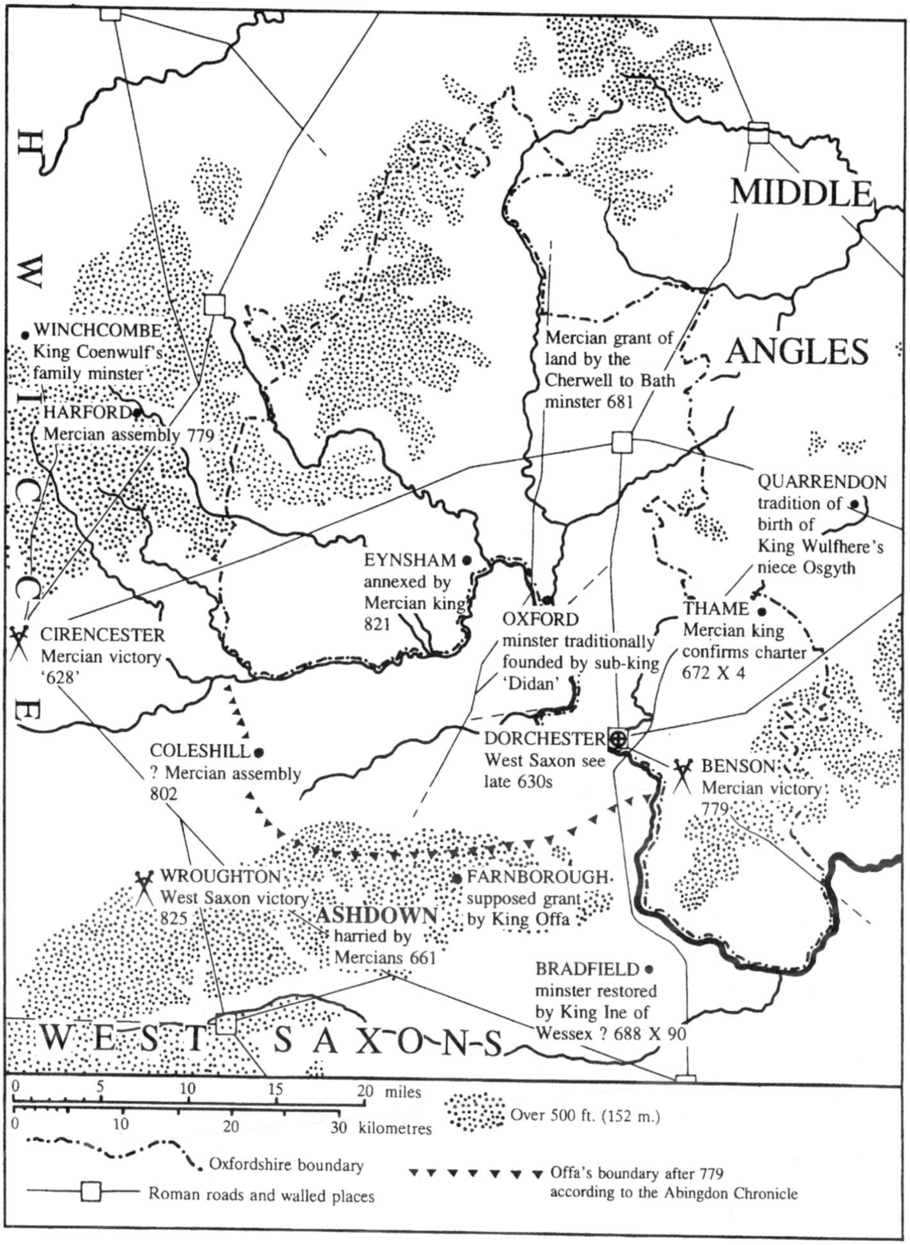
HWICCE
MIDDLE ANGLES
WINCHCOMBE King Coenwulf's family minster
HARFORD Mercian assembly 779
CIRENCESTER Mercian victory '628'
EYNSHAM annexed by Mercian king 821
Mercian grant of land by the Cherwell to Bath minster 681
OXFORD minster traditionally founded by sub-king 'Didan'
QUARRENDON tradition of birth of King Wulfhere's niece Osgyth
THAME Mercian king confirms charter 672 X 4
COLESHILL ? Mercian assembly 802
DORCHESTER West Saxon see late 630s
BENSON Mercian victory 779
WROUGHTON West Saxon victory 825
FARNBOROUGH supposed grant by King Offa
ASHDOWN harried by Mercians 661
BRADFIELD minster restored by King Ine of Wessex ? 688 X 90
WEST SAXONS
0 5 10 15 20 miles
0 10 20 30 kilometres
Over 500 ft. (152 m.)
Oxfordshire boundary
Roman roads and walled places
Offa's boundary after 779 according to the Abingdon Chronicle

35 Mercians and West Saxons in the Upper Thames region, 628-839.

power was contained for almost a decade; it is even possible that he was temporarily displaced by his brother Eowa, ruling as a Northumbrian client.[6] Oswald, in the ascendant, would have been keen to form defensive alliances against his main enemy; this is the obvious context for the baptism and marriage of Cynegils, which would have given the Gewisse much-needed Northumbrian protection against the Mercians.[7] This bulwark collapsed in 642/3, when Oswald was defeated and killed in battle against Penda, and soon afterwards Penda drove the Gewissian king into temporary exile. The Mercian confederation was too huge, its resources too rich and varied, to be contained for long: even Penda's own defeat and death in 655/6 was a mere interlude before his son Wulfhere (658/9–75) resumed the programme of expansionist campaigns.

It looks as though Wulfhere may have held much of the Gewissian territory under tribute, at least at intervals, from early in his reign. The Chronicle says that in 661 he 'harried on Ashdown' (i.e. the Berkshire Downs), and even invaded the Isle of Wight. This campaign may actually have happened slightly later, but it is clear that by the late 660s Wulfhere had thrown existing political authority south of the Thames into disarray; he was in a position to sell the bishopric of London, and we find him ruling Surrey through a Mercian sub-king. Possibly it was only the diversion of Wulfhere's forces against Northumbria in the early 670s that saved the Gewisse from political extinction.[8]

These events provide a context for Bede's account of the see of Dorchester-on-Thames, which runs as follows:[9] Cynegils was succeeded by his son Cenwealh, who unwisely repudiated Penda's daughter whom he had previously married. Penda therefore drove Cenwealh into exile; on his return (perhaps not until 656), he appointed a Frank named Agilbert as bishop of Dorchester to replace the deceased Birinus.

> But the king, who only knew the Saxon tongue, tired of barbarous speech; he intruded into the province another bishop of his own language named Wine, who had also been consecrated in Gaul, and dividing the province into two dioceses, appointed him to an episcopal see in the city . . . called Winchester. Agilbert was gravely offended that the king had done this without consulting him; returning to Gaul, he accepted the bishopric of the city of Paris where he died aged and full of days. Not many years after his departure from Britain, Wine too was expelled by the same king from the bishopric; so he went to the king of the Mercians called Wulfhere and bought the see of the city of London from him for a price, and remained there as bishop for the rest of his life. Thus the West Saxon province was for no short time without a bishop.

Between the lines of this rather unlikely story we can read not the division of the see of Dorchester, but its abandonment: the Gewissian kings and their bishops had found the Upper Thames too hot to hold them, and had decamped to Winchester.[10] In the longer term, however, the removal of the see was part of a re-alignment of which Penda and Wulfhere were not the only cause. If the Gewisse were doing badly in the South Midlands, they were starting to do exceedingly well on the south coast.[11] It may have been only in the seventh century that the Thames Valley Saxons gained control of those Hampshire territories which the late ninth-century Chronicler claimed as their original homelands. Towards the end of the century they annexed the Jutish province around Southampton Water, and in 686 they conquered the Isle of Wight. That year was a landmark, a coming-of-age for the kingdom: thereafter Bede's narrative abandons the archaic term 'Gewisse' in favour of 'West Saxons'. It is no coincidence that archaeology places the beginning of the great international port of Southampton (*Hamwic*), the foundation of their future wealth, at just this time. Winchester and *Hamwic* amply compensated the West Saxons for the loss of Dorchester. They became so thoroughly a Hampshire-based people that they nearly forgot the origins of their ruling dynasty.

The impact of Mercia on the Upper Thames region cannot be over-stressed. Hitherto it had been one of the nuclei of English settlement and expansion; but for Penda, the little country town which is now Dorchester-on-Thames might have become the capital of united England. In the event, the region's status in the emerging world of federations and over-kingships was a marginal one, between the two great power-centres in the valleys of the Trent far to the north and the Itchen far to the south. Yet it was still the gateway of the Thames, the corridor which led from land-locked Mercia to London and a wider northern European world.[12]

THE LAST FURNISHED BURIALS

The Upper Thames region has produced a small but important group of burials from the decades spanning roughly the reigns of Penda and Wulfhere. Since they show new features, including specifically Anglian ones, some archaeologists have been eager to identify them with in-coming Mercians. This could be right, but we must be careful. Society was developing fast, and folk-movements are not necessarily the best explanation for changes in material culture.

36 The Lew barrow. This dramatically sited monument, the origin of the place-name, is one of the most conspicuous landmarks in west Oxfordshire. In 984 Æthelred II gave land 'at the barrow' (*æt hlæwe*) to his scribe Ælfwine.

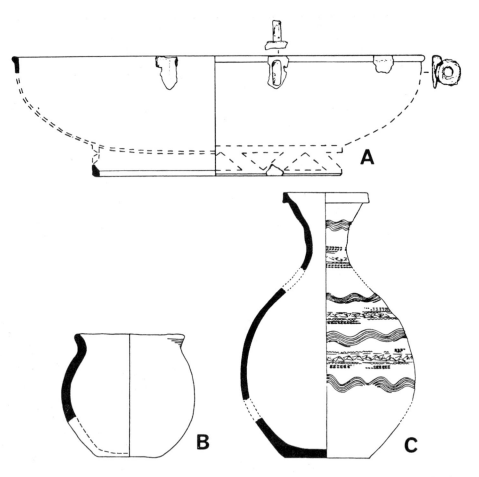

37 Imported and native objects in the seventh-century barrow at Asthall. *A*: Byzantine cast metal bowl (hypothetical reconstruction from fragments). *B*: Anglo-Saxon hand-made pot. *C*: Frankish pottery bottle. Scale 1:3. (Dickinson and Speake 1992, Figs. 16-17)

The most impressive monuments to this period are the scatter of large, prominently sited round-barrows across the uplands of north-west Oxfordshire (Fig. 36), an area largely devoid of cemeteries before 600.[13] The dates of most of these are unknown, but at least four seem to have contained cremations. The great barrow at Asthall[14] covered the ashes of an early seventh-century man who was sent to the afterlife with his horse and a princely range of goods (Fig. 37): an elaborate suite of strap-fittings, a Byzantine cast-metal bowl, an antique silver cup, imported Merovingian pottery, horn or wooden vessels with decorated metal mounts, and a board-game with bone counters. This was someone of the highest status (the only other Anglo-Saxon burial to have yielded a solid silver vessel is the Sutton Hoo ship), and his funeral rite was unequivocally Anglian rather than Saxon. It has also been noted[15] that seventh-century cemeteries are on different sites from earlier ones (Fig. 38), and show a different pattern of grave-

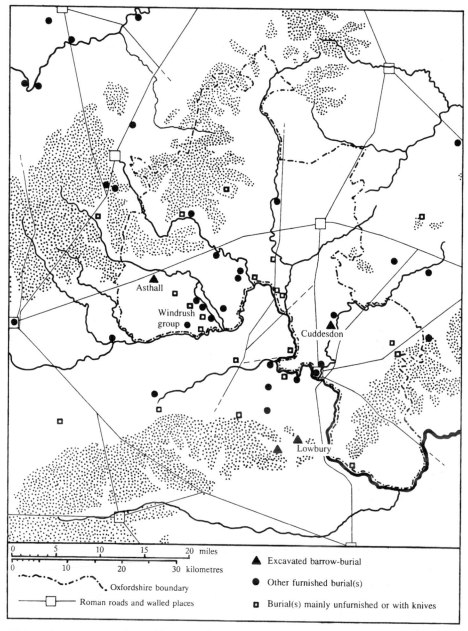

38 Seventh-century cemeteries, and later knife-furnished burials. (Cemeteries after Dickinson 1976, Fig. 53, with minor additions, and omitting uncertain and undated sites.)

goods. Especially striking is the concentration of seventh-century cemeteries in the Lower Windrush, at Standlake, Ducklington, Cokethorpe, Stanton Harcourt and Yelford:[16] some are notably rich, and they point to high-status communities in a zone which does not seem to have had concentrated settlement in the sixth century.

So can we identify the Asthall chieftain and the Windrush communities with Penda's invading armies? Hawkes was confident that 'the later seventh-century colonization of north-west Oxfordshire . . . was carried out by minor aristocracy of the Hwicce, and that the cemeteries give us a precious first glimpse of their initial landtakings'.[17] By that date, however, dress fashions had become universal, and the inhabitants of Ducklington or Standlake cannot be identified as distinctively Anglian: it may have been through changes in the local settlement pattern that these sites replaced the old-established Brighthampton cemetery nearby.[18] Even the slightly earlier and overtly Anglian barrow at Asthall is open to two interpretations: it could commemorate a conquering Mercian prince, but 'if the cultural symbolism is read as an act of "transculturation", that is the incorporation of élite Anglian burial fashions', we might consider a local king 'threatened on all sides by rival kings seeking his subordination, or even a member of the West Saxon dynasty in the early days of its resistance to Northumbrian or Mercian aggression'.[19]

The central question here is whether the Mercian annexation of the region is likely to have involved large movements of people. At a time so long after the original settlements, the reasonable assumption is probably that it did not. Anglo-Saxon kings were bent on military dominance and the annexation of tribute, not on ethnic displacement to create space for their own people: an image of Saxon families trudging away southwards with their cartloads of goods as similar convoys of Anglians moved in from the north would be anachronistic. What mattered was that the people of the Upper Thames, whether Saxon or Anglian, now owed their food-renders and military service to the Mercian over-lord or his deputy, not to the king of the Gewisse.

So while it is not at all unlikely that really top-rank burials such as Asthall are indeed the tombs of a Mercian military élite, ethnic interpretations of even the richest lesser graves seem unnecessary. It is more useful to note the striking changes in both the composition and the incidence of grave-goods. After 600, only a few burials contain more than the simplest objects. At the Yelford cemetery, for instance, twelve of the twenty-six graves were unaccompanied, and at Didcot Power Station the graves contained only simple objects such as knives, shears, a padlock, gaming-pieces and a copper-alloy ring.[20] In contrast to this general poverty, the small minority of properly furnished burials rank with the richest of earlier generations.[21] Occasional mid- to late seventh-century graves, especially in the Windrush group, have gold and garnet jewellery, bags, boxes and girdle-hung items, for instance Standlake grave 8 with its elaborate satchel-mounts and metal cross (Fig. 49).[22] At the same time, isolated barrow-burials show a wider diffusion of the 'princely' mode as the seventh century advanced. A barrow at Lowbury Hill on the edge of the Downs contained a late seventh-century man with his sword, spear, shield and a bronze hanging-bowl, as well as many other small possessions.[23] Such opulent burials, now in a universalised idiom found throughout England,[24] continued up to about 700 and certainly well beyond the Conversion.

Thus by 650 the deposition of grave-goods was confined to a narrow social group for whom it survived as a mark of special status. It may be that we see here a local élite whose power was political and official rather than tribal and customary, and who may have been increasingly hereditary. When the occupant of Standlake grave 8 was buried with a cross on her chatelaine, the Church was already starting to record territorial divisions on parchment for purposes of lordship and taxation. By Wulfhere's reign we are in a recognisably medieval world, of kings and nobles whose wealth depended on systems for exploiting the land and its assets.

KINGS AND UNDER-KINGS

'This was a world in which there were hierarchies of kings, and relativities of kingliness.'[25] The seventh century was an age of amalgamation and absorption: of 'tribal' *ingas*-type groups into local federations, and of local federations into over-kingdoms.[26] Although we cannot be certain, it seems highly likely that even 'great' kings of around the year 600, such as Ceawlin of the Gewisse or Æthelberht of Kent, commanded far smaller areas of territory than mid- to late seventh-century over-kings such as Penda or Wulfhere. The political map of the South Midlands revealed by our earliest texts was drawn during the years of Mercian dominance. Old divisions of the landscape were accommodated to the new requirements, military and domestic, of over-kings: tribal territories became provincial districts, and their focal places became the centres of delegated or itinerant rule.

Thus the landscape had to be organised for the needs of courts which were always on the move. A king and his retinue would circuit around his scattered houses, living off the local food-renders; the bigger the kingdom (and the retinue), the more extensive the circuit. Direct political control, depending as it did on the ruler's personal presence, was therefore subject to practical constraints: Wulfhere, for instance, could hardly spend his whole life circuiting around Greater Mercia. A major kingdom would therefore comprise a core area, subject to a food-render regime and in which the king was frequently seen, and peripheral areas which gave livestock tribute under military sanction, or which were delegated to reliable deputies. The latter would have their own quasi-royal households, and would circuit around their own groups of houses. Hence the 'sub-kings' (*subreguli*) so prominent in the late seventh and early eighth centuries, as Mercian overlords subjected weaker kings or replaced them with their own friends and relatives.[27]

This pattern of life required a network of sites which could accommodate large numbers of people on an episodic basis. It is in the seventh and eighth centuries that we can first recognise the royal centres called *tūnas* in Old English and *villae* in Latin: open-ground sites of the kind that we have encountered at Drayton and Wittenham, comprising domestic and farm buildings centred on a great timber hall (cf. Figs. 30, 63). As the central places of large and stable territories for purposes of law, administration and tax-gathering, they tended to acquire a long-term permanence: Benson is mentioned in the '571' Chronicle annal, and was still the most valuable royal manor in Oxfordshire in 1086 (above, p. 38 and below, p. 108). In the early 670s Wulfhere ratified a sub-king's charter 'in the residence which is called Thame' (below,

p. 61), and although this passed out of royal hands it was still the main place of east Oxfordshire in 1086, and like Benson the centre of a hundred (Fig. 62). Kings Sutton, in later Northamptonshire but the centre of a huge if ill-defined territory extending far into north Oxfordshire, seems another good candidate for an early royal vill.[28] How many other Domesday hundredal manors were already important in the Mercian period is impossible to say, but analogies would support the antiquity of the main outlines of local government as recorded in the tenth and eleventh centuries.

Kingdoms, on the other hand, could be very transient, and recent work has emphasised the artificial character of many of the seventh-century political groups. We cannot be at all certain about the extent of the Gewissian federation around 600, but we can be confident that it bore little resemblance to the provincial boundaries of a century later. By the later seventh century the kingdom of the Gewisse had been carved up, perhaps totally, between new entities: the Hwicce, the 'Ashdown province', Middle Anglia, and a province partly based on the lands of the *Cilternsæte*.

We have already seen that the Hwiccian groups probably gained political coherence in Penda's reign, and that Penda's victories may have given them control of areas, now eastern Gloucestershire, which had first been settled by Thames Valley Saxons. Was the eleventh-century boundary between Gloucestershire and Oxfordshire (also the boundary between Worcester and Dorchester dioceses) the frontier of the Hwicce under Penda, or did they come still further east? Margaret Gelling notes place-name evidence that 'Anglian influence was more marked west of a line roughly parallel with the west boundary of the county and about two and a half to three miles [eastwards] from it, perhaps indicating a strong Anglian element in the Hwicce'.[29] It is also notable that the main woodland area in west Oxfordshire was Wychwood (*Huiccewudu*), 'the wood of the Hwicce',[30] though it could have been so called specifically because it was an outlying resource (just as Watlington is not in the territory of the Wæclingas, nor *Horninga mære* in that of the Horningas: above, p. 35). On balance we should probably trust the evidence of the diocesan boundary, but it remains possible that parts of west Oxfordshire, broadly equivalent to the territories later centred on Bampton and Shipton-under-Wychwood, were once Hwiccian.[31]

Under the year 648 the Anglo-Saxon Chronicle records that King Cenwealh of the Gewisse 'gave to his kinsman Cuthred 3,000 hides of land near Ashdown'.[32] This hidage is perplexingly – perhaps suspiciously - large, exceeding the tenth-century hidage of the whole of Berkshire. Unless the figure has been inflated by mistranscription, the territory must have comprised not just the Berkshire Downs ('Ashdown') and the Vale, but also a large tract of north Wiltshire or west Oxfordshire. If the annal can be taken at face value this was a Gewissian sub-kingdom formed in the worst days of Penda's harassment, when the dynasty's power in the Upper Thames had little more than a decade to run. It is perhaps not surprising that we hear no more of it.

Eastwards and north-eastwards lay the multiplicity of *ingas*-type groups, so prominent in the Tribal Hidage, which stretched over to the borders of East Anglia and which were known collectively as the Middle Angles.[33] The trend of recent scholarship has been to see 'Middle Anglia' as an artificial entity, fought over by Mercians and East Angles in a struggle which, crucially for Mercian expansion in the south, Penda won.[34] In one of the clearest descriptions of delegated under-kingship,

Bede says that in 653 Penda appointed his son Peada, 'an excellent youth most worthy of the name and status of a king', as ruler of the Middle Angles.[35] It is quite possible that they had no corporate identity before this event. But where lay the south-western boundary of Peada's realm? There are persuasive arguments that much of north and north-eastern Oxfordshire was Middle Anglian (Fig. 39): the boundary with Northamptonshire and Buckinghamshire is ragged and artificial, with several county

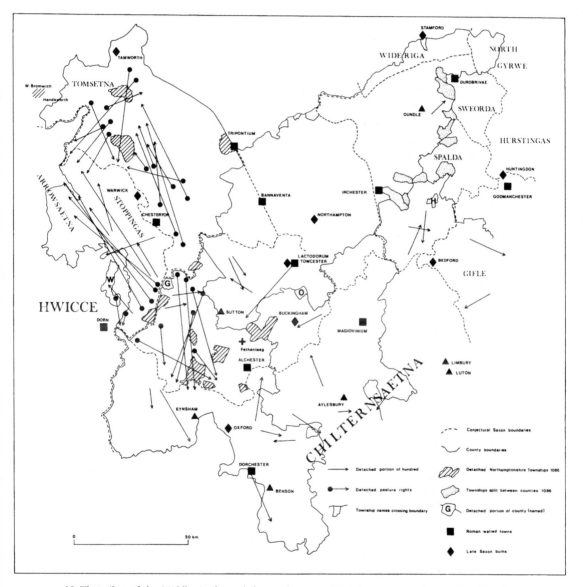

39 The tribes of the Middle Angles and the north-eastern Hwicce: reconstruction by Glen Foard, illustrating the Middle Anglian context of north Oxfordshire. G = Gloucestershire, O = Oxfordshire, H = Huntingdonshire, W = Warwickshire. (Foard 1985, Fig. 5)

outliers and territorial cross-linkages, and the Kings Sutton complex extended well into Oxfordshire.[36] Furthermore, the Middle Anglian *Færpingas* of Bede and the Tribal Hidage have been identified, admittedly on far from conclusive evidence, as the Charlbury district (below, p. 59), which if true would carry the further implication that seventh-century Wychwood was Middle Anglian.[37] From 737 the see of Leicester, which served the Middle Angles, probably included what was left of the old Dorchester diocese. At all events it was to Dorchester that this see returned when Leicester was overrun by Vikings in the late ninth century, which suggests that even central and south Oxfordshire could have been considered Middle Anglian.[38]

One of the larger peoples of the Tribal Hidage were the 'Chiltern-dwellers', the *Cilternsæte*, rated at 4,000 hides. Their name leaves no doubts about where they lived – their territory presumably included southernmost Oxfordshire as well as parts of Buckinghamshire and Hertfordshire[39] – but they never occur again. The sub-king Frithuwold, patron of Chertsey minster in the early 670s, can perhaps be equated with a semi-legendary brother-in-law of Wulfhere who ruled in the Aylesbury region (below, p. 61), and identified as a relative of the Middle Anglian nobleman Frithuric.[40] This hypothesis entails a great sub-kingdom covering Surrey, south-east Berkshire and south Buckinghamshire, which although conjectural is contradicted by no known facts. Such a kingdom, developing out of Middle Anglia around 670, would have been occasioned by Wulfhere's conquests in the Middle and Lower Thames and would have swallowed up much of the *Cilternsæte* province along with former Gewissian and Kentish lands.

These arrangements were very transient. The sub-kingdoms created for Cuthred, for Peada and for Frithuwold belonged to a very specific stage in English political development, and none lasted in its initial form for more than a generation. Nor need the formation of this kind of sub-kingdom have involved the suppression of lesser sub-kingdoms within it, or the alteration of older folk-group boundaries. Thus the question whether there was any part of future Oxfordshire which did not fall within the bounds of either the Hwicce, the Middle Angles or the *Cilternsæte* may be less important than it seems. Whatever the exact political configuration, it could well be that some local ruler, subject either directly or indirectly to the Mercian king, was based in one of the old Gewissian centres at Benson, Dorchester or Eynsham. Just possibly, we can catch a distant echo of such a person in one late and unreliable group of texts.

THE FRIDESWIDE LEGEND:
A SUB-KINGDOM IN THE UPPER THAMES?

The legend of St. Frideswide of Oxford is known only from sources post-dating the re-foundation of her house as an Augustinian priory in the early 1120s.[41] The historian William of Malmesbury visited it soon after this, and wrote a summary of the story. At about the same time an amateurish and simple-minded author wrote a full-length *Vita* ('Life A'). It would be absurd to think that these hagiographical works, written four centuries after Frideswide's death, contain an accurate historical narrative.

40 '*They got into the boat and, guided by the Lord, arrived within an hour's space at the town called Bampton. . . . Then blessed Frideswide, fearing the wicked king's snares, went with her virgins into a certain wood [called Binsey], not far from that town.*' The legend of St. Frideswide's flight from Oxford, recorded in a hand probably that of the early twelfth-century historian John of Worcester. Just below actual size. (Blair 1987a, Fig.1)

It is not impossible, however, that they preserve traditions of people, places and arrangements that really did exist in the late seventh-century Upper Thames.

Malmesbury's story is a very simple one. A princess named Frideswide is pursued, despite her monastic vows, by a young king madly in love with her. He chases her into a wood, from which she escapes to Oxford. The king follows her there, but she prays for divine protection and he is struck blind as he enters the town. Recognising the error of his ways, he begs Frideswide's forgiveness and regains his sight, leaving her in peace to found a monastery in Oxford where eventually she ends her days.

'Life A' is much more elaborate, and contains some important differences. Frideswide's parents are named as Didan 'king of Oxford' and Sefrida his queen. Didan founds and endows the monastery, and Frideswide and twelve companions are established there as nuns. Her suitor is Algar 'king of Leicester', not merely an over-persistent young man but a savage tyrant. He sends messengers to demand Frideswide's hand. Miraculous intervention saves her from the messengers, and they report back to Algar who sets out in person to take her. Warned by an angel, Frideswide goes to the Thames with two companions; they are met by an angelic boatman, who transports them up-river to Bampton where they hide in a swineherd's hut in 'a certain wood called Binsey' (Figs. 40, 47). Meanwhile Algar tries to enter Oxford and is struck blind, remaining, in this version, uncured and unrepentant for the rest of his days. Frideswide stays at Bampton for three years, working miraculous cures. The nuns then return by boat to Oxford, where Frideswide continues her life of prayer and abstinence until her death on 19 October 727.

These narratives seem to be independent and muddled versions of the same body of tradition. The grossest confusion is in the location of Binsey, which in fact lies less than two miles from Oxford: the miracle-stories show that there were legends of Frideswide at both Bampton and Binsey, which the author of 'Life A' has conflated. But at least the action of this drama has a very definite location: in the former Upper Thames heartland of the Gewisse, and specifically in the territories of Bampton, Eynsham and Oxford. The local detail is consistent with likely mid-Saxon conditions. Bampton and Oxford had minster churches, and St. Frideswide's chapel at Binsey stands in an ancient earthwork enclosure (below, pp. 61–4, 67). There was even a notable 'piggery' (*porcheria*) at Bampton in the twelfth century.[42] Most significant is the prominence of the Thames, on whose banks stood both of Frideswide's churches: the story surely belongs to a world in which there was regular river-traffic of a non-miraculous kind between Oxford and Bampton.

Was 'Didan king of Oxford' a real person? The name causes no problems if it can be reconstructed as something like 'Didda' or 'Dæda': Deddington, for instance, is 'Dæda's *tūn*', and Bede knew a priest 'Deda'.[43] This is quite possible, since the author of 'Life A' could have misunderstood a weak genitive in -*n* in a phrase such as *filia Didan regis*.[44] But whatever his name, he is plausible in both time and place. If his daughter died at a mature age in 727, he was roughly a contemporary of King Wulfhere. A territory containing both Bampton and Oxford, but perhaps based on Eynsham half-way between them, is exactly how we might envisage a sub-kingdom in Wulfhere's time; a late memory of it may be the huge 300-hide estate 'at Eynsham' which belonged to the see of Canterbury by the 820s (below, p. 63). Frideswide's name (in its correct form 'Frithuswith', 'peace-strong') may even suggest kinship with 'Didan's' eastern neighbours, the family of Frithuwold and Frithuric who were ruling in Middle Anglia and the Lower Thames. It would be purely through later developments, which eclipsed the old centre while bringing a newer one to national prominence, that a 'king of Eynsham' came to be thought of as 'king of Oxford'.

POWER IN THE THAMES VALLEY, 686–825

After the 680s the West Saxons, the resurgent Gewisse of Hampshire and Wiltshire, were a force to be reckoned with: even the greatest Mercian kings never fully subdued them. Mercia none the less kept its grip on Middle Anglia until well into the ninth century, and even the Thames Valley and the broad vale north of the Berkshire Downs remained Mercian except for interludes. The powerful West Saxon kings Cædwalla (686–8) and Ine (688–726) beat the Mercians back from the lower Thames and south Berkshire, but the basis of the received view that they ruled in the Vale of the White Horse has now collapsed with the re-attribution of the early Abingdon charters.[45] For geographical reasons control of the Vale may well have accompanied control of north Wiltshire, and there Malmesbury received patronage from both sides during the 680s to 700s, though it was evidently more in the West Saxon than the Mercian ambit.[46] The whole area between the Cotswolds and the Berkshire and Wiltshire Downs must have been highly unstable, and under heavy Mercian influence even when Wessex controlled it.

The Mercian overlord Æthelbald (716–57) exerted great influence in the south-east, and even enjoyed some kind of overlordship over the West Saxons.[47] Both the chronology and the geography of his conquests south of the Thames are ill-defined, especially in the earlier part of his reign, and it is unclear how much he had to recover and how much the Mercians had never really lost. There is evidence, for instance, that London had been in Mercian hands during the reign of Coenred (704–9),[48] and it is arguable that the Thames was essentially a Mercian corridor from Wulfhere's reign to Æthelbald's. The Mercian grip on its upper reaches was not, however, wholly secure. In 752 King Cuthred of Wessex 'fought at *Beorhford* against Æthelbald king of the Mercians and put him to flight'.[49] We do not know what territory Cuthred won, but it could well have been the Upper Thames, where his successor Cynewulf was in control a few years later.[50]

Even Offa (757–96), the most powerful of all Mercian kings, seems not to have recovered the Vale region until 779, when he attacked Cynewulf at Benson and 'captured the vill'.[51] The Abingdon chronicler, writing centuries later, thought that Offa's victory gained him the terrain between the Thames and the Berkshire Downs ridgeway, apparently extending westwards to the later Wiltshire boundary.[52] The Downs could well have been Offa's frontier with Wessex, though a later charter[53] ascribes to him a grant at Farnborough, which lies slightly south of the ridgeway. Further west, negotiated land-acquisitions near Bath and Malmesbury show Offa consolidating this frontier in the aftermath of the battle of Benson.[54] South-eastwards his power went much further, running down the Thames to London as Æthelbald's had done before him. In the Middle Thames area he captured various centres, including Cookham, from Cynewulf, perhaps as a result of the Benson victory.[55] In Kent, Sussex and Surrey he had already established a hold which, if intermittent, was stronger than that of any alien king before him. In Offa's England the Thames was a corridor between major elements in a great territorial federation.[56]

The deeds of an eighth-century king, however great, rarely outlived him, but Offa's successor Coenwulf (796–821) was successful in maintaining Mercian power. His own homeland may have been much nearer to Oxfordshire than that of earlier Mercian kings: it has been suggested that he was the heir to Hwiccian princes whose hereditary lands were centred on Winchcombe.[57] This was to be the site of the cult of Cynehelm ('St. Kenelm'), Coenwulf's murdered son,[58] and the dedication to him of the poorly documented but evidently early church of Minster Lovell (below, p. 66) may hint at the extension of this family's influence into what was to become Oxfordshire.[59] In about 821 Coenwulf further consolidated his land-base in the Upper Thames by acquiring a huge, probably monastic estate centred on Eynsham (below, p. 63).

But meanwhile the West Saxon kingdom had been growing, slowly but steadily, to the point where it could end nearly two centuries of Mercian dominance. A very late tradition of a West Saxon victory against Coenwulf in 821, apparently at Cherbury

Camp in the Vale, would if genuine indicate northwards pressure across this long-debated terrain towards the Upper Thames.[60] In 825 King Ecgberht of Wessex fought the Mercian king at Wroughton (Wilts.) and permanently annexed Kent, Surrey, Sussex and Essex.[61] Four years later, in the rather inflated words of the patriotic West Saxon chronicler, Ecgberht 'conquered the kingdom of the Mercians and everything south of the Humber'.[62] This 'conquest' only lasted a year, but the positions of Mercia and Wessex had been decisively reversed. Relations between the two major kingdoms re-adjusted quickly, and hereafter would be set on a more diplomatic course: an alliance of mutual interest in which Wessex was the senior partner. This pattern was to continue through Alfred's reign and beyond.

The fortunes of the Upper Thames between 686 and 825 are in line with earlier rather than later history. Territories remained coherent around their centres, but were kicked like footballs between competing kings; overlords such as Offa and Coenwulf built up huge federations, in an age when dynastic succession was too unstable to permit their survival. Was there any time, during these various boundary changes, when the Thames itself was a frontier? The answer may well be 'No'.[63] The early territory of the Gewisse had been formed around the Upper Thames, and it was probably as an entity that Wulfhere took it over. The north boundary of the short-lived 'Ashdown province' could have been the Thames, but this was an apportioned sub-kingdom with 'friendly' territory northwards. The later Abingdon chronicler thought that the Wessex–Mercia frontier between 752 and 779 was the Thames, but Benson itself, which was evidently West Saxon during these years, lies on the Oxfordshire bank. If Patrick Sims-Williams is right to suggest that the Anglo-Saxon Chronicle annal for '571', which mentions Benson and Eynsham, was shaped with an eye to the events of these years,[64] it seems that Cuthred's victory in 752 gave him part of west Oxfordshire as well as the Vale. It is also possible that two large early estates straddled the Thames between Oxfordshire and north Berkshire.[65]

In the conditions of the time, the natural frontier was not the Thames but the Downs. Above Oxford the river is not wide or deep enough to be an effective barrier against moving armies: any commander would make straight for the ridgeway along the crest of the Downs, as the two Viking invasions were to show. Insofar as controlling the crucial Thames corridor meant controlling land on either side of it, nobody is likely to have been satisfied with it as a long-term boundary.[66] What the river offered was not defensibility but precise demarcation; it emerged as the permanent frontier once Wessex and Mercia reached the stage of settling their differences by negotiation rather than force of arms.

THE FIRST RELIGIOUS CENTRES

In its religious as well as its political narrative, St. Frideswide's legend is a window on the late seventh-century world: a king founds a monastic community on one of his estates, and makes his daughter its first abbess. Between 660 and 750 both Wessex and Mercia saw an unparalleled number of religious foundations, many of them double houses ruled by that generation of princess-saints who have been aptly termed the 'holy cousinhood'.[67] To us these places are most clearly visible in the kingdom of the

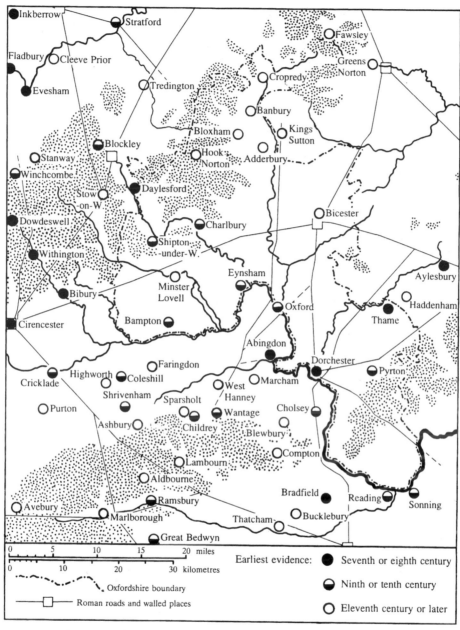

41 Minsters of the Upper Thames region.

Hwicce, where the unrivalled Worcester archive charts their foundation and later history.[68] The evidence for the Oxfordshire minsters (Fig. 41) is far poorer, and we know them mainly from late sources and unreliable hagiographies. None the less, the pattern which emerges resembles that of the Hwiccian lands, and indeed of many parts of England: a network of major religious centres housing wealthy communities of monks, nuns and clergy, which provided devotional, and eventually economic, foci for their surrounding territories. Some of the most important structural changes in the society and landscape of England between the eighth and twelfth centuries can be ascribed directly or indirectly to these establishments, which (to avoid the narrower and anachronistic connotations of 'monastery') will be described here by the vernacular Old English term 'minster'.[69]

It is impossible to know how far the work of Birinus and Agilbert survived the Mercian invasion, but Dorchester itself continued as some kind of religious centre, reappearing briefly in the late 670s as a Mercian see under bishop Ætla.[70] A cathedral, like any other important church, would have had its religious community, and this could well have continued even though episcopal functions ceased. The later re-emergence of Dorchester as a West Saxon bishopric, and as a post-Conquest mother church (below, pp. 111–12, 116), suggest some continuity. Excavations in the north-west corner of the Roman town have revealed a concentration of small rectangular timber 'halls' (Fig. 42) which were twice rebuilt on a larger scale and in stone, the

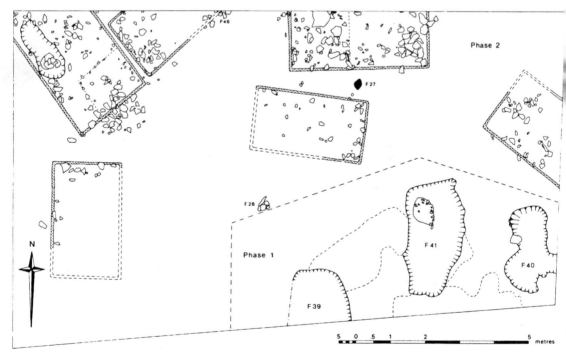

42 Dorchester: timber buildings in the north-west corner of the Roman town, probably associated with the seventh-century cathedral and minster community. (Rowley & Brown 1981, Fig. 5)

sequence spanning (probably) the seventh century to the mid-ninth. These structures lay not far west of the Abbey church, and their resemblance in form, density and evolution to domestic buildings found on other pre-Viking monastic sites is striking.[71] The south-west corner of the town contained a complex of larger-scale timber buildings (Fig.9), and although the evidence is sadly inconclusive a post-Conversion but pre-Viking date seems on the whole most likely.[72] Outside the walls to the north-west, the Bishop's Court site has produced fragmentary settlement evidence and a small seventh-century cemetery, as well as the anthropomorphic lock (Fig. 34).[73] Dorchester may never have lost its status as the mother church of the Upper Thames.

It is unlikely, though, that the systematic endowment of minsters began before the consolidation of Mercian power in the region. Unusually among contemporary rulers, Penda never adopted Christianity. He let missionaries practice in his territories, however, and his son Peada, sub-king of Middle Anglia, converted on marrying the Northumbrian king Osuiu's daughter. An English mission to the Mercians, Northumbrian-influenced and with a Middle Anglian base, was therefore operating in the early 650s. Bede tells us that when Peada was baptized in Northumbria he

> received four priests, who seemed suitable in their learning and way of life to teach and baptize that people, and returned home in great joy. The priests were Cedd, and Adda, and Betti and Diuma, of whom the last was of the Irish race, the others English. . . . These things began two years before King Penda's death. After he had been killed [655/6] and the Christian King Osuiu had taken his kingdom . . ., Diuma, one of the same four priests, was ordained by Bishop Finan as bishop of both the Middle Angles and the Mercians; for there were so few priests that it was necessary for one bishop to rule the two peoples. In a short time he brought many people to the Lord, then died among the Middle Angles in the region called *Infeppingum*.[74]

The fact that Bede bothers to mention it suggests that Diuma's base at *Infeppingum*, wherever that was, was an important centre: a monastery under his control, perhaps his main episcopal church insofar as an Irish bishop would have had one. The name appears as *Færpinga* (glossed 'in Middle Anglia') in the Tribal Hidage, but is otherwise unknown. There is a clue, however, in the early eleventh-century list of resting-places of English saints, in the section believed to copy a lost pre-Viking text.[75] This mentions a St. 'Dioma' or 'Dionia' whose relics lay at Charlbury (*Ceorlincburh*), which it wrongly locates by the Windrush. If this was Diuma, the presence of his bones at Charlbury (which did not continue as a major centre likely to acquire relics later) may well identify it as the centre of the *Færpingas* region. Raised on its bluff overlooking the Evenlode (Fig. 43), Charlbury church is appropriately sited for a seventh-century Irish monastery, and the curvilinear road-pattern of the town may reflect the outline of an early precinct.[76]

Between the eclipse of Dorchester and the foundation (in 737) of Leicester diocese, the Upper Thames area belonged to the Mercian see of Lichfield, established under Wulfhere's patronage in 669. Its first bishop, Chad, was a Northumbrian educated in Ireland, and Irish influence on the emergent church in the South Midlands must have been considerable. Susan Kelly's review of texts long mis-ascribed to Abingdon

43 Charlbury church, raised dramatically on its scarp above the Evenlode. Perhaps an important religious site since the time of St. Diuma.

concludes that the minster of Bradfield, near Reading, was probably founded in the late 660s or early 670s by one Eadfrith son of Iddi, and that fragments can be recovered of a charter, probably in Celtic form, witnessed by three Mercian bishops.[77] This important new evidence suggests, as one might in any case have expected, that minsters founded in north Berkshire during Wulfhere's reign fell within the ambit of the Mercian Irish clergy.

It is rarely easy to see who were the prime movers in monastic foundations. Much of the direction must have come from bishops, and the endowments were usually ratified by over-kings' charters. In many cases the real lay patron was a local sub-king or magnate (for instance Eadfrith son of Iddi, or King 'Didan' of Oxford?), eager to found a minster on his own land and keep it under his family's control. But great kings too saw advantages in spreading a net of minsters over their newly-won lands: royal power-houses in subject territory, ruled over by the over-king's sisters and daughters.

An early eighth-century writer portrays King Wulfhere as a keen monastic founder,[78] and this is borne out by specific local evidence. The minsters at Thame, Aylesbury and Bicester are only known from late sources, but there are indications linking all of them with Wulfhere and his immediate family. In the early 670s, Frithuwold's endowment for Chertsey minster was 'confirmed by Wulfhere, king of the Mercians, for he both placed his hand on the altar in the residence which is called Thame and subscribed with the sign of the Holy Cross in his own hand'.[79] This may mean no more than a household chapel, but post-Conquest sources independently mark Thame out as an ex-minster.[80] So do topographical factors: like so many minsters Thame church is sited in a river-bend, and once again the surrounding road-pattern suggests the outline of an early precinct.[81]

For the origins of Aylesbury minster (in later Buckinghamshire) we have only the fragmentary twelfth-century life of St. Osgyth. This tells us that her parents were King Frithuwold and a sister of Wulfhere, that she was born in her father's palace at Quarrendon, and that she was brought up by her aunt St. Eadgyth at Aylesbury where her church was later established.[82] That Aylesbury was an important religious site is proved by the recent discovery of eighth-century graves, part of a large cemetery inside the Iron Age fort which gives it its name ('Ægel's *burh*').[83] The Osgyth material also introduces us to her aunt Eadburh, yet another saintly sister of Wulfhere, and it has been plausibly suggested that this was the St. Eadburh whose bones were later enshrined not far away at Bicester.[84] This last church (its *chester* name perhaps acquired by transference from the nearby Roman town of Alchester) is again marked out as a minster by late sources, and was finally reformed as an Augustinian priory in the twelfth century.[85]

The existence of early royal minsters at Thame, Aylesbury and Bicester must thus be pieced together from chance references, dubious traditions and much later evidence. As so often, we are left with mere traces of a movement which was of immense cultural significance, and which was part of a rapid and profound change in English civilisation. The decades after 660, the age of St. Wilfrid, St. Cuthbert and Archbishop Theodore of Tarsus, were the golden age of the rich, cosmopolitan life of early Christian England. Never again, probably, was so much land and money devoted within such a short space of time to the expansion of the English Church. Where Oxfordshire is concerned the art and the learning are lost to us; there are only traces of contacts with a wider and more exotic world, such as Æthelmod's gift in 681 of 'land by the Cherwell' to the Frankish-founded double minster at Bath.[86]

It is of course to this world that the Frideswide legend relates. Her community was one of a series of important Thames-side minsters on the second gravel terrace, where earlier Anglo-Saxon settlement had been so prolific. The first clear references come no earlier than the start of the eleventh century: the entry *Đonne resteð Sancta Fryðeswyð on Oxnaforda* in the list of saints' resting-places, a grant in 1004 to 'a certain minster situated in the town called Oxford where the most blessed Frideswide rests', and a note of her feast on 19 October in an Abingdon Abbey calendar.[87] The topographical and archaeological evidence, however, has been accumulating, and the importance of the town which was later to grow up around Frideswide's church gives it a special interest.

Oxford stands on a large, flat peninsula of the gravel terrace (Fig. 55),[88] bounded by a great loop of the broad, many-channelled Thames to the west and south and by the

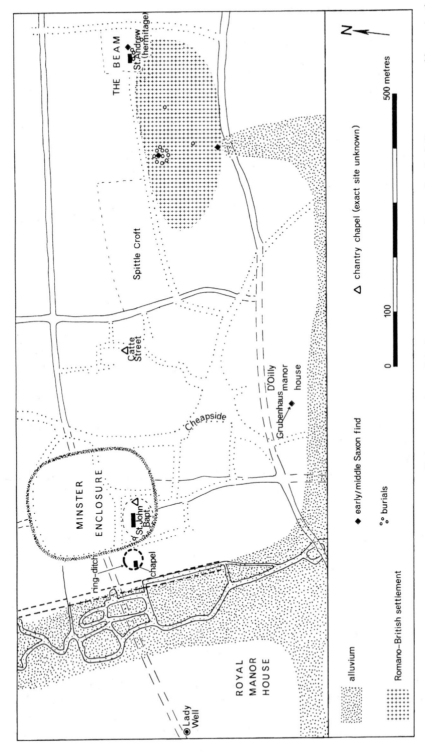

44 Bampton: an axially-planned religious complex. A series of holy sites in and around the later town preserve traces of a complex ritual alignment, presumably associated with St. Beornwald's monastic community. South-east of the main enclosure is the large triangular market-place, evidence of post-Conquest urban growth.

THE BEAM

St. Andrew (hermitage)

Spittle Croft

Catte Street

Cheapside

D'Oilly

Grubenhaus manor house

MINSTER ENCLOSURE

ring-ditch

St. John Bapt.

chapel

ROYAL MANOR HOUSE

Lady Well

N

◆ early/middle Saxon find

△ chantry chapel (exact site unknown)

°° burials

alluvium

Romano-British settlement

0   100   500 metres

Cherwell to the east. At the extreme southern edge of the gravel is the Romanesque priory church (now Oxford cathedral) which replaced St. Frideswide's minster. Hard up against its cloister ran the Trill Mill Stream, a relict channel of the Thames which must have formed the south boundary of the first ecclesiastical precinct.[89] This had largely dried up by the early centuries AD, but in apparently the eighth century its northern edge was re-cut and lined with stakes. This seems to have been associated with an artificial raising of the water-level, whether for defence, mill-power or navigation.[90]

Along the north bank of this stream, overlooking the Thames floodplain, there may have stood a line of churches, perpetuated into the later middle ages as the priory church and as the parish churches of St. Aldate and St. Ebbe.[91] 'Life A' of St. Frideswide mentions an 'original' dedication to the Holy Trinity, St. Mary and All Saints, perhaps a garbled memory of three churches of which St. Mary's, where the saint was believed to have been buried, preceded the Romanesque priory church.[92] No remains of any early church have yet been found, but a cemetery to the south and west of the cathedral has produced late Anglo-Saxon burials, some on beds of charcoal.[93] The west precinct boundary may well be marked by a north–south ditch, V-shaped and containing seventh- to eighth-century pottery, which underlay a late Anglo-Saxon road to the west of St. Ebbe's church (Fig. 86).[94]

Up-river from Oxford lies Eynsham, a minster which in its origins may have been much more important. We have already seen that the Bronze Age enclosure on the edge of the gravel terrace contained some sixth- to seventh-century buildings (above, p. 27), and over these a group of ground-level timber structures was built during the seventh to tenth centuries.[95] Finds included three eighth-century coins, which are rare on ordinary domestic sites, as well as a large slab of plaster from the wall of a high-quality timber building with close-spaced squared posts. Given that these structures directly underlay the abbey buildings of 1005 (below, pp. 114–16) a monastic use seems likely, and two texts support this. The first is the agreement of c. 821 by which the archbishop of Canterbury relinquished to King Coenwulf of Mercia, in return for the Kentish minsters of Reculver and Minster-in-Thanet, a 300-hide estate at *Iogneshomme*, almost certainly Eynsham.[96] The wider context is the series of bitter wrangles over monastic property which were such a feature of the late eighth and early ninth centuries (below, pp. 67–8), and although not stated explicitly it seems highly likely that this huge estate was centred on a minster. The second text, dated 864, is a grant by the Mercian king of five hides at Water Eaton, the grantee to pay 30s. 'to Eynsham to that church' after one year,[97] which looks very much like compensation for the dispersal of monastic lands. Taken together, the archaeological and written evidence make a compelling case for an extremely rich minster at Eynsham, which the see of Canterbury had presumably acquired at some point in the seventh or eighth century.

Bampton was the highest minster on the Thames water-way. It occupies a gravel promontory in a bend of the Shill Brook, a stream which feeds into the Thames between the Leach and Windrush confluences. This minster is first mentioned in the 950s, by which time it housed a religious community venerating the relics of an otherwise unknown saint named Beornwald.[98] So far it has not yielded such clear archaeological evidence as Eynsham, but it possessed a linear sequence of religious sites of remarkable complexity (Fig. 44).[99] The main church occupies one corner of a large oval enclosure which, like those already mentioned at Charlbury and Thame, is reflected in the road-pattern; in this case excavation has shown that the road overlies an Anglo-Saxon boundary ditch, four metres wide. Immediately westwards stands a late eleventh-century chapel, built within the circuit of a Bronze Age barrow-ditch (Fig. 31) which may also be respected by the great oval enclosure. Westwards again, beyond the stream, was a holy well; further out to the east, but axially aligned on the main church, was a twelfth-century chapel dedicated to St. Andrew. Although no one of these sites is demonstrably of pre-Viking origin, the general configuration resembles the linear groups of churches which characterise major religious establishments in both England and Gaul between the seventh and ninth centuries.[100] St. Andrew's chapel stands on the edge of a large Iron Age and Roman site, in a location known by the fourteenth century as the 'Beam'. This exceptionally interesting minor place-name seems to be the origin of the name of Bampton itself (*beām tūn*, 'the *tūn* by the beam'). Whatever the 'beam' was – presumably some kind of post or obelisk – it was a focus for ritual activity long before the chapel: many burials have been found nearby, one of them accompanied by a seventh-century bronze pin. There are hints here of that most elusive of sequences: Christian adoption of a pagan Anglo-Saxon religious site.

Only one early minster is known to have stood on the Berkshire bank of the Upper Thames. Abingdon is a community about which we know less than has hitherto been assumed:[101] it now seems that the early charters transcribed in the Abingdon Chronicles are in fact the archive of the lost minster at Bradfield. None the less, the garbled traditions in the Chronicles may contain germs of truth. The minster stands on the great estate of *Earmundesleah* (Fig. 33), one of the early endowments of Bradfield, so it seems possible that it was founded as a cell of that community. The witness-list from the putative Celtic charter by which Bradfield was established around 670 includes the name of one Æbbe. Susan Kelly has suggested[102] that this otherwise unknown lady may have given her name both to Abingdon itself (Æbbe's *dūn* or hill) and to the small Anglo-Saxon church of St. 'Ebbe' in Oxford, perhaps part of the St. Frideswide's complex (above, p. 63). This ingenious idea may have recovered for us another member of the 'holy cousinhood', prominent in the early religious life of the Upper Thames.

But the problems do not end there. Abingdon lies in the Thames floodplain and is anything but a *dūn*, whereas in the tenth century *Abbandun* survived as a name for part of Boars Hill.[103] The Chronicles tell a complicated story that the minster moved from the hill to the valley site, which had previously been called *Seovechesham*. This name is plausible (its first element also occurs in nearby Seacourt, *Seofecanwyrthe*), but the narrative could be a rationalisation of something more straightforward: that the *dūn* had given its name to the whole surrounding territory including *Seovechesham*, for instance, or that there were two linked religious communities, one on the hill and the other by the Thames. The Chronicle also contains a parallel story that the abbess Cille (a member of the family which we must now identify as proprietors of Bradfield) built her nunnery at *Helnestoue*, in other words 'Helen-stow' or the area around St. Helen's in Abingdon, and that the nuns subsequently moved to the top of Wytham hill where they remained until ejected by Offa. Extracting genuine history from this hotch-potch is probably a lost cause, though the association of river-side with hill-top sites does possibly conform to genuine patterns of eighth-century monasticism (below, p. 67). At least it looks as though the forgers who appropriated the Bradfield archive were also faced with genuine Abingdon traditions, recalling a minster of some complexity.

Archaeology supports this conclusion.[104] The likely nucleus is not the later Abbey but the church of St. Helen, tucked into the south-west corner of the late Iron Age valley-fort at the confluence of Thames and Ock. This promontory site is inherently convincing, and early 'archaeologists' explored it to good effect. 'In this town', wrote the thirteenth-century Chronicler, 'crosses and other images are found buried here and there'. An especially prized relic was the 'Black Cross', believed to have been made from a nail of the Crucifixion, which had been dug up at St. Helen's. A sketch of this object in the Chronicle (Fig. 45) reveals its true identity: a cruciform disc-headed pin, closely resembling eighth-century examples from monastic sites such as Whitby and Flixborough.[105] 'The Black Cross', Gabrielle Lambrick wrote, 'constitutes independent evidence of the most convincing kind for the existence of an early Christian establishment of some description on this site; all unknowingly, the monks chose to emphasize, and to illustrate, the one item in their discoveries at Helenstow which confirms for the modern archaeologist the essential truth of the traditions.'[106] Together with a fine ornamental mount from nearby Culham (Fig. 45), possibly a stray from the same community,[107] it shows that eighth-century Abingdon shared the rich 'minster culture' known to us mainly from sites in northern and eastern England.[108]

The Thames-side minsters are a well-defined and on the whole well-recorded group. The valleys of the Cherwell, Evenlode and Windrush contained other minsters, but few of them are mentioned before the Conquest. In the Cherwell Valley, Banbury,

45 The early eighth-century 'minster culture' at Abingdon. *Left*: The 'Black Cross of Abingdon', as drawn in the thirteenth-century Chronicle. Size unknown. *Right*: Gilt-bronze mount found at Culham. Actual size (Hood & Speake 1987).

Cropredy, Bloxham and Adderbury were important churches in the eleventh to thirteenth centuries, all at major manorial centres of the bishop of Lincoln and the earl of Mercia and all controlling chapelries.[109] In no case is there any earlier evidence for minster status, though the topography of Bloxham is suggestive (Fig. 70), and at Cropredy the river-confluence associated with St. Freomund's cult has a huge round enclosure and place-names containing the Old English terms *preost*, 'priest' and *ancra*, 'hermit' (below, p. 75 and Fig. 51). Adderbury, 'Eadburh's *burh*', recalls other *burh* names which denote early monastic sites ruled by women,[110] and in later hagiography it was identified as the home of St. Eadburh of Bicester (below, p. 74). This odd concentration of ill-recorded minsters along the Cherwell extends a pattern evident in the neighbouring part of Northamptonshire (Fig. 41); the structure of the region is complex and puzzling in other ways, and may reflect the breakup of a very large territory centred on Kings Sutton.[111]

On the Evenlode above Charlbury was the royal hundredal manor of Shipton-under-Wychwood. Its church stands out clearly as a minster: it controlled several chapelries, and burials from the area between the church and the river have been dated on radiocarbon evidence to the ninth century (Fig. 46).[112] On the Windrush, Minster Lovell was actually called *Minstre* in 1086; both the dedication to St. Cynehelm (above, p. 55) and the post-Conquest use of the church as a Benedictine cell[113] are further indications of its status, though there is no hint of a mother-parish. At Hook Norton there are tenuous suggestions of a small minster serving the former royal vill, possibly on a different site from the present parish church.[114]

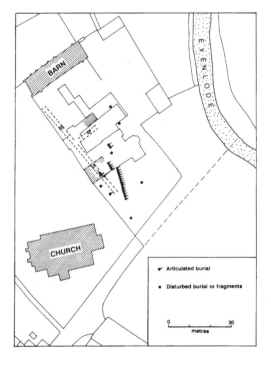

46 Shipton-under-Wychwood: archaeological evidence for centralised burial practice. Ninth- or tenth-century graves underlying the Prebendal House show that the cemetery serving the minster parish was much larger than the present churchyard. Its contraction presumably reflects the decline of mother-church rights and the appearance of dispersed manorial graveyards from the tenth century onwards. (Blair 1992b)

In all these cases the evidence is unsatisfactory and tantalising. Some could be early and important (Adderbury and Cropredy look promising), but several may well be later and lesser foundations, resulting from changes in administrative and tenurial geography up to and beyond the Viking invasions.[115] More work is clearly needed.

A notable feature of nearly all the minsters of the region was their proximity to water-transport. The Thames-side communities were either directly on the river itself (Oxford, Abingdon), or on streams feeding into it (Bampton, Eynsham, Dorchester). Charlbury and Shipton overlooked the Evenlode, Minster Lovell the Windrush, Thame the Thame, Banbury and Cropredy the Cherwell; Bicester is on a stream feeding into the Ray, and Adderbury and Bloxham are on one feeding into the Cherwell. This is part of a wider pattern, evident throughout England and especially well-illustrated by the series of important minsters which run down the Thames from source to estuary.[116] It is hard to believe that the minsters did not develop the water-fronts for profit: these locations emphasise their centrality in the economic systems which were growing around them in the seventh and eighth centuries, and which ensured the re-birth of many of them as small towns between the tenth and twelfth (below, pp. 119–21).

This was a world in which religious life centred on minsters, not on parish churches: if 'one-priest' churches existed before the tenth century, we have no knowledge of them.[117] None the less, the mother-parishes would have contained a range of devotional foci such as outlying graveyards, holy wells (abundant in Oxfordshire) and perhaps free-standing crosses.[118] Minsters should not be conceived as single, enclosed nuclei, but rather as complex entities pervading their dependent territories. We have already noted the elaborate linear sequence at Bampton; others could have consisted of paired sites (Bloxham and Adderbury, Cropredy and Prescot?), or have had outlying components such as cells, hermitages or processional stations.[119] Thus the improbable-sounding stories in the Abingdon Chronicle about monastic communities on Boars Hill and Wytham Hill may contain a grain of truth. One suggestive site is Binsey, north-west of Oxford and less than two miles from Wytham Hill. Here, according to twelfth-century legend, St. Frideswide and her companions paused for a period of seclusion in 'a place entangled with many kinds of trees, called *Thornbiri* in the Saxon tongue because of the many different species of thorns there, lonely and most suitable for devotion', and a well sprang up in answer to her prayers.[120] Binsey church and its holy well stand on the north edge of an oval enclosure (Fig. 47), presumably *Thornbiri*, where excavations in 1987 revealed a perimeter ditch and stone revetment associated with scraps of early Anglo-Saxon pottery; an early eighth-century coin (Fig. 52) was found somewhere nearby.[121] Could these be examples of the 'remoter houses', used by ecclesiastics for Lenten retreats, which are mentioned in some eighth-century texts?[122]

Minsters remained important throughout the Anglo-Saxon period, but the extraordinary power and wealth which they enjoyed between the late seventh and mid-eighth centuries was never to come again. For kings of Wulfhere's generation they were a new and exciting means of widening horizons and extending royal power; for kings of Offa's they were entrenched, bound up with secular interests, and consumers of much-needed resources. The patronage of royal and noble families had been the original source of their wealth, and the communities had no real protection against the political and military needs of kings or the consequences of dynastic feuds.

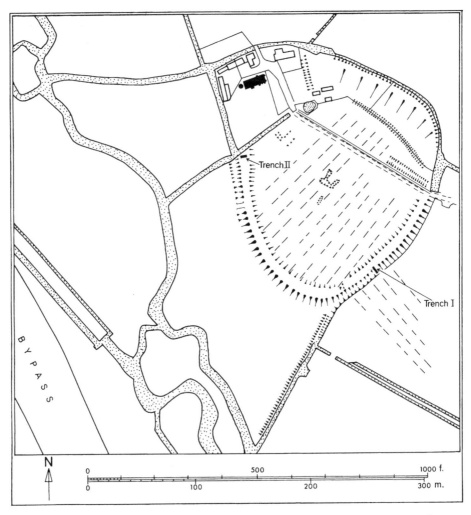

47 Binsey: the earthwork enclosure ('Thornbury'), with Binsey chapel and St. Frideswide's well on its northern edge. (Blair 1988d, Fig. 4)

A family minster was exactly that: if the patrons needed the land which they had once bestowed, they had few qualms about taking it back again. Thus the endowments of the minsters, built up so high by 750, gradually decayed over the next three centuries. In Oxfordshire, Eynsham best illustrates this common experience: the 300-hide estate was appropriated by the Mercian king around 821, we have a record of the alienation of five hides in 864, and by 1005 only thirty hides remained to the minster.[123] Furthermore, the locations of many minsters and their incipient economic role made them strategic centres worth controlling. Offa's annexation of the Middle Thames was conceived by a slightly later Canterbury writer as the capture of 'Cookham minster and many other towns' (*coenobium Coccham et alias urbes quamplurimas*).[124] Too important for their own good, the minsters had become pawns in a political and dynastic game.

THE CHURCH IN LAY SOCIETY: PAROCHIAL AUTHORITY, BURIAL ARRANGEMENTS AND THE CULTS OF SAINTS

By 800, therefore, the Oxfordshire landscape was sprinkled with important churches. The minsters had been founded by kings and great nobles, and were inhabited by their relatives; their affinities were with an élite social group. Were they, therefore, of relevance only to that group, or did they have some part to play in the wider world of lay society? This question, which is a general rather than a local one, is still debated by historians. The view to be offered here, inevitably a personal one, is that minsters did indeed influence secular life profoundly, acting as foci not just for devotional life but also for a wider and growing range of social and economic activities.

Before the existence of parish churches in the modern sense of the term, it seems that parochial authority and pastoral care were exercised from minsters at the centres of great 'mother-parishes', many times larger than later parishes but equally well-defined. Proving this assertion involves working backwards from later evidence.[125] Local studies have shown that ex-minsters often preserved traces of their former status into the late Middle Ages, in the form of links binding them to the small churches which had been built within their ancient parishes. Typically they received payments from the lesser churches, or could insist that parishioners brought their dead (and their burial-fees) to the mother-church graveyard. Most historians accept that a law of the 960s, enjoining thegns who built churches on their private estates to continue paying tithes to 'the old minster to which obedience pertains', refers to this two-tier arrangement.

By piecing together these scattered clues, it is possible to go some way towards reconstructing the first parochial system. No systematic reconstruction of Oxfordshire's mother-parishes has yet been attempted, but Fig. 48 plots some relatively well-studied examples in the western and central parts of the county.[126] What is rather impressive about this map, like similar maps from other parts of England, is the close correlation between recorded Anglo-Saxon minsters and later medieval mother churches exercising parochial rights over several daughters. The picture is of course very incomplete, since many of the more peripheral chapels broke away so early that their original affiliations are unrecorded; we are left with the remnants of an obsolete pattern.

For present purposes the central problem is how far back this system can be shown to have existed. The law mentioned above proves that in parts of England it was established, indeed under attack, by the 960s. It is possible, but surely improbable, that hundreds of ancient minsters were pressed into service in the tenth century to form new parochial centres. Economy of hypothesis suggests rather that these places had been in some sense parochial centres from the start, a view consistent with such slight literary evidence as we have for pastoral care in seventh- and eighth-century England. What kind of pastoral care, and how much, is another matter. The gulf between priest and peasant must have been greater in a world where priests were concentrated in minsters than in one where they were scattered through the countryside in village churches. Contact must have relied to a large extent on the diligence of the priests, perhaps operating through satellite holy sites. But whether or not the minster-priests came to the people, there are persuasive indications that the people did sometimes come to the minsters. Three kinds

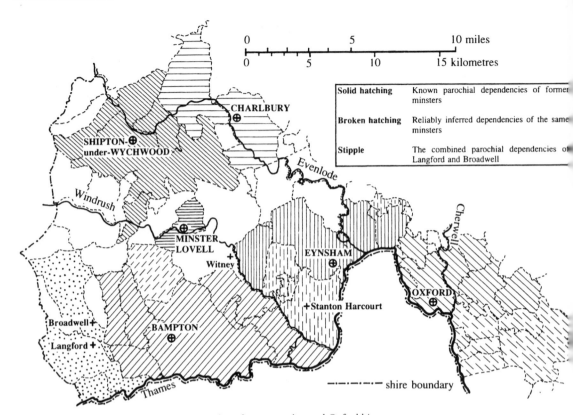

48 Some minsters and mother-parishes of western and central Oxfordshire.

of contacts and influences can be explored through the Oxfordshire evidence. One of these, the growth of about half the medieval market towns of the county around minsters, is a principally late Anglo-Saxon phenomenon which belongs to the next chapter. The others are the Christian impact on burial arrangements between the seventh and tenth centuries, and popular devotion to the cults of the local saints.

Changes in burial practice should in theory be the clearest possible guide to the growth of Christianity. The 'Age of Conversion' was broadly the age when grave-goods were abandoned, but archaeologists have become less and less sure about cause and effect.[127] Grave-goods were never explicitly banned by the Church, and we have seen that they continued in high-status graves through the whole seventh century. That conversion did not necessarily involve forsaking one's ancestral cemetery, or the grave-goods appropriate to one's rank, is shown by overtly Christian objects found in a few of the latest furnished graves.[128] The concentration of local examples in west Oxfordshire (Fig. 49) is suggestive, though the sample is perhaps too small to mean very much. These are graves of high, but not the highest, status: they show that at least a (presumably influential) minority of the inhabitants of some parts of the region were in some sense Christian. Here is tangible support for Bede's very explicit statement that the priests whom Peada brought to Middle Anglia 'were gladly heard, and many

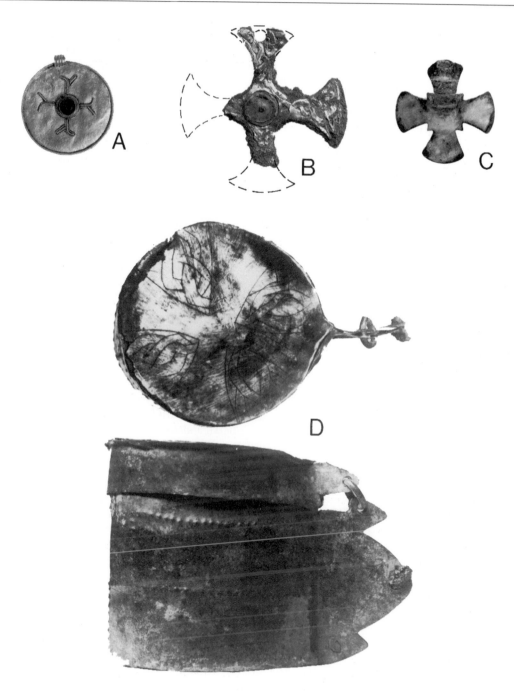

49 Converts of St. Birinus or St. Diuma? Christian objects from mid-seventh-century female graves in the west Oxfordshire area. *A*: Gold bracteate with filigree cross, from Ducklington grave 2 (Ashmolean Museum). *B*: Pendant cross of sheet-bronze and silver foil, found among the girdle mounts in Standlake I grave 8 (Ashmolean Museum). *C*: Silver pendant cross, from necklace in Lechlade grave 1182 (Cirencester Museum). *D*: Bronze 'thread-box' with cruciform decoration, from North Leigh (Ashmolean Museum); one interpretation of such containers is that they were personal reliquaries. Actual size.

both of noble and of common (*infirmorum*) folk, renouncing the filth of idolatry, were daily washed in the font of faith'.[129]

By the late Anglo-Saxon period, minsters enforced burial monopolies within their 'mother-parishes' and were surrounded by graveyards. The origins of this rigorously centralised system, and the process by which it superseded the 'late pagan' cemeteries, are still very unclear. At least some of these large minster graveyards existed relatively early, and shrank as the status of the churches declined: Aylesbury and Brixworth, on the fringes of the region, are particularly good examples.[130] In Oxfordshire, Shipton-under-Wychwood (Fig. 46) and Charlbury are clear cases of minster graveyards which have contracted since the late Anglo-Saxon period; Marcham, a probable minster in north Berkshire, may be another.[131] None the less, the overall pattern remains very unclear: at Bampton, for instance, it seems topographically unlikely that the main churchyard was ever very large, despite the huge parish which it served.

If it could be proved that the minster graveyards were in active use by the late seventh century, we might assume a general shift to them from the 'late pagan' cemeteries. This is not, however, what archaeology seems to show us. Among the minster graveyards just mentioned, there is radiocarbon evidence for burials at Brixworth and Aylesbury from the eighth century, at Shipton-under-Wychwood from the ninth, and at Oxford and Bampton from the ninth to tenth.[132] Only a few burials were dated in each case, so all these graveyards could have started earlier; but if they were in heavy use during, say, 650–750, it is perhaps a little odd that no evidence for it has yet come to light. So where were the children and grandchildren of the last occupants of 'pagan' cemeteries buried? The answer may be that archaeologists have failed to recognise graveyards of the seventh to tenth centuries which were not beside churches, but which were used for Christian burial and which could well have been controlled by the minsters.

The only way of dating groups of unaccompanied, west–east inhumations is by taking radiocarbon samples, which is expensive and rarely done. The Oxfordshire Sites and Monuments Record contains (1993) some fifty reports of finds of unidentified human burials, any or all of which could be Anglo-Saxon. Luckily, a few 'post-pagan' burials are not wholly unaccompanied: small iron knives, and occasionally buckles, continue to occur when other artefacts cease. This must be because they were regarded as items of dress: they merely show that the dead were buried clothed. It is well known that the latest 'final-phase' graves often contain knives and buckles,[133] but it has been insufficiently realised (mainly because grave-goods are the preserve of early Anglo-Saxonists) that this phenomenon is not the tail-end of furnished burial but a trend set for the future. It looks, in fact, as though a few knife-burials among otherwise unfurnished graves may be characteristic of mid- to late Anglo-Saxon graveyards.

Isolated knife-burials, mostly orientated, have been found at Brize Norton, Cokethorpe, Frilford, Kidlington, Oxford (Crick Road), Radley and Great Tew.[134] These look like simple versions of the isolated 'special' burials characteristic of the early seventh century, and they probably date from the seventh or early eighth centuries rather than later; the Kidlington grave, with its distinctive seax (long knife), is certainly eighth-century.[135] Groups of between two and five skeletons, some in each case with knives, at Cassington, Oxford (Kingston Road), Whitchurch and Woolstone,[136] may be fragments of larger cemeteries. A clearer view is provided by the more completely excavated sites at Dorchester (Bishop's Court Rectangle) and Appleford, each comprising eight, possibly more, orientated burials; one of the Dorchester graves had a seventh-century seax and a knife, and two of the Appleford graves had knives.[137]

These finds prove the existence of ostensibly Christian-rite cemeteries containing occasional knife-burials, but are hard to date. More helpful, because supported by radiocarbon determinations, are the cemeteries at Beacon Hill, Lewknor, and Chimney near Bampton (Fig. 5).[138] At Lewknor thirty-nine graves were excavated, two containing knives; radiocarbon samples gave date-ranges between the mid-eighth and late ninth centuries, and one knife is of a type introduced in the seventh century and in use until at least the ninth. The Chimney cemetery is very large, perhaps containing thousands of bodies. The few graves there which have been excavated include one knife-burial; three unfurnished burials from different parts of the site yielded radiocarbon date-ranges between the mid-tenth and mid-eleventh centuries, though it cannot be assumed that the knife-burial was necessarily as late as this.

The particular interest of Chimney is that it has a historical context: the land was given (or confirmed) to the minster-priests of Bampton in the 950s, and remained attached to Bampton church thereafter.[139] This is therefore an unequivocal case of a minster controlling a dependent cemetery which lay three miles distant. Earlier, a similar dependence on the minster (or its episcopal predecessor) can surely be assumed for the Dorchester cemetery, which lay in the grounds of Bishops Court beside the Roman town (Fig. 8). So a cemetery did not have to adjoin a minster in order to lie within its purview.

It may be that burial at the minster was at first the privilege of the wealthy: ordinary people were buried in a penumbra of small, scattered cemeteries within the mother-parish, even if the minster-priests performed their funerals.[140] Rather than a sudden, single-stage move from 'pagan' cemeteries to churchyards, we should envisage a slow transition as grave-goods were abandoned, orientated burial universally adopted, and funeral arrangements brought more and more thoroughly under the minster-priests' control.[141] Perhaps it was only from the tenth century, when the new phenomenon of manorial churches prompted the defence of established rights, that people at large were forced to bring their dead to the minsters and the scattered cemeteries were abandoned. But from the seventh century onwards, the Christian practices observed in the scattered cemeteries can only have been mediated from the minsters.

A very different approach to relations between religious communities and the laity is through the study of local saints. We have already seen that several minsters in the region had their own saints, most of whom lived in the seventh or eighth centuries: Birinus at Dorchester, Diuma at Charlbury, Osgyth at Aylesbury, Eadburh at Bicester, Frideswide at Oxford, Beornwald at Bampton. Recent research has emphasised the tenuous, sometimes accidental nature of the surviving evidence for local cults: it is quite possible that many more have been forgotten (the hypothetical 'St. Æbbe of Abingdon' may be a case in point), and that *every* minster had its saint.[142] This points to a localised element in religious devotion, but leaves uncertain how wide a section of the population it involved: these saints were mainly aristocrats enshrined in aristocratic communities, and some historians argue that their cults were high-status affairs irrelevant outside the walls of minster or palace.

Our only access to early popular cults lies through the texts which contain stories of the saints' lives and miracles. This is a difficult body of material, and the minor English 'Lives' are still very little studied. Most of them have been so re-worked and embroidered by professional, mainly twelfth-century hagiographers as to make them highly unattractive as historical sources, and it is conventional wisdom to discard them as worthless. Paradoxically, stories of just this kind from more vernacular cultures, notably those of Wales and Brittany, have been taken much more seriously because they lack the veneer of sophisticated invention and are held to be products of 'oral' or 'traditional' societies.[143] Legends of some of the Oxfordshire saints survive in twelfth- and thirteenth-century sources, and it may be worth examining them for traces of cults at a rustic level.

Nearly all the stories involve journeys which the saints make – living or dead – between named and identifiable places (Fig. 50). We have already considered St. Frideswide's miraculous travels between Oxford, Bampton and Binsey (above, pp. 53–4). St. Osgyth of Aylesbury, born in her father's palace at Quarrendon (so holy a spot that the grass never grew there afterwards), visited her aunt St. Eadburh at Adderbury and accidentally fell in the Cherwell.[144] Just over the county boundary into Northamptonshire and Buckinghamshire were the three places associated with the infant prodigy St. Rumwold. At the moment of his

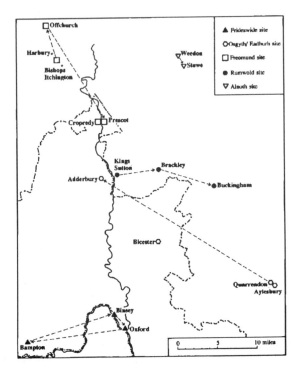

50 The early Christian folklore of Oxfordshire and its region: legendary and miraculous migrations of saints.

birth he declared his Christian faith and demanded baptism; he then preached a sermon, and died at the age of three days after instructing that his body should be moved at yearly intervals through three successive graves at Kings Sutton, Buckingham and Brackley.[145]

St. Freomund of Cropredy has a legend so bizarre and outrageous that it is worth dwelling on.[146] The story makes him a son of King Offa, who abandons a career of heroic asceticism to help the English against the Vikings, but is beheaded by an English traitor. The corpse picks up the head, forgives the murderer, and walks to a site between Harbury and Itchington (Warwicks.) where it becomes inanimate. The repentant murderer and his friends collect the head and body, and bury them in a lead coffin within the precincts of the royal palace at Offchurch. Sixty-six years later a vision directs three crippled girls to the site, where they find the grave marked by a column of light. Instructed by an angel, they carry the lead coffin to 'a place surrounded by marsh between the Cherwell and the *Brademere*, where those rivers meet, situated about three miles from Banbury', and deposit it in a spot indicated by a snow-white carved stone. They plant a willow-rod as a marker, and leave for the night. Returning next morning, they find that the rod has grown into a huge tree, and reassured by a vision they return home cured. Grass and flowers grow around the willow; no animal can approach or bird settle, but the peasants find that hay made from the grass cures sick animals, and know that the spot is holy. Meanwhile, in the church of the Holy Sepulchre in Jerusalem, a pilgrim called Albert is told in a vision to seek a place on the Cherwell where five priests keep a house, and find a precious treasure buried under a willow-tree in a nearby meadow. At first he ignores it, but an angel urges him on: 'Under one of the roots you will dig up a tomb, decorated within with precious treasure, in which you will find the body of the holy martyr Freomund; under the same martyr's tomb you will find a sow with thirteen piglets, but you will not see how she comes in or goes out.' Everything happens as predicted, and crowds of sick people gather around the tomb for healing. With the help of the bishop of Dorchester (St. Birinus!), Albert and the priests try to carry the corpse to 'the nearest monastery', but when they reach *Ridic* (Cropredy) it refuses to go further. So a chapel is built on the spot, and the bishop elevates the corpse from its old tomb into a shrine with silver lamps.

What suggests that such stories may contain more than just the fantasies of twelfth-century hagiographers is their strong sense of place and their lively detail. There is repeated reference to places and landscape features which the writers or their sources must have known: Frideswide's refuge in the piggery of Bampton, her miraculous well at the thorn-grown earthwork of Binsey, the palace site at Quarrendon where no grass grew, the three burial-sites of Rumwold and those of Freomund.[147] The Freomund story in particular shows a rich bucolic imagination: the magical willow-tree, the wonder-working hay, the sow and piglets buried under the tomb. The place 'between Cherwell and *Brademere*' is easily located (Fig. 51) and the nearby farm Prescot ('priests' *cot*') must be the dwelling of the five priests.[148] Place-associations could sometimes have been introduced to support property claims (though no such are recorded in any of these cases), and some elements belong to the standard stock-in-trade of hagiographers; but there is a deeper layer which looks like genuine rural folklore. That folklore tells us nothing reliable about the seventh and eighth centuries;

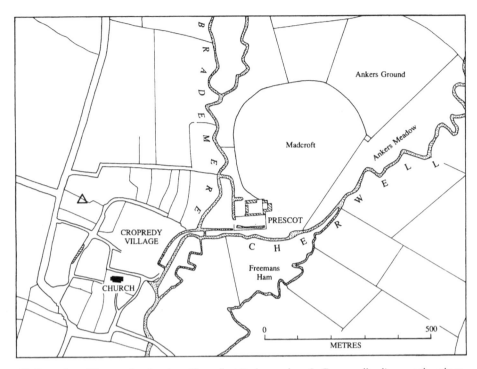

51 Cropredy and Prescot: the place *inter Charewelle et Brademere* where St. Freomund's relics were thought to have rested. The round outline of 'Madcroft' is suggestive, as are the names 'Ankers Ground' and 'Ankers Meadow' which probably contain Old English *ancra*, 'hermit'. 'Freemans Ham' may mean 'Freomund's Ham'. The triangular symbol marks late Anglo-Saxon settlement material found in 1993.

what it does suggest is that the cults of seventh- and eighth-century saints became rooted in the popular culture of their districts. These cults, like the Welsh and Breton ones, were 'remembered in local, oral traditions attached to healing springs and notable landmarks and objects', and like them they indicate 'intensely localised lay devotion'.[149]

Saints of this kind would have been the focus of popular rituals, expressing both the centrality of the relic-holding churches and the coherence of their parochial communities. This area of Anglo-Saxon rural life is almost wholly lost to us, but Bampton, where St. Beornwald's relics were enshrined by *c.* 950, preserves a distant trace of it. In about 1120 a daughter church was licenced at Alvescot, within the mother-parish, on condition that the chaplain should visit Bampton church on a series of feasts: St. Beornwald's day; Christmas; Palm Sunday; Easter; the Rogation Days; Pentecost; the Nativity of St. John the Baptist.[150] This is a sequence familiar to folklorists: the division of the year into a 'non-ritual' half from midsummer to midwinter, and a 'ritual' half containing festivals which normally ran from Christmas to the Nativity of St. John (24 June).[151] At Bampton, whether by chance or by design, the sequence began and ended with specifically local feasts: St. Beornwald's day fell on 21 December and must have initiated the Christmas festivities, while the main church was dedicated to St. John the Baptist. The inclusion of the Rogation Days suggests that on those occasions at least, the chaplain was expected not only to visit the mother church but also to participate in processions for blessing the crops or beating the bounds. What we seem to have here is an affirmation of the integrity of the ancient parish by means of a cycle of feasts and processions, attended by the subordinate clergy and initiated by the festival of the local saint himself.

Although we can never know how many of the practices visible in the tenth to twelfth centuries existed in the seventh to ninth, it was clearly during that earlier period that the foundations of pastoral and funerary provision and of local cultic practice were laid down. There were many occasions, both in the liturgical year and in the individual life-cycle, which would have brought ordinary people to their local minster. Other points of contact suggest themselves: the giving of alms on the anniversaries of the rich; the sanctuary which holy sites offered to fugitives from the law; the stimulus to trade and commerce created by establishments which needed luxury goods, which enjoyed legal privileges and which were central to the communications system. The minsters were indeed 'aristocratic' in their membership and life-styles, but they were anything but detached from the flow of ordinary life around them.

EXPLOITING THE LAND

The amalgamation of small territorial units into big ones during the late sixth and seventh centuries must have had its impact on the people who lived on the land, especially on their duties to those above them. Society was becoming less 'tribal', more hierarchical and political. Over-kingship meant that resources had to be managed from a distance, through officials, at just the time that the English were starting to become literate. Thus began the slow evolution from folk-custom to bureaucracy, each stage making use of what existed already. The old *ingas*-type regions formed the basis of the territories grouped around royal vills, which developed in turn into the hundreds which were the units of local government and law-enforcement in the tenth and eleventh centuries (below, p. 108). From the seventh century a different kind of social institution, the private estate, began to develop out of the same matrix. Common to all systems of dividing up the land, whether for government, for taxation or for exploitation, was one basic unit of assessment: the hide.

We have already encountered the hide as the 'land of one family', a large farm supporting a peasant proprietor and his household within a kin-group structure. By the late seventh century, when we meet it in charters and the Tribal Hidage, it had become formalised as a conventional unit, normally unaffected by changes in population structure or productive capacity. Its essence was the assessment of obligations, whether to pay tax, perform labour services or fight in the army. The food-renders which supported an itinerant court as it moved around the royal vills were exacted on a basis of hides. Thus the laws of King Ine of Wessex (between 688 and 694) define the food-rent owing from ten hides as 'ten vats of honey, 300 loaves, twelve ambers of Welsh ale, thirty of clear ale, two full-grown cows or ten wethers, ten geese, twenty hens, ten cheeses, an amber full of butter, five salmon, twenty pounds of fodder and 100 eels'.[152]

This is the classic description of an early medieval tribute regime, involving extensive rather than intensive exploitation of large, multi-vill territories which were lightly settled and farmed and which contained substantial non-arable resources.[153] It suited the needs and circumstances of the time, so it is not surprising that when, after the mid-seventh century, kings started to grant estates to monasteries and eventually to laymen, they should be constructed along similar lines. The so-called 'multiple estate' was a bundle of townships, already named, hidated and defined within a hierarchical system of royal control, which were carved out of the territory serving a royal vill and re-grouped around a new (initially monastic) centre. In Steven Bassett's words, 'the notion of the manor, and of the landlord-tenant relationship, developed as kings ceded land to private persons and to the Church, whose idea of control was more proprietary. Land was being privatised.'[154]

The organisation of groups of hides was startlingly regular, and can be traced from the earliest to the latest texts. Late Anglo-Saxon Oxfordshire was divided symmetrically into twenty-four 100-hide hundreds (below, p. 103), and King Coenwulf's acquisition of exactly 300 hides at Eynsham in about 821 offers a strong hint that this symmetry was not a tenth-century innovation. In Gloucestershire, Warwickshire and Worcestershire, Steven Bassett has argued that the definition of secular territories and minster parishes in the seventh and eighth centuries followed 50- and 100-hide multiples.[155] Given this orderly framework it is not so surprising that when large estates were created, and progressively subdivided into smaller and smaller groups of component townships, they followed similarly regular lines.[156] In Oxfordshire, as in many shires, the tendency for land to be held in units of five, ten or twenty hides is quite clear from the Domesday data of 1086.[157] The following table, which correlates the hidages in all genuine Oxfordshire charters up to 970 with the equivalent hidages in Domesday Book, shows agreement in a majority of cases as well as an overwhelming preference for round-figure assessments:

Date	Place	Charter hidage	1086 hidage	Reference
670-1 or 681	Slæpi	40	?	S.1168
681	by the Cherwell	20	?	S.1167
841	Wychwood [Spelsbury]	10	10	S.196
864	[Water] Eaton	5	5	S.210
887	Brightwell [Baldwin]	6	2+2=4	S.217
887	Watlington	8	8	S.217
940	Culham	15	Not in D.B.	S.460
956	Cuddesdon	20	18	S.587
956	Tadmarton	20	20	S.584
958	Ducklington	14	4+7+3=14[158]	S.678
958	Wootton	20	5+5=10	S.675
966	Newnham [Murren]	10	10	S.738
969	Witney	30	30	S.771

Later cases of round-figure charter hidages which remained unchanged in 1086 are Ardley and Cuxham (each five hides in 995), Shipton-on-Cherwell and Yarnton (respectively five hides and ten hides in 1005) and Whitchurch (ten hides in 1012).[159]

Some figures, of course, do not agree, but usually this is more convincingly explained by fragmentation or changes in estate boundaries than by assuming re-assessment of the hides. These hidages are a striking product of the 'in some ways oddly orderly world of early England';[160] whenever they were imposed, they certainly moulded the development of land-management throughout the Christian Anglo-Saxon period.

We have virtually no evidence for administration and landlordship in Oxfordshire between the seventh and ninth centuries, and certainly nothing that contributes to the general picture. Although charters show that estates as small as five or ten hides existed by the mid-ninth century, there can be little doubt that the landscape was still dominated by large, multi-township territories. These can only be guessed at from the tenth-century and later evidence reviewed in the next chapter. The king's vills of Benson, Bampton, Kirtlington, Headington and Shipton-under-Wychwood, and the bishop of Dorchester's vills of Dorchester, Thame, Banbury, Charlbury and Cropredy, were the centres of big land-complexes in 1086 and can probably be assumed to have controlled much bigger ones before late Anglo-Saxon fragmentation.[161] The lost vill of Hook Norton was the focus of a block of royal land which may have spread across north Oxfordshire and included the later comital manors of Bloxham and Adderbury.[162] The old 'pre-manorial' territories were still the core of the land-management structure, though already they had been much reduced by the creation of great ecclesiastical estates such as the 300 hides of Eynsham, and fragmentation into still smaller manors was probably starting to gather pace by 850 (below, p. 133).

Manorialisation affected the peasantry very gradually, if in the end fundamentally. Great estates continued to be run on a tribute-render basis, the purpose of which was to meet the immediate needs of lords, not to exploit the peasants to full capacity. Christopher Dyer has noted the discrepancy between the small amounts of food-rents listed in West Midland charters and the large size of the estates that owed them. Although there would certainly have been demands beyond those stated, it may be 'that lords did not squeeze their tenants very thoroughly, or tackle the management of their estates with much vigour. After all, unless there was a market for surplus agricultural produce, there was not much point in accumulating large quantities of perishable foodstuffs beyond the immediate needs of the consuming households.'[163] But the requirements and opportunities of landlords were slowly changing. Resident proprietors, of whom the earliest and most important were the communities housed in the minsters, were more sedentary than royal courts: their tables had to be laden day by day. And as markets and coinage developed, production of surpluses became a more attractive proposition.

Place-names offer some hints of more systematic management between the seventh and mid-tenth centuries. Two types compounded with *tūn* '(farmstead', 'estate') may be relevant to the early stages of the shift from a food-render regime to organised production on demesne farms: 'directional' names (Norton, Sutton, Weston, Aston), and names describing specific crops, livestock and features.[164] The first group are by definition satellite places, and they suggest a kind of integrated estate economy in which production in dependent vills was organised from a monastic or royal centre. North Weston and Aston Sandford have the appropriate geographical relationship to Thame; Brize Norton and Aston Bampton to Bampton; Sutton to Eynsham; Chipping Norton and Steeple Aston (less unambiguously) to Charlbury. Whether the mills, marshes, moors and vegetables recorded in the various Miltons, Marstons,

Moretons and Wortons were likewise components of complex estates is less clear, but one name of special interest is Barton (*beretūn*, literally 'barley-farm'), which comes to have the sense of 'home-farm'. The demesne centre of the Abingdon Abbey estate by the eleventh century was Barton Court, and it is clearly no coincidence that a Barton lies less than a mile east of the royal vill of Headington (Fig. 55).[165] Dating is as usual imprecise, though Aston Bampton existed by 958.[166] Minor *tūn* names were not common before the mid-eighth century, and a recent study of Shropshire suggests that the directional names are 'part of the material which might be considered to be evidence for a particularly tight Mercian administrative organisation' there.[167]

The peasants of Mercian Oxfordshire are invisible to us, but just a trace of them may be preserved in place-names including the element *ceorl*, 'peasant farmer'. Charlton-on-Otmoor was a *tūn* occupied by ceorls; it was ceorls who used the *ceorla graf* at Wheatley, the *ceorla pytte* at Pyrton, and the island and *feld* of *Cherleia* (Sandford-on-Thames) and *Cherlefeld* (Henley).[168] A ceorl is often defined as a 'free' peasant, but how free these ceorls were is uncertain. It has been pointed out that many 'Charltons' are near royal centres (in the present case Kirtlington?), and this may be another kind of *tūn* which was a normal component of certain complex estates; a Gloucestershire charter of *c.* 900 grants another *ceorla graf* along with the land and states that the ceorls themselves 'shall belong to Prestbury'.[169] Whether or not English 'free' peasants had ever been wholly free (which is debatable), it is possible that they were becoming rather less so during the eighth and ninth centuries.

The twilight of Mercian rule in the South Midlands was the dawn of sustained economic growth: over the next two centuries the estate structure, the patterns of farming and settlement, of trade and transport, would all be transformed. But crucial steps towards an integrated market economy at local, regional and international levels were already being taken in the reigns of Æthelbald and Offa. In this process the Upper Thames region seems to have had a special role, as a focus of long-distance exchange systems.

THE UPPER THAMES IN THE MERCIAN ECONOMY

Mercia was rich in resources, poor in outlets. The wealth and power of Kent and East Anglia in the earlier seventh century had owed much to their proximity to Gaul and Gallic trade. Access to the Channel and the North Sea must have been a major goal of Mercian kings from Penda onwards, especially with the growth of Frisian commerce and the coastal ports ('wics') of north-west Europe towards the close of the century. This was surely the great unstated factor in Mercia's struggles for the Middle Anglian territories in the seventh century, and for the Thames and south-east England in the late seventh and eighth. Just before 700 the foundation of two great international emporia, London (*Lundenwic*) and Southampton (*Hamwic*), set off ripples of change which spread further and further inland. At least one minster on the Thames estuary had a fleet of ships by the 730s, part of a trade network that could have extended up-river as well as outwards to the Continental ports.[170] Thus the economy of greater Mercia depended on interaction between two zones: political power and natural resources to the north and west,

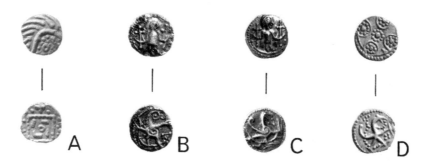

52 Examples of secondary sceattas. *A*: 'Porcupine', found at Binsey. *B*: 'Bird and branch', found at Abingdon. *C*: 'Bird and branch', found at Dorchester. *D*: Southampton (*Hamwic*) type with 'bird and branch' reverse. Actual size. (Ashmolean Museum)

commercial sophistication, merchants and markets to the south and east. The peculiar importance of the Upper Thames region is that it was where these two zones met.

Our great – and rapidly growing – source for the economy of eighth-century England is its coinage. In the 680s the northern Frankish realm, Kent and Essex switched almost simultaneously from the old, now heavily debased gold 'thrymsas' to a new currency of silver pennies known to numismatists as 'sceattas' (Fig. 52).[171] These crude, unimpressive-looking little coins are much more important than the thrymsas, for they were struck in vastly greater numbers. The size and purpose of this currency have been much debated, but the current acceleration of finds seems to be supporting the view, propounded above all by Michael Metcalf, that it was of huge volume and wide circulation, the mark of a developing economy organised for trade.[172] Sceattas found in England have been grouped in three phases – 'primary' (*c.* 680–710), 'intermediate' (mainly Continental, *c.* 695–740) and 'secondary' (*c.* 710–60) – and in numerous types and sub-types. Towards the mid-century a silver shortage caused debasement and the sceattas petered out, to be replaced after a short interval by the 'broad pennies', of higher value and artistic quality, struck by Offa and his contemporaries.

The location of mints and the plotting of find-spots have much to tell us about the commercial development of the South Midlands. The 'primary' and 'intermediate' phases can be seen as a monetary tide, slowly creeping in from the south-east and the east coast, in which Frisian merchants provided the dominant stimulus.[173] Some coins may already have been coming up the Thames, but the main influx to the region was through the Middle Anglian areas north-eastwards, where Frisian and East Saxon sceattas circulated in roughly equal proportions. It is clear, in fact, that the line of trade and communication from the East Midlands along the Clay Vale and the Icknield Way, conspicuous in the tenth-century pottery imports (below, p. 121), was already important by 700. Near Aston Rowant, an Oxfordshire village on the Icknield Way, was buried around 710 a hoard of some 350 sceattas, the largest ever found in England. Only a quarter of the coins were English, the rest coming mainly from the Rhine mouth area, and the owner may have been some Frisian merchant travelling to the Upper Thames region along the Chiltern-edge route.[174]

The 'secondary' phase, after about 710, saw coinage used over a greatly increased area. Many more mints operated and production was localised, though a tendency for groups of related designs to be produced at different centres suggests links between mints. It looks as though international and inter-regional trade had stimulated money transactions at a local level, and that local rulers were meeting the demand. At Shakenoak in the Evenlode valley, seventh-century weaving debris (above, p. 22) was associated with three early eighth-century sceattas,[175] suggesting that woollen cloth may have been bought from the farm with cash. Furthermore, coins start to reflect the balance between the sources and outlets of Mercian produce. In Metcalf's words:

> Several midlands issues of sceattas show a dual distribution pattern. They are found in the region for which they were struck, and also in the emporia of the Wantsum channel in East Kent, but not much in between. Cross-Channel trade was the principal motor of the money economy in the eighth century, and the relatively large numbers of coins found there shows that merchants transacted much business at Channel ports such as Fordwich, Richborough, Reculver – and, of course, London and Southampton. The coins also suggest that, during the second quarter of the eighth century, merchants were travelling inland, for example to and from south Mercia and the Channel ports, or to and from the Cotswolds and the Channel ports. One must suspect that Mercian wool was entering international trade. No doubt a range of other commodities was exchanged too.[176]

Of special interest here are the 'bird-and-branch' series (sceatta types 23b–d). These fall into three distinct groups, all with the same basic design: on one side a standing figure holding two crosses, on the other a crested bird pecking at the berries of a vine or branch. Three examples of Type 23b have been found close together in the Upper Thames, at Abingdon, Dorchester and Moulsford (Fig. 52 B–C), and two of the remaining four come from *Hamwic*.[177] The even rarer Type 23c occurs as single finds from Eynsham, Walbury Camp (Berks.), Handford (Dorset) and *Hamwic*,[178] and the impression of a West Saxon link is strengthened by the use of the 'bird-and-branch' reverse on types minted in *Hamwic* (Fig. 52 D). Type 23d, by contrast, shows a totally different distribution pattern, heavily concentrated in the south-east.

In 1972 Michael Metcalf suggested that the 'London-connected' type (23d) on the one hand, and the 'Abingdon–Dorchester' types (23b-c) on the other, were dual issues of Æthelbald of Mercia in the 730s, struck respectively in London and at some inland mint which could well have lain in the Upper Thames.[179] Unfortunately this attractive theory has run into problems. The re-dating of a French hoard has forced the beginning of the 'bird-and-branch' series back into the 710s or early 720s, when Æthelbald was still to some extent overshadowed in southern England by the powerful kings Ine of Wessex and Wihtred of Kent. The hypothesis of linked Mercian mints in London and the Upper Thames would still be tenable, since we have a very poor idea of who controlled London in these years.[180] However, the emerging distribution pattern of Type 23d now puts its source in eastern Kent, not London, which associates it with King Wihtred (690-725) and leaves us with the odd conclusion that the Mercian and Kentish kings were deliberately striking similar coinages.[181] Whatever the answer to this puzzle, the Upper Thames–*Hamwic* axis of Types 23b–c remains

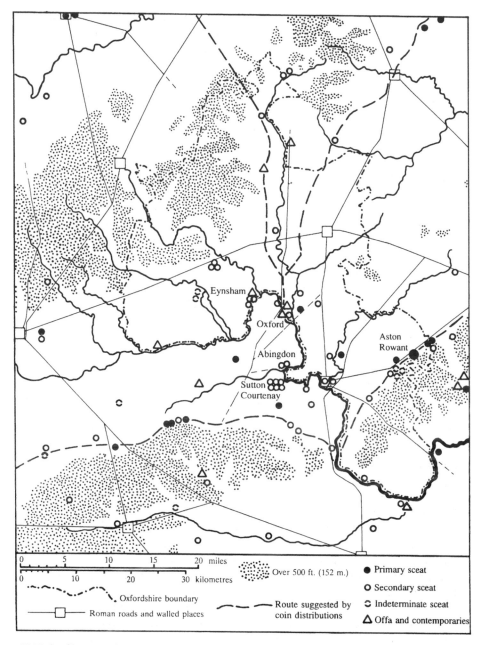

53 Finds of late seventh- and eighth-century coinage in the Upper Thames region. (Finds reported up to May 1993; data from D.M. Metcalf)

unimpaired. To quote Metcalf again, 'if there was, exceptionally, an inland mint in the Abingdon–Dorchester area, its *raison d'être* may have been in the context, not of the east–west route up the Thames Valley, but of the north–south route from *Hamwic*'.[182]

Such arguments based on the diffusion of specific types can be supplemented by mapping gross distributions of sceatta finds, distinguished chronologically (Fig. 53). Recovery by metal-detector enthusiasts (currently the main source) introduces distortions of its own, but the picture of the Upper Thames region which is starting to emerge shows definite change over time. Nearly all the 'primary' sceattas have been found near the west–east route out of Middle Anglia along the Chiltern scarp-foot and thence westwards along the north edge of the Berkshire Downs. The distribution of 'secondary' sceattas consolidates this pattern, but also extends it to areas where 'primaries' are scarcely ever found. Most notable is the concentration of 'secondaries' along the valleys of the Kennet, the Cherwell and above all the Thames, with clusters from the neighbourhoods of Eynsham, Oxford and Sutton Courtenay.

It is important to admit how little we know about what these patterns mean: they are showing us merely a section of the economy that was in some sense becoming 'monetarised', not the whole economy. Even so, a real change does seem to happen soon after 710: previously money had only been lost by people traversing the region on west–east routes, but now it was lost in a series of places on the Thames and its feeders, some of which had recently been selected as sites for minsters. Coins of Offa and his contemporaries suggest a further development: four of the eleven were found near the Banbury Road, a significant route in view of the emergence of Oxford during the late eighth and ninth centuries. In all this there is a message: we do not really understand it yet, but it is likely to prove of fundamental importance.

The coin evidence thus suggests that merchants from the south-east and further afield were taking a strong interest in commodities produced in, or obtained through, the Upper Thames region, but tells us nothing of what they were. Wool may have been the most important export then as centuries later, followed perhaps by hides, minerals from central Mercia, and even slaves from its still-expanding western frontiers. More locally, grain and timber may already have been shipped down-river. The details of how any of this was organised elude us. For one commodity only, Droitwich salt, do we have any chance of reconstructing local transport and marketing patterns. This is more useful than it seems: the system for distributing salt may be a reflection of traffic in much more important commodities.

The salt-springs of Droitwich, in the land of the Hwicce, are one of the very few industrial sites in England for which it is possible to show continuous activity from the Iron Age through into the high Middle Ages.[183] By the eighth century this major source of inland salt was controlled by the Mercian kings, and charters record salt-rights allocated for the benefit of royal and ecclesiastical estates.[184] Later, Domesday Book shows rural manors holding *salinae* in Droitwich. Although most numerous in the Bromsgrove area, these places were not confined to the kingdom of the Hwicce: they extended north-westwards into Herefordshire, and south-eastwards into Oxfordshire (Great Rollright and Bampton) and Buckinghamshire (Princes Risborough). References in Anglo-Saxon and later texts to 'salt-streets' and 'salt-ways', supplemented by place-names, reveal a system of overland routes which in many cases linked the Domesday centres (Fig. 54).

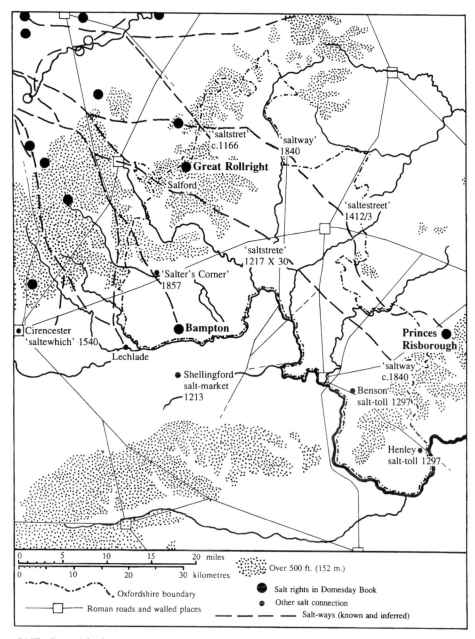

54 The Droitwich salt trade: the south-eastern sector of the distribution network.

How far this later evidence reflects arrangements dating back to the Mercian supremacy might be questioned: Droitwich salt continued in production, and its distribution network could have been extended. On the other hand, all the manors with known Droitwich links lay in greater Mercia (there are none in Berkshire, for instance), while Great Rollright, Bampton and Princes Risborough represent the fringes of a pattern whose Hwiccian core is attested by good eighth-century evidence. In outline if not in detail, it was an essentially Mercian system.

Integral to this system were regular deliveries of salt to the manors entitled to receive them. By a reciprocal arrangement, such places in the woodland area around Bromsgrove sent loads of firewood to Droitwich to fuel the boiling-vats.[185] On practical grounds it has been suggested that the more distant manors discharged this duty in cash rather than in kind, and both Princes Risborough and Bampton seem to have commuted their firewood renders by the post-Conquest period.[186] The actual carriage of firewood over such distances in the eighth and ninth centuries may be less implausible than it sounds: the supply was guaranteed and free, and the salt-wagons presumably had to return to Droitwich. The recipient estates probably consumed much, but not all, of the output. On a great royal manor such as Bampton large quantities of produce would have been salted, whether to store or to sell. Bampton had a 'piggery' as well as the most profitable Domesday fisheries in Oxfordshire,[187] and one might speculate whether the Upper Thames sustained a trade in salted pork and fish.

The distribution network shows a certain logic, hinting at the sale of surpluses both before and after they reached the main centres. It is possible to trace three salt-ways across Oxfordshire, all of them continuing routes better recorded in Worcestershire and Gloucestershire.[188] The first ran from Broadway and Blockley (Glos.) into west Oxfordshire, and then southwards via 'Salter's Corner' (Widford) to Bampton. The second branched off the first near Moreton-in-Marsh, ran south-eastwards through Salford near Great Rollright, skirted Woodstock and Oxford to the east along *Saltstrete* (Shipton-on-Cherwell), and headed towards the Chilterns (there is a 'Saltway' in South Weston) in the general direction of Maidenhead, perhaps branching to Princes Risborough via Thame. The third entered north Oxfordshire from Brailes (Warwicks.), skirted Banbury and Bicester via *Saltstret* (Swalcliffe), 'Saltway' (Banbury) and *Saltestreet* (Stratton Audley), and presumably continued to Princes Risborough.

The convergence of routes on Lechlade and Bampton suggests recognised Thames crossings, or, just as likely, freighting-points for water transport. Much later, the down-river journey is reflected in salt-tolls levied at Benson and Henley in 1297, and in the 'salt-rent' paid by Sonning tenants.[189] On the other hand, the circuitous courses of the salt-ways – starting from Droitwich, bifurcating and then converging again – suggests the possibility of sales along the way, supplying the countryside with salt in small quantities. Roadside markets at places such as Stow-on-the-Wold, Enstone or Thame may therefore be envisaged. The salt being sold *c.* 1200 at Shellingford (Berks.) at 'a certain gathering called a vigil which was there from the Conquest of England'[190] had clearly come from Bampton, six miles due north. Thus the salt-routes may reflect a local market network as well as a long-distance transport system.

Fragmentary though it is, the evidence for trade and communications in the Mercian period pinpoints very clearly the major routes leading into the Upper Thames area (from Middle Anglia along the Icknield Way, from the north along the Banbury Road, from Hwiccian territory along the salt-ways), and those leading out of it (across north Berkshire to *Hamwic*, down-river to *Lundenwic*). The stretch of the Thames between Bampton and Dorchester was the meeting of all the ways of the South Midlands. Of the various overland routes to it, there may have been an increasing emphasis towards the end of the eighth century on the one that came from the north out of central Mercia: from Offa's citadel at Tamworth, through Coventry and Banbury, and then down the Banbury Road to the broad Thames crossing which may already in Offa's time have been known as the 'oxen-ford'.

THE FORD BY ST. FRIDESWIDE'S MINSTER

The location of Frideswide's church at the head of the most important long-distance crossing on the Upper Thames is no coincidence. It illustrates the phenomenon, discussed more fully in the next chapter, of the 'monastic town', created by organic commercial and industrial growth at the gates of a minster. Oxford itself is so far the only place in Oxfordshire to have yielded evidence, albeit far from conclusive, for urban origins in the late eighth or ninth century. Before the Vikings came, it may already have been starting to acquire its special position among Upper Thames centres.

Did the church or the settlement come first? St. Frideswide's, on its gravel promontory at a meeting of rivers, occupies a classic minster site, whereas Oxford is not the most obvious point at which to cross the Thames. The floodplain is extremely wide there, containing many braided river-channels separated by islands of gravel and alluvial clay: the crossing from Oxfordshire to Berkshire is interrupted at intervals by water and reed-swamp over more than a mile (Fig. 55).[191] Yet the name which we use today clearly does refer to a crossing. First recorded in about 900 as *Oxnaforda*, 'ford of oxen', it is directly comparable to Shifford and Swinford (the 'sheep-ford' and 'swine-ford') further upstream. It is probably safe to assume that the stock was in all cases driven from north to south, out of the rich agricultural lands of Mercia to the market outlets of Wessex and *Hamwic*. It is a question why three separate crossings should have been attributed respectively to sheep, swine and oxen. The names must reflect drovers' practice, and the 'oxen-ford' could have been so called because only long-legged beasts were able to use it.

A hidden but powerful influence on the Oxford crossing is the presence of two Roman roads, cutting obliquely across the Thames–Cherwell confluence and converging on Frilford to the south-west. The more northerly served an extensive Roman settlement in the North Oxford area; the other left the Dorchester–Alchester road near Headington Quarry, crossed the Thames channels near modern Donnington Bridge and at Redbridge, and continued over Boars Hill.[192] The Redbridge section partly survives as an ancient causeway; its small, spaced-out flood-arches resemble those of the Norman Grandpont, but they could just possibly be Roman. Somewhere near this point, the late Anglo-Saxon bounds of Kennington and Hinksey mention a 'stone ford' (*stanford*).[193]

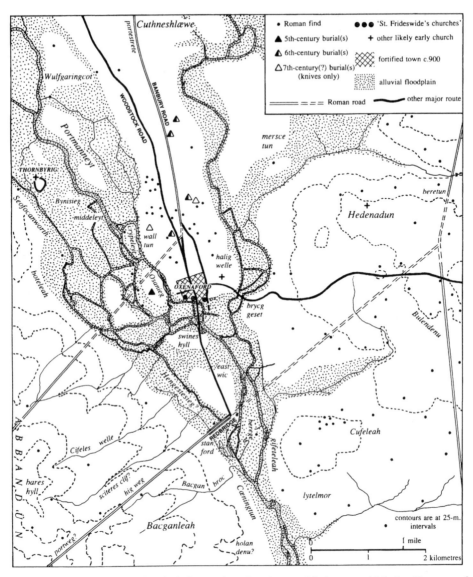

55 The topographical setting of Oxford, showing how the minster and ford were established amid a nexus of Roman and later roads crossing the floodplain.

Two south-bound routes meet at Oxford: the Banbury Road coming ultimately from central Mercia, and the Woodstock Road coming ultimately from the land of the Hwicce. Since at least the tenth century these have converged on one river-crossing down the urban axis of Cornmarket and St. Aldate's,[194] but they did not always do so. Cornmarket is the natural course of the Woodstock Road, but the Banbury Road has been deflected artificially south-westwards to meet it at the

North Gate of the town. Its earlier southwards course seems to have followed Parks Road, Catte Street and Oriel Street, to meet the Trill Mill Stream to the south-east of St. Frideswide's church. There it crossed a well-built paved ford, observed briefly in 1863 but otherwise buried some twenty feet below Christ Church Meadow,[195] before presumably converging on the line of Grandpont further south.

It must be a serious question how far the Anglo-Saxon road-pattern in this crucial corner of Oxfordshire was conditioned by the Roman one. Given the apparent size of the Roman settlement in north Oxford it seems highly likely that a road ran southwards from it, along roughly the line of Parks Road and Grandpont, to the Redbridge crossing. Support for this recently emerged during deep mechanical excavation, which revealed a lost river-channel, silted up by the Anglo-Saxon period, with a metalled ford across it.[196] Thus the ford found near St. Frideswide's in 1863 could have been either Roman or Anglo-Saxon. The basic configuration of the through-route may have been much the same in Roman, Anglo-Saxon and later medieval times: down the Banbury Road, southwards to Redbridge, then kinking sharply south-south-westwards over Boars Hill. This makes excellent sense if a Roman stone causeway survived at Redbridge to be used, and it does so too in terms of the eighth-century economy. The Roman road via Frilford and Wantage was the obvious course southwards to *Hamwic* and Winchester, along much the same route that saucer-brooches may have travelled from the Upper Thames to the south coast in the sixth century (above, p. 8).[197] We do not know whether oxen were regularly driven from the heart of Mercia to the heart of Wessex, but if they were they would have crossed the 'oxen-ford'.

The channelling of south-bound traffic over one ford may have been associated, whenever it happened, with political and fiscal control, with engineering works to improve the crossing, or with both. Thanks to a series of excavations by Brian Durham of the Oxford Archaeological Unit, the 'oxen-ford' has gradually been acquiring archaeological reality. The first excavation (in 1970-1) located, at the north end of the crossing, a feature which was interpreted as a major causeway from Offa's time: a bank of dumped alluvial clay some thirty-two metres wide which was 'mixed into the lake-bed deposit as if it had been trampled, and could be broken apart as if it had been deposited in irregular lumps'.[198] However, work elsewhere in the Thames floodplain has revealed natural alluvial deposits of similar material, raising the possibility that the 'bank' profile was in fact sculpted from one of these.[199] The uncertainty is unfortunate, and we must hope for a new exposure of the 'Mercian causeway' which can be examined *in situ* by a soil scientist.

Apart from this question of royal engineering, the clay bank is less important than the features and objects which accumulated above it.[200] The bank was heightened slightly, a north–south gully lined with wattle fences was dug into it, and a fence was set up in the reed-swamp along its west edge (Fig. 56). These features conform to the alignment of the modern road, and must relate to an earlier (but much broader) carriageway on the same course. Debris in the gully may indicate flax-retting,[201] which would suggest that linen cloth was being made nearby. Meanwhile a dramatic, though intermittent, increase in river-silting against and over the clay bank suggests major interruptions to the flow of the river, presumably because of obstacles such as

56 Ninth-century wattle fencing at the Oxford crossing of the Thames, set into the 'clay bank' and covered by thick river alluvium. (Oxford Archaeological Unit)

weirs and causeways. Into this thick deposit of silt were inserted a series of close-spaced wattle fences at right-angles to the causeway, perhaps groins to prevent erosion, as well as several large stakes. Trapped in and under the silt were artefacts[202] including some 300 potsherds, a small iron knife, a spindle-whorl, an arrowhead, a key, a bone skate and some worn-out leather shoes (Fig. 57). Clearly this is the debris of occupation, and one fragment of leather-cutting scrap shows that shoes were being made as well as worn. It must none the less be a moot point whether these objects, found only 150 metres south-west of St. Frideswide's church, belonged to a lay settlement at the head of the ford or to the monastic inhabitants themselves.

There are two possible ways of dating this earliest settlement at the 'oxen-ford': form and fabric analysis of the pottery, and scientific determinations. The pottery is dated by Maureen Mellor to the late eighth or early ninth century.[203] The three radiocarbon samples, from one of the fences lining the gully and from a fence and a stake in the overlying silt layer, all produced date-ranges (calibrated, at 68 per cent

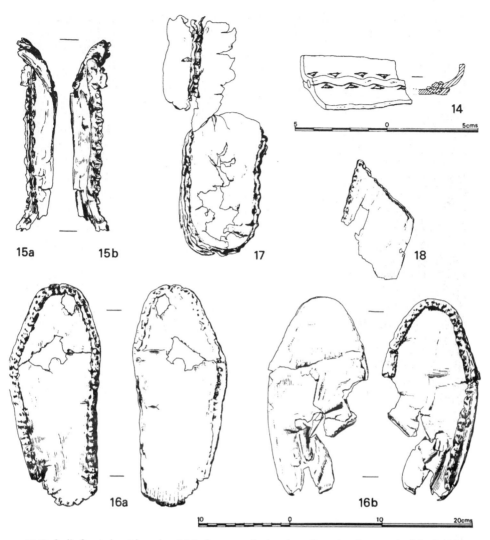

57 Oxford's first industrial products? Ninth-century leather shoes from the silts over the 'clay bank' in St. Aldate's. Shoe-making was still a major occupation in Oxford in the early twelfth century. (Durham 1977, Fig. 36)

confidence level) centred roughly in the mid-ninth century.[204] The gully-fence, the earliest feature, has a range between AD 760 and 980, but this can be narrowed to 760–*c*. 870 (if we allow a minimum of thirty years for seventy centimetres of silt to accumulate) because the date-range for the stake post-dating the silt ends in 900. Two pottery samples from the silt layers produced thermoluminescence date-ranges (68 per cent confidence) of AD 688–812 and 631–779.[205] These ranges are all compatible and suggest that the whole sequence, from the first activity on the clay bank to the building of fences on the silting, should be placed broadly between the mid-eighth and mid-ninth century: at much the same time, in fact, that people were losing coins of Offa along the line of the Banbury Road.

What emerges as reasonably certain is that earth-moving and construction works of some magnitude took place at the Oxford river-crossing in the reign of King Offa or King Coenwulf, and that these works were followed by an intensification of settlement. But who carried them out: the monastic community at St. Frideswide's, or the Mercian king? The former is by no means impossible: if the suggested reconstruction of the precinct (p. 63) is correct the main road passed straight through it, and the ford could have been part of outworks which also included boundary banks and gates to control access. But if the clay causeway is really artificial it indicates engineering on a massive scale, more suggestive of the royal 'bridge-work' which is specified as a public burden in Mercian charters from the mid-eighth century onwards.[206]

This raises the further question of whether there could already have been some kind of defended settlement at the north end of the ford. The idea that Offa's Mercia was equipped with a network of fortress-towns at bridgeheads, foreshadowing the *burhs* of King Alfred's Wessex, has recently attracted much interest, and a good case has been made for the eighth-century origins of some West Midland towns, notably Hereford.[207] This has important implications for the shire as well as the city, for the surrounding 50-hide or 100-hide units could have been responsible for maintaining such a fortress, constituting a proto-Oxfordshire.[208] Until further discoveries are made an agnostic position seems best: we have no direct evidence that there was a Mercian *burh* at Oxford, nor any that there was not. But the scale of the works does at least suggest that the crossing was of considerable importance, perhaps strategic as well as economic, by the 820s.

The relations between king and monastic community which made these operations possible are irrecoverable, but analogies suggest only too clearly what they are likely to have been. Offa seized Cookham, and Coenwulf harrassed the Archbishop of Canterbury into giving up Eynsham (above, p. 63); would they have left a site so strategically important and commercially promising as Oxford in autonomous monastic hands? We can never know for certain, but it seems highly likely that St. Frideswide's was one of those minsters which Mercian kings thought too important to be left to their own devices. The great river-crossing was the cuckoo in the community's nest, bringing as it did the traffic of an increasingly busy world through their very gates.

CHAPTER THREE

OXFORDSHIRE IN THE WEST SAXON KINGDOM

The events of the 820s left Wessex ascendant over Mercia, but they did not instantly create a new political dispensation in the South Midlands. The 840s were evidently a time of accomodation, in which the ambiguous status of northern Berkshire was acknowledged on both sides. A charter of 844 relating to Pangbourne shows the king of Mercia, and perhaps also the bishop of Leicester, exercising authority in that area, which was governed by a Mercian ealdorman named Æthelwulf.[1] On the other hand, King Æthelwulf of Wessex made grants in the Vale in 840 and 856, and in 849 his son, the future King Alfred, was born at Wantage.[2] West Saxon control of the Vale was evidently consolidated when King Burgred of Mercia (852-74) married King Æthelwulf's daughter Æthelswith,[3] and seems to have been effected by Ealdorman Æthelwulf changing lords and taking his ealdordom with him: in 860 we meet him leading part of the West Saxon army against the Vikings.[4] Bishops of Mercian sees never again had authority over Berkshire, which was absorbed into Winchester diocese and transferred *c.* 909 to a new West Saxon see eventually fixed at Ramsbury.[5]

It was thus by negotiation, not conquest, that the Thames at last emerged as the definitive frontier between the two realms. The lands that were to become Oxfordshire lay on the Mercian side of that frontier, and the autonomous kingdom of Mercia was to outlast both the Vikings and King Alfred. The story of Oxfordshire's absorption into Wessex is a complex and in some ways very obscure one, in which Viking invasions played an important but by no means decisive part.

THE VIKING RAIDS AND THEIR AFTERMATH

Scandinavian pirates had been a nuisance to the English since Offa's time. Seaborne raiders, however ferocious, were unlikely to affect inland regions, but after 865 raiding rapidly escalated into invasion, with the arrival of the first Danish 'great army' and the conquest of Northumbria and East Anglia.[6] The fatal year for the Upper Thames region was 870–1, when Danes already stationed in East Anglia and a newly-arrived army moved inland and converged on Reading, where they set up a fortified camp in the premises of the old minster at the Thames–Kennet confluence (below, p. 99).

The occupation of Reading amounted to an invasion of Wessex, and West Saxon troops quickly moved against it. Their leaders were the local ealdorman, King Æthelred I, and the king's brother Alfred ('the Great'). The outcome is described in vivid detail by Alfred's biographer Asser: a battle such as had been fought on the Berkshire Downs a century or two earlier between West Saxons and Mercians, fought there now between West Saxons and Vikings:[7]

> In the year of the Lord's Incarnation 871 . . . the Viking army of hateful memory left East Anglia, went to the kingdom of the West Saxons, and came to the royal estate called Reading (situated on the southern bank of the river Thames, in the district called Berkshire). On the third day after their arrival there, two of their earls, with a great part of the force, rode out for plunder, while the others constructed a rampart between the two rivers Thames and Kennet, on the right-hand [southern] side of the same royal estate. Æthelwulf, ealdorman of Berkshire, confronted them with his followers at a place called Englefield, and battle was joined there resolutely on both sides. When both sides had held out there for a long time, and when one of the Viking earls had been killed and a great part of the army overthrown, the others took to flight and the Christians won the victory and were masters of the battlefield.
>
> Four days after these things had happened there, King Æthelred and his brother Alfred combined forces, assembled an army, and went to Reading. When they had reached the gate of the stronghold by hacking and cutting down all the Vikings whom they had found outside, the Vikings fought no less keenly; like wolves they burst out of all the gates and joined battle with all their might. Both sides fought there for a long time, and fought fiercely, but alas, the Christians eventually turned their backs, and the Vikings won the victory and were masters of the battlefield; and the Ealdorman Æthelwulf mentioned above fell there, among others.
>
> The Christians were aroused by the grief and shame of this, and four days later, with all their might and in a determined frame of mind, they advanced against the Viking army at a place called Ashdown. . . . But the Vikings, splitting up into two divisions, organised shield-walls of equal size. . . . When the Christians saw this, they too split up the army into two divisions in exactly the same way, and established shield-walls no less keenly. But as I have heard from truthful authorities who saw it, Alfred and his men reached the battlefield sooner and in better order . . . The battlefield was not equally advantageous to both contending parties. The Vikings had taken the higher position first, and the Christians were deploying their battle-line from a lower position. A rather small and solitary thorn-tree (which I have seen for myself with my own eyes) grew there, around which the opposing armies clashed violently, with loud shouting from all, one side acting wrongfully and the other side set to fight for life, loved ones and country. When both sides had been fighting to and fro, resolutely and exceedingly ferociously, for quite a long time, the Vikings (by divine judgement)

58 A superb English sword of about the time of King Alfred, found near Abingdon. Slightly below actual size. (Ashmolean Museum; Hinton 1974, No. 1)

were unable to withstand the Christians' onslaught any longer; and when a great part of their forces had fallen, they took to ignominious flight. One of the two Viking kings and five earls were cut down in that place, and many thousands on the Viking side were slain there too – or rather, over the whole broad expanse of Ashdown, scattered everywhere, far and wide.

The sequel was not quite so glorious for the English. Other engagements during 871 were won by the Danes, reinforced by the arrival of yet another army at Reading. At this critical stage Alfred succeeded his brother as king, and was forced to gain a breathing-space by buying off the invaders. Vacating Wessex, the Vikings moved to London, where the Mercians (in the Chronicle's ominous phrase) 'made peace' with them.[8] It was now Mercia's turn to be invaded: in 874 King Burgred fled, to be replaced by the collaborator and Viking puppet Ceolwulf II. A new assault on Wessex began in 875-6 with the occupation of Wareham, and in January 878 a full-scale invasion was launched from Mercian bases. These were the months of crisis for Alfred, who was taken completely off guard and held at bay in the Somerset marshes, but in May he rallied the West Saxon forces and defeated the Vikings near Edington. Driven back to his camp at Chippenham, the Danish leader Guthrum capitulated and made peace on Alfred's terms.

This famous story leaves us with two big questions: how were frontiers drawn as a result of Alfred and Guthrum's peace, and how much autonomy, if any, was Mercia able to salvage in the years which followed? These issues are crucial to the fate of the Upper Thames area during the decade or two after 878, for which we are dependent on some laconic annals in the Anglo-Saxon Chronicle, a handful of charters, and the text known as 'the treaty of Alfred and Guthrum'. A radical new interpretation of the last has just been proposed by David Dumville.[9] How his analysis will stand up to criticism remains to be seen; at present it is the most sophisticated and comprehensive explanation of some very intractable evidence, and it will be accepted for the purposes of the discussion which follows.

The Dumville hypothesis dates the 'treaty' to 878, and identifies the frontier which it establishes between the two kings as the frontier between greater Wessex and occupied Mercia, much of it still marked by the Thames (Fig. 61). Alfred recovered the provinces which had been absorbed into Wessex during the ninth century (Berkshire, Surrey, Sussex, Kent, Essex, parts of Hertfordshire and Bedfordshire), while Guthrum retained the south-eastern tongue of mid-ninth-century Mercia (Oxfordshire, Buckinghamshire, Middlesex, and the rest of Hertfordshire and Bedfordshire). From the English point of view it was thus a specifically West Saxon treaty, leaving the Mercians to make their own peace as best they could. This they seem to have done during the following year, while the army which had vacated Chippenham after Alfred's victory was encamped on Mercian soil at Cirencester. In 879 this army left Mercia to settle in East Anglia, and its puppet Ceolwulf II disappeared from the scene (presumably not through natural causes).[10] His successor was one Æthelred, a shadowy but important figure to whom surviving sources give the title *dux* or ealdorman, but whom Mercians would surely have regarded as their king.[11]

Thus the early 880s found a Mercia under Æthelred which, though still only partly freed from its unwelcome Danish guests, was no West Saxon province. What remains very uncertain is precisely how much of the territory which Guthrum kept under the treaty of 878 he relinquished to Æthelred by the deal struck in 879.[12] In 884 a Mercian council met at Princes Risborough, on Guthrum's side of the frontier,[13] and it was at about this time (exactly when is unclear) that a Mercian bishopric was re-established at Dorchester-on-Thames to replace Leicester, still in enemy hands. The possibility that Oxfordshire, Buckinghamshire and Middlesex were already liberated from the Danes before 886 must colour our view of the Chronicle's statement that in that year 'King Alfred occupied London, and all the English people that were not under subjection to the Danes submitted to him, and he then entrusted the borough to the control of Ealdorman Æthelred'.[14] Did Alfred capture London from the Vikings (as is always assumed) or from Æthelred?[15] In either event, was it this victory which persuaded Æthelred to accept Alfred's overlordship, a relationship at once confirmed by the return of London to his keeping and his marriage to Alfred's daughter Æthelflæd?

Even after 886, Mercia was not a West Saxon province but once again the junior partner in an alliance. Æthelred and Æthelflæd ruled Mercia, the Oxfordshire region included, semi-autonomously;[16] they acknowledged Alfred's overlordship in their charters (such as the grant of land at Pyrton in 887, issued by Æthelred as *dux et patricius* of the Mercians with King Alfred's consent[17]), but even this concession ceased after his death in 899. Probably Mercia and Wessex were already in an alliance of mutual interest against the East Midland Vikings which left the re-consolidation of former Mercian land to Æthelred: thus in 888 he granted land at Walden (Herts.), which had lain on Alfred's side of the 878 boundary. The implication must be that 'Alfred and Guthrum's frontier' quickly became an irrelevance, as Mercia slowly expanded back into old Middle Anglian territory with West Saxon approval.[18]

So matters remained until 911, when Æthelred died and Alfred's son and successor Edward the Elder (899–24) 'succeeded to' the lands dependent on London and Oxford.[19] These would surely have been the Mercian enclave which was ringed by the West Saxon shires of Berkshire, Surrey and Essex, in other words Oxfordshire, Buckinghamshire, Middlesex and south Hertfordshire. Edward and his sister Æthelflæd, Æthelred's widow, continued in fruitful alliance against the Danes, but it is unclear whether the transfer of territory from Mercian to West Saxon control was an expedient agreed between them to bring the lands bordering the Thames under a single command,[20] or an act of aggression. At all events the extension of the English frontier protected Oxfordshire from further recorded Viking incursions, apart from a raid on the Hook Norton area in the north-west of the county in 913.[21] But on Æthelflæd's death in 918 Edward moved decisively against Mercian independence, deposing her daughter and heir and absorbing her kingdom into his own.[22]

There is some reason to think that the lands north of the Thames, including what was to be Oxfordshire, were assuming a distinct identity within both the Mercian realm and the emergent kingdom of England, foreshadowing the later division between 'West' and 'East' Mercia. It has been suggested that Æthelfrith, one of three sub-ealdormen in late ninth-century Mercia, may have ruled this area under Æthelred and Æthelflæd.[23] If so, his ealdordom was perhaps the same south-eastern sector which King Edward was to annexe in 911; it may already have seemed rather peripheral to the Hwiccian territory, equivalent to Worcester diocese and containing Æthelflæd's headquarters at Gloucester, which was emerging as the new heartland of post-Viking Mercia.[24]

59 Late Anglo-Saxon weapons: two swords and three seaxes found in the Thames between Chimney and Wallingford. *Find-spots, from left to right*: Ten Foot Bridge, Chimney (usually called the 'Shifford Sword'); New Bridge, Standlake; Wittenham; Shillingford; Wallingford Bridge. Scale 30 centimetres. (Reading Museums and Art Gallery; photograph by J. Farmer)

The status of Oxfordshire within the unifying tenth-century kingdom is often hard to trace, but its affiliations remained Mercian. Æthelfrith's son Ælfstan may have continued to govern a territory resembling Oxfordshire and Buckinghamshire until his own death, probably in 934.[25] Thereafter this region sometimes had its own ealdorman, and at other times was grouped with the rest of Mercia;[26] the ealdordom of all Mercia which King Æthelred II created in 1002 for his much-hated henchman Eadric Streona would almost certainly have included it. It was at *Wudestoce on Myrcena lande*, 'Woodstock in the land of the Mercians', that Æthelred II issued two of his law-codes.[27]

Did the Vikings leave any permanent mark on Oxfordshire during their brief presence? Their transience is emphasised by the lack of Scandinavian place-names, which start to become prolific only a little way to the north-east;[28] this was not a region where the invaders settled down. Archaeological evidence is sparse, and entirely military in character. A form of burial now known to be characteristic of the 'great army', in which a packet of coins was deposited with the dead warrior, has been encountered twice in the region: in the churchyard of St. Mary's minster at Reading, presumably a relic of the 870–1 camp, and under a barrow at Hook Norton, buried in 875 or a little later during Guthrum's occupation.[29] Burials of two men at Sonning, and of a man and a horse at Reading, were accompanied by Viking-age swords;[30] they could well be further relics of the 870-1 campaign, though the Scandinavian practice of furnished burial occurred later on the Thames, as a find from Oxford testifies (below, p. 170).

A different matter is the remarkable quantity of Viking-age and late Anglo-Saxon weapons that have been recovered from the river between Oxford and Reading, with two outliers upstream at Chimney and Standlake (Figs. 58-9): somewhere in the region of ten swords, eight seaxes and thirty spearheads.[31] The sequence starts in the Viking period (there are virtually no pagan Anglo-Saxon weapons), but many of the items are probably English, and date from well into the tenth or even eleventh century. This is part of a wider phenomenon, however, and it is hard to believe that the huge quantity of ninth- and tenth-century weapons from English rivers can all be casual losses; several of the swords (including one or two from the Thames) have been ritually 'killed' by bending, which recalls the ancient Scandinavian tradition of making ritual deposits in rivers and bogs.[32] Did the English learn from the Vikings a practice of dropping weapons in the river at peace-making or oath-taking ceremonies?

THE FOUNDATION OF OXFORD

Around the year 900 a grid-plan town, with ramparts, gates and streets, was built at the north end of the 'oxen-ford', enclosing the church or churches of St. Frideswide's minster. This and thirty-two other places are listed in a document called the Burghal Hidage, dated variously to between the early 880s and 919, and are usually interpreted as a defensive system established by King Alfred to protect Wessex from Viking raids.[33] This is part, but only part, of the story: the *burhs* were not all built at once, they were not all West Saxon, and many of them were a good deal more than fortresses. There are strong grounds for thinking that Oxford was built by Mercian rulers as a Mercian town.

The uniformity of the Burghal Hidage is belied by the very different kinds of place which it lists, ranging from complex towns like Winchester to simple forts like Sashes or Eashing. Archaeology proves that many of the larger *burhs* were towns from the start, with streets and boundaries defining property inside them.[34] They were urban in an urbanising age, the product much less of short-term defensive needs than of the long-term economic growth which first became conspicuous in burgeoning Danelaw towns such as York, Lincoln and Norwich, and which moved gradually westwards.[35] The techniques of formal town planning were re-invented before Alfred: the plan of late eighth-century Hereford foreshadows (on a small scale) early tenth-century Oxford, for instance, and some of the West Saxon towns may have been laid out by Alfred's father. And the *burhs* were not alien intrusions, but grew from local roots. Many were at royal estate centres or minsters, or near incipient commercial foci.[36] Oxford would probably not have been sited where it was but for the earlier developments around St. Frideswide's and the ford; if built in a Wessex-dominated world, it was a product of the organisation and economy of the Mercian kingdom.

The Burghal Hidage cannot be used to date the foundation of Oxford, for its own date remains very controversial. The strongest evidence that the town existed by Alfred's death in 899 comes from two very rare silver pennies by a moneyer named Bernwald (Fig. 60): one with the king's name ÆLFRED dividing the legend

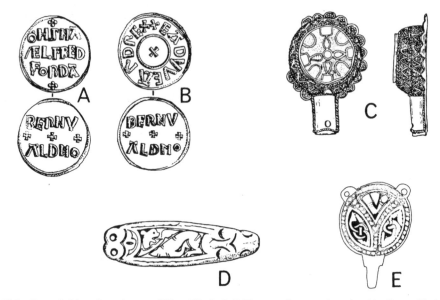

60 Small metal objects from the age of King Alfred. *A–B*: The two silver pennies minted by Bernwald, the first bearing the mint-name *Ohsnaforda* (after Lyon 1976, Fig. X). *C*: The Minster Lovell jewel (Ashmolean Museum; Hinton 1974, No. 22). *D*: Copper-alloy strap-end found at Souldern (Ashmolean Museum; Hinton 1974, No. 31). *E*: Nielloed silver hooked tag found near Bampton (Ashmolean Museum; *Oxo.* lviii (1992), 341). Actual size.

OHSNA/FORDA, the other in the name of Edward the Elder. These have been much debated, not least because most surviving specimens are Viking imitations with the name corrupted to 'Orsnaforda'. However, numismatists now seem satisfied that the 'Ohsnaforda' penny and its counterpart are genuine coins struck in the late 890s and early 900s.[37] Since *hs* is phonetically equivalent to *x*, and attested as a West Saxon spelling,[38] the likelihood is overwhelming that this is merely an eccentric form of the expected 'Oxnaforda'. Not all Anglo-Saxon mints were in fortified towns, but those which first appeared in Alfred's later years were essentially part of the expanding burghal system. It looks as though 'Ohsnaforda' was in some sense in the same league as the new mints of Winchester, Exeter and Gloucester,[39] though unlike those it was not a place with Roman walls.

According to the Burghal Hidage, Wessex's northern frontier was protected by a series of strongholds spaced out along the Thames from its source to its estuary: Cricklade, Oxford, Wallingford, Sashes, Southwark. Alone among these, Oxford lay on the Mercian side of the river, and the question must be asked whether it was built and controlled by the semi-autonomous rulers of Mercia. Æthelred and Æthelflæd never struck coins in their own names, so it is immaterial that Bernwald's pennies bear the names of West Saxon kings. Oxford was defended on the south as well as on the north, and recent excavation suggests that the Thames was gathered into an artificial channel along its south side to form a water defence.[40]

One other town on the Mercian bank which had certainly been re-occupied by the 890s, even though the Burghal Hidage ignores it, is London. The Anglo-Saxon Chronicle tells us that in 886 Alfred captured London and entrusted it to Æthelred of Mercia, and that on Æthelred's death in 911 'King Edward succeeded to London and Oxford and to all the lands which belonged to them'.[41] It might be inferred that the two north-bank towns thus named in one breath had a common history, and there is at any rate no doubt that the site of Oxford, like London, was in Mercian territory between 886 and 911. Taken together, the lack of any reference to Oxford in 886, the 'Ohsnaforda' pennies and the 911 annal point persuasively to a foundation in the 890s in a Mercian context; a later date is only possible if the Oxford in which the pennies were struck and which Edward annexed was a non-burghal place. One further piece of evidence is relevant here: the first block of planned streets within the walls of Roman London seems to have been laid out between 888 and 898, and it adjoined a wharf called 'Æthelred's-hythe' after its Mercian lord.[42]

If Oxford began as a Mercian town, its true founder may well have been Æthelflæd, Lady of the Mercians. This remarkable daughter of King Alfred ruled Mercia in name from 911, and perhaps in reality for several years earlier: it has been suggested that her husband Æthelred may already have been incapacitated by 892.[43] Æthelflæd, who probably extended the defences of Hereford and who certainly built some later *burhs* on the northern Mercian frontiers,[44] had been brought up by the greatest of all medieval town planners. It was surely from her father's team of surveyors and engineers that she and her husband recruited the expertise to set out the streets of Oxford and London, even if they did so in the vain hope of preserving an autonomous Mercia.[45]

THE FORMATION OF OXFORDSHIRE

By Alfred's time his own kingdom of Wessex had long been divided into shires, and Asser could write of the king's birth in 849 'at the royal estate called Wantage in the district known as Berkshire (*Berrocscire*)'.[46] The Thames formed a precise north frontier for Wessex as it did for Berkshire, and was re-affirmed as such in 957-9 when Wessex and Mercia were temporarily divided once more.[47]

North of the river, matters were very different. Not one of the Mercian shires is mentioned by name before 1006, whereas three-quarters of them occur between then and 1016. The analyses of C.S. Taylor and J. Whybra have made a very strong case that the shiring of Mercia was a comprehensive administrative act, perhaps carried out by Eadric Streona in 1007.[48] Thus the formal existence of Oxfordshire can be dated with confidence to just before the first references to it, as *Oxnaford scire* in 1010-11 and *provincia Oxnafordnensi* in 1012.[49]

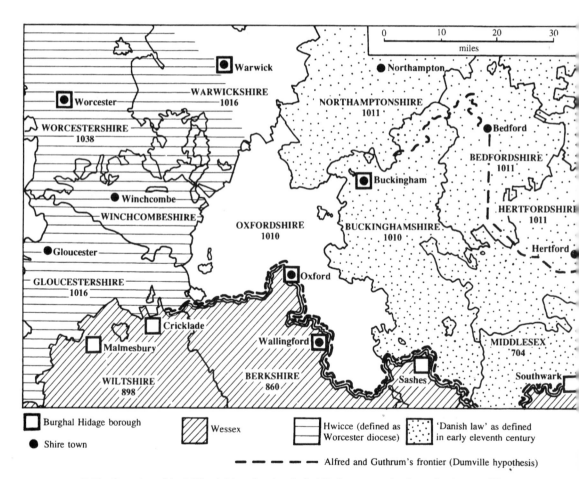

61 The formation of the Midland shires, showing Oxfordshire's status as a border region between Wessex, 'old Mercia' and territories on the periphery of Danish settlement.

The reorganisation of the lower tiers of local government was equally thorough: symmetrical, 100-hide hundreds were gathered into groups of twelve to make up the new shires. A compilation known as the County Hidage (admittedly of uncertain and probably later date) lists hidages for several Mercian shires which conform exactly or approximately to multiples of twelve hundreds: 2,400 hides for Cambridgeshire, Gloucestershire, Oxfordshire and Shropshire, 1,200 hides for Bedfordshire, Worcestershire, Herefordshire and Cheshire.[50] In some of these shires the individual hides recorded in Domesday Book can be added up to totals close to the County Hidage assessments, and this works best of all for Oxfordshire with its 2,412 Domesday hides. Moreover, the Domesday descriptions of the Oxfordshire royal manors assign to them groups of small (i.e. 100-hide) hundreds, which had only recently been amalgamated to form the large hundreds used in 1086 and thereafter (below, p. 108). The regular fiscal assessment of Oxfordshire thus reflects regularity on the ground: manors were added together to make up 100-hide bundles, twenty-four of which went into the making of Oxfordshire.

The foundations of this system certainly pre-date Eadric Streona. As already noted, local estates were assessed in round numbers of hides well before the Viking period, including the huge 300-hide estate of Eynsham; the grouping of land into 100-hide units was therefore practiced in the area long before it became Oxfordshire (above, p. 78). The symmetry of the Mercian shires was under-pinned by an older symmetry of their components: the main royal estates of the Upper Thames may already have been administrative centres for groups of 100-hide units at the time of the Viking invasions.

It was near a chosen few of these places that the burghal towns were built in the late ninth century, by a process of selection that must have involved re-structuring and amalgamation. Thus Purton/Braydon (as a 'host' for Cricklade), Headington (for Oxford), Cholsey (for Wallingford) and Cookham (for Sashes) were selected, whereas Faringdon, Bampton, Abingdon, Benson, Reading and so on were passed over. The Burghal Hidage lists the numbers of hides which 'belong' to the various boroughs, 1,300 or 1,500 (depending which text is preferred) in the case of Oxford.[51] An appendix to one text explains what 'belonging' means in defensive terms: each hide provides one man, who defends a four- to five-foot length of the rampart. So manning the walls of Oxford absorbed the military levies from rural estates totalling 1,300 or 1,500 hides. These could have been defined on the ground as thirteen or fifteen hundreds, in other words just over half the hundreds that made up Domesday Oxfordshire. It is possible that these were the 'lands which belonged to' Oxford annexed by Edward the Elder in 911, though the context perhaps suggests a looser usage in which the whole south-eastern Mercian territory was identified with London and Oxford.

The transformation of this strategic system into the eleventh-century shires would have involved a second stage of amalgamation, as administrative and legal functions were centralised at selected towns.[52] This is essentially what happened in the East Midlands, where the shires developed out of groups of wapentakes assigned to the boroughs.[53] The reorganisation of 1007 could thus have formalised an evolving system. A suggestion that something like a sheriff already existed comes from a charter of 995, in which Æthelred II describes how 'Æthelwig my reeve in Buckingham and Wynsige the reeve in Oxford' buried victims of a feud at Ardley.[54] This intervention in a place which lies near the county boundary, and about half-way between the two shire towns, suggests that Æthelwig and Wynsige were effectively sheriffs rather than town-reeves, managing royal business within burghal districts that were about to become shires. After 1007 Oxfordshire would have had stable boundaries more-or-less identical to those of the pre-1974 county. In 1059, for instance, Edward the Confessor's charter for Saint-Denis (Fig. 75) locates Taynton 'in the territory and county of the town which is called Oxford' (*in territorio et comitatu urbis que Oxenaforda dicitur*).

When the shire boundaries did finally crystallise, they preserved some anomalies.[55] In Domesday Book some twenty Oxfordshire manors are listed in the folios for other shires. Clearly mistakes could be made when the returns for whole fiefs were split up to be rearranged by shire, but several of these anomalies are recorded later and must be genuine. Some of them must arise from short-term tenurial links (Widford was in Gloucestershire because it belonged to St. Oswald's at Gloucester, while Langford was transferred to Berkshire *after* 1086 because of its manorial connection with Faringdon). The number of manors in north-eastern Oxfordshire which were outliers of Northamptonshire, Buckinghamshire and Warwickshire is none the less striking, and suggests very ancient links with Middle Anglian territory (above, pp. 51–2).

The most complex part of the boundary was at the Thames–Cherwell confluence, where the broad floodplain and multiple streams offered no clear line (Fig. 55). Geologically the natural junction of Thames and Cherwell was between Kennington and Littlemore, well below Iffley Lock, and the modern course of the Thames above this point was indeed still called *Cearewyllan* in the late tenth century.[56] Around 900, however, the configuration was altered by the gathering of the waters into a new cutting tight around the south wall of Oxford (above, p. 101). In the later Middle Ages this channel continued the line of the Shire Lake Ditch and marked the county boundary, though it cannot necessarily be assumed that it had done so from the beginning.[57] The status of the gravel islands in the floodplain south of Oxford, including the southern suburb along the 'oxen-ford', was thus ambiguous: by the thirteenth century they lay in Berkshire (indeed, its shire court sometimes met on Grandpont), but were regarded as part of the city.[58] It may be that this area had originally belonged to St. Frideswide's minster, but was absorbed into the Berkshire estate of Abingdon Abbey.[59] The island called *Berege* (Fig. 55), enclosed by the original Thames–Cherwell confluence, was disputed between Abingdon and the men of Oxfordshire in the tenth or eleventh century; it was remembered at Abingdon that the matter was settled by launching down-river a round shield bearing a sheaf and a taper, which duly floated around the east side of the island.[60]

A larger question is why Oxfordshire itself assumed such an untidy, sprawling shape (Fig. 61). The simplest answer may be that it was defined as the hinterland of its broad Thames frontier, on the north bank of which Oxford was the only burghal town. The western boundary was already established as that between 'West' and 'East' Mercia, in other words between the Hwiccian heartland and the old south-eastern ealdordom (above, p. 97). The boundary *within* this ealdordom, between Oxfordshire and Buckinghamshire, is not quite so obvious. Equitable allocation may be a factor: the southwards-sprawling tongue of Oxfordshire's Chiltern hundreds is untidy, but to have assimilated it to the Buckingham territories would have given a very small Oxfordshire and a very large Buckinghamshire. Another reason, social rather than organisational, is suggested by the eleventh-century inclusion of Buckinghamshire among the shires subject to 'Danish law', whereas Oxfordshire remained under 'Mercian law'.[61] Essentially this was a matter of cultural identity: Buckinghamshire was that much closer to Danish-settled areas, and by the end of the tenth century it may have seemed in some senses more Danish. If so, it was as an ambiguous border zone that Oxfordshire was eventually defined: north of the West Saxons, east of the Hwicce, and south-west of the Anglo-Danish peoples.

FROM ÆTHELRED THE UNREADY TO WILLIAM THE CONQUEROR

The years from the 990s to the 1060s show an often perplexing mixture of political disaster and economic growth. The main force for change was the return of the Vikings under King Swein of Denmark, their attacks escalating until, in 1016, England accepted the rule of Swein's son Cnut. The government of Æthelred II ('the Unready') may have been corrupt and incompetent, but it faced impossible odds. Huge sums of money had to be raised in 'Danegeld' to buy brief respites, milking landlords of the profits that agrarian growth would otherwise have brought them. Viking pressure on the east coast and East Midlands was relentless; Æthelred had few resources there with which to buy support, and a large section of the inhabitants were of Danish descent, not necessarily averse to the idea of a Danish king.[62]

Thus Oxfordshire was increasingly exposed to infiltration from the north-east, and violence from almost any direction. The disasters of the first decade of the century, when Viking armies roamed at will across southern England, are recounted in the despairing annals of the Anglo-Saxon Chronicle. In 1006

> after midsummer the great fleet came to Sandwich, and did just as they were accustomed, ravaged, burnt, and slew as they went. . . . And then towards Christmas they betook themselves to the entertainment waiting them, out through Hampshire into Berkshire to Reading; and always they observed their ancient custom, lighting their beacons as they went. Then they turned to Wallingford and burnt it all, and were one night at Cholsey, and then turned along Ashdown to *Cwicelmeshlæw* [Scutchamer Knob on the Ridgeway, a landmark and meeting-place] and waited there for what had been proudly threatened, for it had often been said that if they went to *Cwicelmeshlæw* they would never get to the sea. They then went home another way. The English army was then gathered at the Kennet, and they joined battle there, and at once they put that troop to flight, and afterwards carried their booty to the sea.[63]

In 1009 the Danes went through the Chilterns to Oxford, burnt it, and returned to their ships along the Thames. The next year Oxfordshire was raided again, and finally, in 1013, Swein received submission and hostages from the citizens of Oxford on his way to Winchester and the heart of the kingdom.[64]

The effects of Danish invasion and settlement are most obvious in Oxford itself (below, pp. 167–70), but they are apparent in the countryside too. In about 1010 King

Æthelred gave land at Horton and Beckley to a Dane named Toti, ironically in return for 'one pound of pure gold' for paying the Danegeld.[65] Spreading outside their zones of established settlement, the Danes were putting down roots in English England. Naturally these roots grew tougher after Cnut's conquest. In 1017 he divided England into four parts, placing Mercia, East Anglia and Northumbria under the control of 'earls'. These men were not unlike the ealdorman with wide territorial powers who had emerged during the tenth century, but a few years later Cnut appointed one Godwine to an earldom of all Wessex, launching the career of an over-mighty subject who would not make life easy for later kings.

After Eadric Streona's execution in 1017 his Mercian ealdordom, including Oxfordshire, seems to have been given to Leofwine, an Englishman and already ealdorman of the Hwicce.[66] But earls with Danish names, who may or may not have been subordinate to Leofwine, are also mentioned: Hakon (Worcestershire), Hrani (Herefordshire) and Eglaf (Gloucestershire). It is possible that Eglaf's sub-earldom included Oxfordshire, where an eleventh-century Worcester source blames 'villainous Danes' for seizing the manors of Heythrop and Kiddington 'by their tricks and frauds and secular power'.[67] In any case there can be no doubt that Cnut's regime involved oppressive military occupation, maintained by 'housecarls' or professional Danish troops. At Wallingford, just down-river, Domesday Book mentions fifteen acres 'where the housecarls lived', and there is strong circumstantial evidence for a Danish garrison in Oxford itself (below, pp. 168–70).[68]

Danish rule in England was never overthrown; it just faded away. After Cnut's death in 1035 he was succeeded by his sons Harold I and Harthacnut, but on the latter's death in 1042 the English nobles brought back the old royal house in the person of Edward ('the Confessor'), son of Æthelred II. The Danish earldoms in the West Midlands, created for short-term political needs, did not long outlast Cnut, and such evidence as we have suggests that the impact of the regime on the local society of the area was relatively superficial.[69] There are indications, though uncertain ones, that Cnut-period Danish magnates such as Osgod Clapa and Tofig the Proud acquired, and retained, Oxfordshire estates.[70] Domesday Book may show us some others, men with Scandinavian names who still held Oxfordshire manors in 1066: Haakon at Nuneham Courtenay, Merton and Piddington, Kettill at Somerton, Thorkell at Chalgrove, and possibly three or four others. But these were exceptions: by 1066 most West Midland thegns were Englishmen, and those of Norse descent had been assimilated into an essentially English society.[71]

The greater Mercian earldom, shorn of Herefordshire, descended from Leofwine to his son Leofric, who occurs as co-president of the Oxfordshire shire court in 1050–2.[72] Shortly afterwards Oxfordshire seems to have been transferred to the earldom of King Edward's nephew and protégé Raulf, to whom a writ of 1053 × 7 concerning Taynton is addressed.[73] Leofric and Raulf both died late in 1057, and it was probably then that the shire was re-absorbed into the Mercian earldom which descended to Leofric's son Ælfgar. It is clear from Domesday Book that both Ælfgar (who must have died shortly after 1062)[74] and his own son Eadwine included Oxfordshire in their earldoms.[75]

But shortly before King Edward's death there was a change: three writs of 1065-6 address Gyrth, son of the former Earl Godwine of Wessex, as earl in Oxfordshire.[76]

This is symptomatic of one of the main facts of English political life on the eve of the Norman Conquest: the rise of the sons of Godwine, above all of Earl Harold who was soon to have a brief career as king.[77] In Oxfordshire as elsewhere, Domesday Book reveals land-grabbing by the Godwinesons which Gyrth's official position may well have facilitated. By 1066 Harold had acquired big manors at Langford and Shipton-under-Wychwood totalling twenty-five hides, of which probably the first and perhaps also the second had been official comital manors attached to the earl's office.[78] A further thirty hides in the shire were also held by Harold, and some twelve by his brother Tostig. Oxfordshire was a county in which the assets of the Leofricsons (the family of the old earls of Mercia) and the Godwinesons were more or less equal.[79] Both were extremely powerful, and the life of the shire in the decade or so before the Conquest must have been dominated by dynastic politics.

SHIRE, HUNDREDS AND HUNDREDAL MANORS

The structures of local government under Cnut and Edward the Confessor, recorded for us above all by Domesday Book, developed unbroken from the system that West Saxon kings had built up during the tenth century. The essence of this system was a hierarchy of units – tithing, hundred and shire – with defined responsibilities and regular meetings.[80] Members of tithings (notionally groups of ten households, in practice defined in relation to local settlement patterns) were mutually responsible for peace-keeping and law-enforcement. Hundred courts, assemblies of the free men of the hundred, met monthly to transact local business, settle disputes, and deal with such matters as trading and cattle theft. The shire court (which in the present case would have been the court of Oxford's burghal district until *c.* 1007) was the chief assembly of local magnates and thegns, normally meeting twice-yearly to deal with a wide range of business including geld, military service and other royal exactions. In the eleventh century it was generally presided over by the ealdorman or earl and the bishop. The sheriff (i.e. 'shire-reeve'), the king's chief administrative, judicial and financial officer in the shire,[81] would have been present, but so would other reeves representing both royal and noble interests. This was now a developed and commercialised society, and the local courts would have seen a good deal of hard bargaining and manipulation by landowners and their agents.[82]

A lease of Great Tew in 1050–2[83] gives us a glimpse of the Oxfordshire shire court. The witness-list begins with Bishop Ulf of Dorchester, Earl Leofric of Mercia, the abbots and communities of Abingdon and Eynsham, and 'Vagn and all the earl's housecarls (*eale þæs eorles huscarles)*'.[84] Then follow the names of thirteen thegns, the portreeve of Oxford, the earl's reeve and 'all the townsmen' (below, pp. 139, 154). What emerges clearly from this is the prominence of Earl Leofric, turning up to the shire court in the doubtless forbidding company of his Danish household troops. He could have been a more evident power in Oxfordshire than the king, and in the absence of any reference to a sheriff one wonders whether the 'earl's reeve' was exercising the shrieval functions. If so, Oxfordshire would have resembled nearby Warwickshire, where the sheriff was very much the earl of Mercia's man.[85]

The divisions of the land and of the people in eleventh-century Oxfordshire were a mixture of old and new elements. We have already seen that the shire as defined around 1007 seems to have comprised 2,400 hides, in other words twenty-four regular hundreds, but an amalgamation into fewer, larger hundreds had occurred by the time of our post-Conquest sources. Domesday Book shows that by 1086, and probably by 1066, the 'soke' (jurisdiction) of groups of hundreds had come to be attached to important manors which were acting as hundredal centres: three hundreds to Wootton, two to Bampton, four-and-a-half to Benson and so on, totalling twenty-two of the expected twenty-four original hundreds (Fig. 62).[86]

The hundredal system was both communal, involving popular assemblies, dispute-settlement and peace-keeping, and seigneurial, involving the finances and jurisdictional rights of the lords of the hundredal manors (in Oxfordshire the king, the earl and the bishop of Lincoln). The profits of justice from the groups of hundreds went to the central manors, and it is only this that Domesday Book, a record of assets, is concerned to mention. Since the underlying pattern of small hundreds had mostly disappeared by the time that legal records start, it is only visible to us in patches (as in the Chilterns, where the four-and-a-half hundreds of Benson can be identified as Ewelme, Pyrton, Lewknor, Langtree and Binfield hundreds), and is impossible to map. The assemblies were not held at the manorial centres, but on open, upland sites often marked by barrows. Thus the two hundreds of Headington were named after Bullingdon Green ('bull's valley'?) in Horspath and *Shotteslawa* ('Sceot's barrow') near Great Chesterton; one of the Kirtlington hundreds met at Ploughley ('baggy barrow'), and one of the Shipton ones at *Chenewardesberge* (Cyneweard's barrow').[87]

The main hundredal manors were of course royal, some of them long-standing *villae regales* where itinerant Mercian and then West Saxon kings had stayed for centuries: Benson (valued at £85 in 1086), Bampton (£82), Shipton-under-Wychwood (£72), Headington (£60) and Kirtlington (£52). We have occasional glimpses of court life at some of these places. In 887 Ealdorman Æthelred gave away 'six men who formerly pertained to the royal vill of Benson'.[88] Royal assemblies were held at Kirtlington in 943–7 and 977, and Æthelred II issued a charter at Headington in 1004.[89] Other centres may have disappeared long before Domesday Book. Hook Norton is said to have been a *regia villa* in 913, and there is a certain amount of topographical and archaeological evidence to bear this out.[90] Another could be Culham, though the Abingdon tradition that kings from Offa onwards had a palace there is late and unreliable.[91] It is tempting too to wonder if Minster Lovell (above, p. 55) could have remained an important and perhaps royal place, if only because it is the source of the Minster Lovell jewel (Fig. 60): a sumptuous gold and enamel mount of *c.* 900, comparable to the Alfred Jewel.[92]

If old royal vills could vanish new ones could appear, especially when they suited the king's pleasures. Wootton is the odd man out among the Domesday hundredal manors because of its very low valuation (£18), and as recently as 958 King Eadgar had granted it away to a royal thegn.[93] A clue may lie in the name Wootton, 'the *tūn* in the wood', which is a counterpart to Woodstock, 'the stockade in the wood'. Probably the whole complex on the edge of Wychwood had been developed during the last century or so as a royal hunting-ground, very likely by Æthelred II who issued laws at Woodstock on two occasions (above, p. 99). Headington also adjoined good

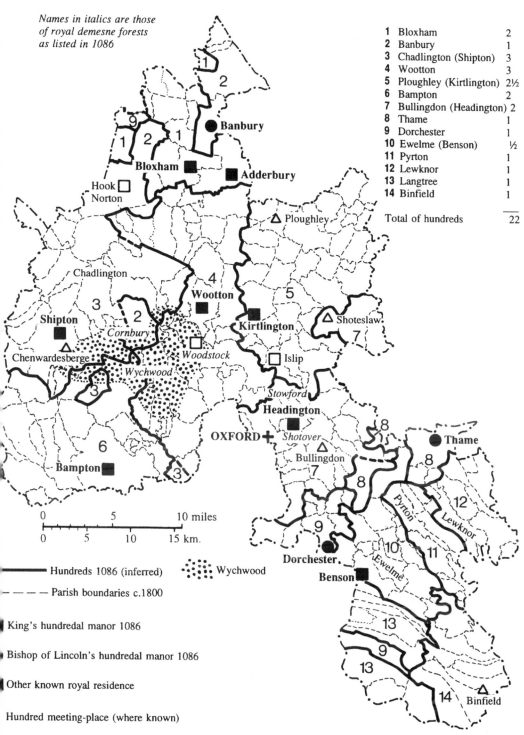

Names in italics are those
of royal demesne forests
as listed in 1086

1	Bloxham	2
2	Banbury	1
3	Chadlington (Shipton)	3
4	Wootton	3
5	Ploughley (Kirtlington)	2½
6	Bampton	2
7	Bullingdon (Headington)	2
8	Thame	1
9	Dorchester	1
10	Ewelme (Benson)	½
11	Pyrton	1
12	Lewknor	1
13	Langtree	1
14	Binfield	1
	Total of hundreds	22

0   5   10 miles
0   5   10   15 km.

——— Hundreds 1086 (inferred)   ∴∴∴ Wychwood

— — — Parish boundaries c.1800

King's hundredal manor 1086

Bishop of Lincoln's hundredal manor 1086

Other known royal residence

Hundred meeting-place (where known)

62 Administration and kingship in eleventh-century Oxfordshire: hundreds, hundredal manors and royal hunting-grounds. The list in the top-right corner indicates the numbers of original 'small' hundreds which made up the Domesday 'great' hundreds. County outliers, omitted in the interests of clarity, are shown on Fig. 39.

hunting country, and Domesday Book mentions the king's 'demesne forests' of Shotover, Stowford, Woodstock, Cornbury and Wychwood.[94] These were not necessarily a Norman innovation; Shipton-under-Wychwood had woodland 'in the king's park' (*in defen' regis*) which had already produced 50s. yearly in King Edward's day.[95] Such enclaves would have been carefully maintained, and perhaps even extended; a recent pollen core from Shotover dates the post-Roman regeneration of the woodland to the *late* Anglo-Saxon period.[96] Islip, north of Stowford, may perhaps have been a hunting-lodge frequented by Æthelred and his queen, for Edward the Confessor was born there between 1002 and 1005.[97] Most Anglo-Saxon kings found hunting more congenial than high politics, and the shire's yearly payment of £10 for a hawk and £23 for dogs[98] would have been enthusiastically claimed.

The king's manors had to support multifarious officials, servants and hangers-on when the need arose, so it is not surprising that tenurial sources, above all Domesday Book, show a tendency for court personnel to acquire land near them. It was surely the proximity of Kirtlington that caused Hugolin, Edward the Confessor's chamberlain, to hold the manor of Tackley.[99] Bampton was the focus of grants by Æthelred II to his scribe Ælfwine in 984, and by Edward the Confessor to his household chaplain (later bishop) Leofric.[100] Around Bampton's 'north *tūn*' (Brize

63 Reconstruction, from excavated evidence, of the late Anglo-Saxon royal hunting-lodge at Cheddar, Somerset. Woodstock in the time of Æthelred II would have looked much like this. (Longworth & Cherry (eds.) 1986, Fig. 112)

Norton) were holdings of fifteen 'thegns' or royal servants, as well as one for the king's goldsmith Theodoric.[101] The routine duties of some of the 'thegns' may be preserved in later sergeanty services: providing a falcon, guarding the door of the king's hall, even supervising the court prostitutes.[102]

Three other hundredal manors, Dorchester, Thame and Banbury, were in a different category, for they controlled the three hundreds of the bishop of Dorchester. These were based on a massive block of episcopal land nearly as large, and perhaps nearly as ancient, as the king's own lands, including the ancient centres of Charlbury and Cropredy as well as the head manors.[103] These hundreds are demonstrably regular, totalling almost exactly 300 hides. They were probably apportioned as an episcopal 'triple-hundred', obliged to provide a ship and its crew of sixty men, like the bishop of Worcester's 'ship-soke' of Oswaldslow.[104]

The third power in the county was of course the earl. The twin hundredal manors of Bloxham and Adderbury, worth £67 in 1086, had been held before the Conquest by Earl Eadwine.[105] Another pre-Conquest comital manor had been Broadwell,[106] and since this interlocked topographically with Langford (Fig. 48), which Earl Harold of Wessex had acquired by 1066, we can probably reconstruct the two as a single compact estate of some 50 hides which had been held by former Mercian earls.

MINSTER CHURCHES: PROSPERITY AT A REDUCED LEVEL

The old minster churches mostly survived the Viking invasions, but by the late tenth century the world around them had changed.[107] The great territories which they had originally controlled were now broken up into numerous small manors, whose lords were busily founding private churches. This inevitably reduced the minsters' standing, as did the progressive reduction in their endowments from the late eighth century onwards through a combination of lay exactions and political disruption. Yet as the senior churches of their regions they still remained very important, the foci for a range of secular as well as religious activities.

The late ninth and early tenth centuries are not usually considered an age of monastic revival, but this, in a broad sense and on a modest scale, is what they were. King Alfred's grandfather and father had gained by their reputation of being good friends to the church, and in their turn his son and daughter founded, endowed and reformed religious establishments within their respective spheres of influence. These lacked the vast wealth and varied composition of the early minsters; nor were they 'monastic' in the narrow sense in which that word would later be understood. They were communities of clergy, not necessarily very ascetic or communal in their lifestyles, but fulfilling liturgical and pastoral functions that most contemporaries would have considered worthy and useful.[108]

In Mercia, Ealdorman Æthelred and the Lady Æthelflæd were notable patrons of minsters, especially at Gloucester where Æthelflæd built a magnificent church, later known as the 'golden minster', to house St. Oswald's relics and her own tomb.[109] They it must have been who re-founded the cathedral of Dorchester-on-Thames, which had not been an episcopal seat since the 670s, to replace the Viking-occupied see of Leicester. Although religious life had probably never wholly ceased at Dorchester, this was an important event which restored to the Upper Thames something of its ancient character of a provincial centre. We should assume buildings of suitable magnificence, and Nicholas Doggett has suggested that fragments of a large late Anglo-Saxon church survive in the existing twelfth-century structure.[110] In the south-west corner of the Roman town the sequence of large timber buildings seems to have continued into the late ninth or tenth century.[111]

The Mercian rulers also patronised a church at *Readenoran* (later Pyrton) belonging to the community of Worcester, to which Æthelred gave fourteen hides and six men from the Benson estate complex in 887.[112] The scale of this endowment suggests that Pyrton church was a minster of some kind. There is no later evidence that it had a larger-than-average parish, though in 987 the tenant of the subordinate township of Golder was obliged to pay church-scot, an acre's crop and an acre's hay to Pyrton, and his heir was to 'have true friendship with the lord of the church'.[113]

St. Frideswide's emerges into the clear light of history in 1004 (above, p. 61).[114] By this time the minster probably housed secular priests – 'the canons of St. Frideswide's' have their own entry in Domesday Book – but its fortunes since the Viking invasion are unknown. If Æthelflæd was indeed the founder of Oxford as a town, however, it is distinctly likely that she took an interest in the minster which she found there: at Chester and Gloucester her urban renewal went hand in hand with monastic renewal.[115] One clue that this may have been so is the presence at Oxford of a second minster, outside

64 Late Anglo-Saxon grave-slab found in Oxford High Street, possibly from the nearby church of St. Peter-in-the-East. (Ashmolean Museum)

the east rampart of the original *burh*. The church of St. Peter-in-the-East appears in Domesday Book as of more-than-average status, with its own entry listing two geld-free hides and their stock;[116] later it had a large mother-parish outside the city, including the chapelries of Holywell and Wolvercote.[117] The apostolic dedication is appropriate to a minster, and the crypt of the existing twelfth-century church is equipped for displaying an important relic.[118] The presence of two or more minsters seems a characteristic feature of the late Anglo-Saxon Mercian towns; Æthelflæd's minster at Gloucester was also dedicated to St. Peter and was also just outside the town wall.[119]

Bampton is the only other Oxfordshire minster with evidence for royal patronage in this period. In a charter of 1069, the boundary-description of its estates is prefaced by a note that 'these are the bounds of the lands which King Eadwig gave to the holy man at Bampton and the community'.[120] The 'holy man' was presumably St. Beornwald (above, p. 63), and this lucky if casual reference proves that his relics were still being venerated by a religious community at Bampton in the reign of Eadwig (955–7). We cannot know whether the grant was made by a formal diploma (though small grants to secular minsters certainly could involve charters),[121] nor whether it gave new endowments or confirmed existing ones, but it demonstrates continued support for the minster attached to one of the main royal centres in the Upper Thames.

These cases illustrate monastic patronage along traditional lines. But by now there was a new impetus in the English Church, which after the 940s rapidly gathered momentum with royal support. A movement to reform religious communities along strict Benedictine lines had been spreading across Europe since the beginning of the century, and by the time it reached England it brought with it a wealth of scholarship, liturgy, art and architecture developed in the great monasteries of France and Germany. Injections of wealth and land gave the English Church a chance to become cosmopolitan as it had not been since the eighth century. But although the reformed monasteries might rival their pre-Viking predecessors in religious observance, learning, wealth, power and opulence, they could not do so in numbers: they were a favoured and restricted group enjoying the patronage of a narrow court circle. Thus in the Upper Thames region only two of the old minsters – Abingdon and Eynsham – are known to have been reformed as fully-fledged Benedictine houses; a third and more shadowy case – Cholsey – may have been a completely new foundation.

Abingdon has pride of place, both as one of the first English minsters to be reformed and because its first abbot was the great St. Æthelwold, chief architect of the Benedictine Reform and future bishop of Winchester. Later Abingdon tradition held that the decayed old minster had been appropriated as a royal residence by King Alfred, improbably cast as 'like Judas among the Twelve, . . . rendering a very poor return to the Conquering Lord through whom he had obtained victory over the Danes at Ashdown'.[122] Certainly Abingdon was a royal possession during the next half-century: King Æthelstan received a Frankish embassy there in 926, and in 955 King Eadred gave it to Æthelwold with the forty hides that still remained to it. The reformed abbey quickly gained numerous manors, especially in the Vale, and when Æthelwold left it to become bishop of Winchester in 963 it was immensely rich and influential.[123] His monastery was built to the north-east of the old religious site at St. Helen's, though still within the area of the late Iron Age valley-fort. It is doubtful if any of the excavated remains are pre-Conquest, but the account in the Abingdon

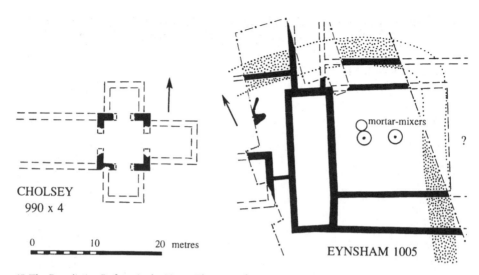

65 The Benedictine Reform in the Upper Thames. *Left*: Reconstruction, based on the surviving tower, of the monastic church built by Æthelred II at Cholsey (after R.D.H. Gem). *Right*: The excavated cloister of the monastic complex built at Eynsham *c.* 1005 by Ealdorman Æthelmær. The underlying Bronze Age ditch is indicated with stipple; see Fig. 24 for its location in relation to the town. (Oxford Archaeological Unit)

Chronicle suggests that Æthelwold's church was a rotunda of a type derived from the palace chapel at Aachen.[124] Its magnificent furnishings included precious objects made by Æthelwold himself, and a famous collection of relics.[125]

If Abingdon was one of the first houses of the English reform, the other two were among the last. In the early 990s, allegedly for the soul of his murdered brother Edward, Æthelred II founded (or possibly re-founded) a minster at Cholsey, on a commanding site near Wallingford on the Berkshire bank of the Thames. Encapsulated in the existing twelfth-century church is a late Anglo-Saxon central tower, presumably Æthelred's (Fig. 65).[126] A familiar landmark from the railway between Oxford and London, it stands as the most substantial surviving monument to the English Benedictine Reform.

Eynsham was re-founded in 1005,[127] the last Reformed house in England before Cnut's conquest and the only one within the boundaries of Oxfordshire. The old minster and its remaining thirty hides were family property of Æthelmær the Fat, ealdorman of the western shires. This scholarly nobleman patronised the great homilist and grammarian Ælfric, a monk in his own monastery of Cerne (Dorset) and the foremost English writer of the age. In 1005 Æthelmær lost favour at court, and it has been suggested that he re-founded Eynsham in that year to serve as a congenial 'retirement home', safely outside his own former ealdordom.[128] At all events Ælfric was brought up from Dorset to become the first abbot of Eynsham, which thus for a brief few years in the 1000s became one of the cultural centres of England. The Oxford Archaeological Unit's recent excavations have been spectacular, revealing the very cloister which Æthelmær built and in which Ælfric

66 Eynsham Abbey: 'mortar-mixer' (shown half excavated) from the construction of the 1005 cloister. This residue was left by mixing mortar with a wooden paddle which was rotated around a post set in the central hole. (Oxford Archaeological Unit)

67 Architectural decoration at two Oxfordshire minsters. The fragment of plinth with blind arcading (one-quarter actual size) was discarded in a late eleventh-century pit at Eynsham Abbey, and may come from one of Æthelmær's buildings of 1005. The relief-decorated tile from St. Frideswide's, Oxford (half actual size) has affinities with tiles from other important religious sites of the late tenth and early eleventh centuries. (Oxford Archaeological Unit and Ashmolean Museum; Biddle & Kjølbye-Biddle 1988)

68 Two early eleventh-century ivories from the Eynsham Abbey excavations. *Left*: Fragment of casket-panel with two tiers of blind arcading. *Right*: Figure of St. John the Evangelist from a crucifixion group (cf Fig. 80), perhaps intended for a book-cover. This piece is unfinished, and was presumably being made within the community. Actual size. (Oxford Archaeological Unit)

lived, as well as a fragment of its architectural sculpture and two contemporary ivories (Figs. 65-8).

The eleventh century was not, on the whole, a happy time for the local minsters. Only Abingdon flourished, to remain one of the great South Midland monasteries until Henry VIII's time. Cholsey has no recorded abbots after the 1010s, and seems to have reverted to a secular state by the Conquest.[129] Eynsham is similarly obscure after Ælfric; it still had an abbot and community in the early 1050s,[130] but by the time of Domesday Book it was only vestigially monastic (below, p. 179). St. Frideswide's survived, and may indeed have been reformed for secular canons in 1049, but it seems for a time to have been annexed by Abingdon Abbey; by 1086 its lands had been reduced, and it was to be a perquisite for royal servants over the next generation.[131] The same might be said of Bampton minster, which Edward the Confessor gave to his clerk Leofric.[132] These originally free-standing communities were doomed, like so many others, to lose their autonomy to high-ranking absentees and see their revenues diverted to other uses.

Yet they still survived as religious communities of one sort or another, as did other Oxfordshire minsters (such as Dorchester and Bicester)[133] for which the evidence is even scantier. Sorely reduced though they were, the ancient minsters continued to stand out from the mass of ordinary churches, and their control over their mother-parishes remained considerable until at least the Conquest. The survival of a minster-based pastoral system is the other side of the coin from the growth of one based on manorial churches, and the chronology of this is very unclear (below, pp. 137–8): in 1066 the Oxfordshire minsters may still have retained much wider parochial rights than they were to have when sources start to become prolific a century later. And if the minsters were declining as religious centres, they had an assured place in the developing medieval world as economic ones.

EXCHANGE, INDUSTRY AND PRODUCTION: THE UPPER THAMES REGION AND ITS RESOURCES

The central fact of the tenth and eleventh centuries is growth. A larger and more diverse population lived in a more organised and exploited landscape. Certain changes are tangible: the nucleation of settlements, the fragmentation of land-holdings, the formation of open field-systems, the emergence of towns, the re-growth of a coin-based economy after the disruptions of the Viking period, the proliferation and diffusion of pottery types. These are the outward and visible signs of more elusive trends: social ranking, intensified exploitation of the peasantry, the production of agrarian surpluses, the expansion of local markets and long-distance transport.

By the late eleventh century we can identify several places in the Upper Thames which in one way or another can be called 'towns', even though our sources often refrain from doing so. Many settlements never dignified with such words as *civitas*, *urbs* or *burgus* had features which an economist or geographer would recognise as more than rural, and their number was certainly growing during the tenth and eleventh centuries. Other places, never urban in the sense of containing merchants, industries or large concentrations of people, were components in a growing exchange network: it is impossible to know how many villages which received royal licences to hold markets between 1150 and 1350 had in fact been holding them for centuries. Below the few well-defined towns, a wider range of places can be associated with some kind of commercial or proto-urban activity.[134]

We must begin with the 'hard' evidence, selective though it is: the Burghal Hidage, mint-signatures on coins, and Domesday Book. Patterns of local and inter-regional trade do not respect county boundaries, so Fig. 69 is an attempt to map this evidence for the whole Upper Thames region.[135] By 1086 the four boroughs of Cricklade, Oxford, Wallingford and Buckingham were substantial towns, all containing mints. Conspicuous in the Domesday record, and much discussed, are the arrangements by which town houses were attached to rural manors, creating groups of satellites in proportion to the status of the focal towns. Thus Oxford, Wallingford and Cricklade had many dependencies, Winchcombe had several, Calne had two and Reading one. It used to be thought that these links between town and countryside identified the original garrison territories of the *burhs*, but most historians would now agree that the pattern was an evolving rather than a static one; at Oxford at least it is clear that some links were relatively new in 1066 (below, p. 158). It is likely enough that the lords of manors obliged to maintain the *burhs* when they were first set up were also the original urban landlords, but the nexus would have expanded as commercial links did: nobles and gentry with business in a town would acquire houses there.

The arrangements plotted on Fig. 69 suggest a hierarchy: the satellites of Cricklade, Winchcombe, Reading and Calne were contained within their own shires, whereas those of Oxford and Wallingford spread across Oxfordshire, north Berkshire and

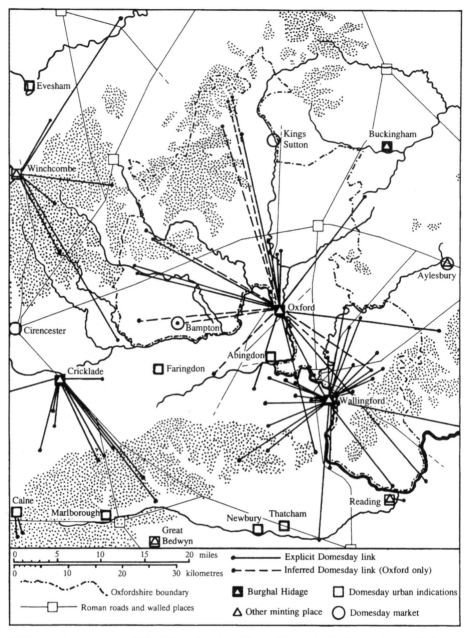

69 Towns and markets in the Oxfordshire region: the evidence of Domesday Book and of late Anglo-Saxon mints.

Buckinghamshire, and overlapped considerably in the Chiltern and Otmoor region. By 1066 the king's tenants in Wallingford owed carrying services, by horse or river, as far as Blewbury, Reading, Sutton Courtenay and Benson.[136] Clearly the influence of these centres on the whole Upper Thames area had become very considerable. This must be the reason for the decline of Dorchester, the oldest historic centre of the region. Caught between Oxford, Wallingford, and the growing monastic town of Abingdon, there was simply no room for it: in the early 1070s it was considered one of those 'villages' from which it was necessary to remove cathedrals and re-locate them in towns.[137]

There is then a second stratum of places where Domesday Book mentions town houses (*hagae*), burgesses or markets. Four of these places — Reading, Winchcombe, Great Bedwyn and Aylesbury — were also mints at one time or another before 1066.[138] A line of settlements with Domesday evidence for proto-urban status runs down the Kennet valley from Calne to Reading, on the fringe of the developing West Saxon heartland. There were nine *hagae* in the *villa* of Faringdon, and Abingdon had 'ten merchants dwelling before the gate of the church'.[139] In Oxfordshire itself, Domesday only credits one place apart from the shire town with any kind of urban attribute: Bampton had a market worth 50s.[140]

This is certainly a minimal record. The maxim that Domesday Book should rarely be used as negative evidence applies above all to its urban data, which are notoriously bad. Once records start to become plentiful in the thirteenth century, many other places can be recognised as small market towns, and a well-integrated network of markets for rural produce can be reconstructed.[141] It cannot be proved that this system existed before the Conquest, but nor is there any justification for assuming that the basis of it did not. The existence by 1000 of big towns such as Oxford and Wallingford, pulling in produce from a wide territory, suggests a penumbra of smaller exchange centres feeding and fed by them.[142]

Oxford, Reading, Winchcombe, Calne, Great Bedwyn, Aylesbury, Abingdon, Faringdon and Bampton have one thing in common: they were the sites of Anglo-Saxon minsters. The same is true of Banbury, Bicester, Charlbury, Eynsham and Thame, which emerge as small towns in sources of the late twelfth and thirteenth centuries.[143] The minsters were in fact the basis of the medieval market network: some 40 per cent of the markets recorded in the Upper Thames region during the thirteenth and fourteenth centuries were at minster places, and only about a quarter of the known minsters are not known ever to have had markets. This pattern can be identified down the whole length of the Thames Valley, and is increasingly being recognised throughout England.[144] Thus the economic role of the minster sites, already clear in the pre-Viking period (above, p. 67), developed and diversified: they were still the foci of commercial life in the thirteenth century and after. It is symptomatic that the town of Bicester grew up not, as one might expect, on the site of Roman Alchester, but around St. Eadburh's minster two miles to the north-east.[145]

The topography of such places is often distinctive. Eynsham, Bampton and Bloxham (Figs. 24, 44, 70) are cases where a core settlement, formed out of the original ecclesiastical enclosure, was enlarged as the lay community grew by the addition of streets and house-plots.[146] There are other local examples of this widespread pattern,

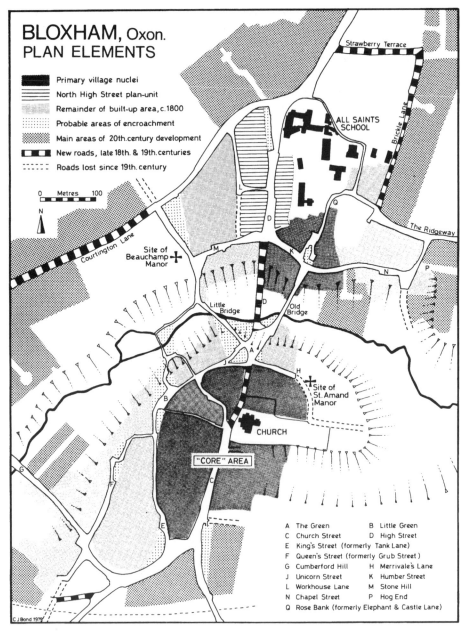

BLOXHAM, Oxon.
PLAN ELEMENTS

- Primary village nuclei
- North High Street plan-unit
- Remainder of built-up area, c.1800
- Probable areas of encroachment
- Main areas of 20th. century development
- New roads, late 18th. & 19th. centuries
- Roads lost since 19th. century

0   Metres   100

A   The Green   B   Little Green
C   Church Street   D   High Street
E   King's Street (formerly Tank Lane)
F   Queen's Street (formerly Grub Street)
G   Cumberford Hill   H   Merrivale's Lane
J   Unicorn Street   K   Humber Street
L   Workhouse Lane   M   Stone Hill
N   Chapel Street   P   Hog End
Q   Rose Bank (formerly Elephant & Castle Lane)

C J Bond 1979

70 Bloxham: the core of this complex settlement is an oval enclosure, probably in origin ecclesiastical, in the bend of a river; compare the Bampton enclosure shown on Fig. 44. (Bond 1985, Fig. 9.8)

such as Thame, Charlbury, Lambourn and Ramsbury.[147] Sometimes the early precinct retained into the late Middle Ages the character of a town within a town, with its own distinctive pattern of life. At Bampton the church was flanked by the rectory to its west and by vicarages on the other three sides; grouped tightly around were fifty cottage tenements held of the rectory manor, perpetuating a characteristic type of proto-urban settlement.[148] The influence of the old ecclesiastical pattern on the new economic one was formative, and justifies coining 'minster-town' as a generic term for this type of English local centre.

As settlements and trading-places expanded, there must have been more and more coming and going between them. The terms 'port-way' and 'port-street', meaning 'road to a major market', are applied at various times to Akeman Street, to the Roman roads across Otmoor and Boars Hill, to the Banbury Road and to the road from Witney to Bladon; in some at least of these cases the 'port' was clearly Oxford (below, p. 154). A 'wain-way' and a 'hay-way' crossed the high ground south of the Thames,[149] the latter for carting hay from the river-side meadows to farms on Boars Hill. Place-names and charter-boundaries record some major through-routes and a prolific variety of minor local roads, often with fords across the numerous streams and rivers.[150] One little crossing over a west Oxfordshire stream, called 'stone ford' in 958 and 'stone bridge' in 969 (Fig. 77), has been excavated: it consisted of a rubble ramp leading down on to a shallow cobbled ford.[151] We cannot know how long most of these roads had existed, but it is very possible that the network of local tracks grew as part of the general expansion of the man-made landscape from the ninth century onwards.

As at all periods, the most important highway was the Thames itself. Although alluvial silting may have made the upper reaches less navigable by 1000 than they had been two or three centuries earlier, it has been argued that the proliferation of mill-weirs had a contrary effect by making the river deeper and slower.[152] Later evidence demonstrates use of the Thames above Oxford: King John allowed merchandise to be shipped down-river from Radcot to London, and in 1317 grain was regularly shipped from Bampton to Oxford.[153] It is a measure of the increased volume of traffic on the difficult stretch from Oxford to Wallingford that between 1052 and 1065, at the request of the men of Oxford, Abingdon Abbey cut a navigation channel across the meadow between Abingdon and Culham.[154] Anglo-Saxon canals are a neglected topic; others may have existed on the Thames, such as the *lade* in the Shifford charter-bounds of 1005.[155]

By 950 Oxfordshire was no longer part of a politico-economic system run from Mercia, and contacts with the Central Midlands may have tended to atrophy. But as finds of eighth-century coinage have already made clear (above, p. 81), a natural line of communication to the Oxford region was from the north-east, along the Clay Vale and the Icknield Way, and here commercial links expanded during the last Anglo-Saxon century. These links have principally been revealed by the study of pottery types.[156] The commercially precocious East Midlands produced an increasing volume of pottery for regional export, including pre-eminently the fine yellow-glazed and unglazed wares from Stamford. At a lower level, the coarse shelly types known generically as 'St. Neot's Ware' are found widely over Cambridgeshire, Huntingdonshire, Hertfordshire and Buckinghamshire, the Vale of the White Horse and southern Oxfordshire marking their south-westerly limit. Both Stamford and 'St. Neot's' types are found in Oxford, the latter perhaps especially favoured by Danelaw immigrants (below, p. 167).

Rich in clay deposits and firewood, Oxfordshire developed a major pottery industry of its own. Maureen Mellor's work has identified a local tradition of coarse hand-made shelly wares ('Fabric B'), found on Oxford sites between the eighth and early eleventh centuries and widespread in the surrounding countryside.[157] During the earlier eleventh century these products, already facing stiff competition from the 'St. Neot's' imports, gave way to another locally-made fabric with calcarious gravel tempering ('Fabric AC') which continued in production beyond the Conquest. No kiln sites have yet been found, but it is likely that production was decentralised and largely determined by the sources of raw materials. The gravel-tempered wares can be shown on geological grounds to have been made north of Oxford, and it seems highly likely that they should be associated with the *ollaria* (glossed *potaria*) which Domesday Book locates at Bladon.[158]

The distribution pattern of the shelly wares is potentially very significant, though currently open to dispute. Pottery of this type has been found in the Upper and Lower Thames (though not in its middle reaches), and above all in London, where excavations show that it had a virtual monopoly between the late ninth and early eleventh centuries (Fig. 71).[159] If the vessels found in such quantities in London really did come from Oxfordshire, the implications for the commercial importance of the region, and for the volume of down-river trade on the Thames, are enormous. The problem is that the vessels found in London are more varied than those found in Oxfordshire, and unlike the local finds they are wheel-made.[160] However, the latest mineralogical analysis of the London fabrics concludes that 'a source in Oxfordshire, probably in the valley of a stream or river overlying or cutting through Jurassic shelly clays, is likely'.[161] These issues are relevant to very much more than pottery studies, and they need to be resolved.

A lesser but still significant Oxfordshire industry was quarrying. The name of Standhill, on the Portland Beds east of Oxford, commemorates a 'stone-quarry' (*stangedelf*) mentioned in 1002, and the same term occurs about a dozen times as a field-name.[162] North Oxfordshire ironstone was used in the late Anglo-Saxon churches of Tredington (Warwicks.) and Swalcliffe.[163] Most significant was Taynton, on the Great Oolite formation of the Cotswold edge, where the Domesday entry mentions a *quadraria*.[164] E.M. Jope has shown that Great Oolite, much of it probably from Taynton, was used for architectural details over a wide area of the south-west Midlands; a notable example is the Taynton and Burford stone used for the quoins and belfry details of the tower of St. Michael's-at-the-North Gate, Oxford (Fig. 96).[165] It is unclear how far this pattern can be pushed back before the mid eleventh century: the expansion of quarrying may in fact be a phenomenon of the very late Anglo-Saxon period, when the boom in church-building fuelled a demand too big to be met by the plundering of Roman ruins.[166]

The river was the meeting-place of agrarian and commercial activities. More corn meant more mills (all water-powered at this date); mills required the digging of leats and the building of banks and weirs, which in turn provided new opportunities for both transport and fishing.[167] As with navigation-channels, we may have under-estimated the number of Anglo-Saxon mill-leats on the Thames. At Abingdon the leat

71 'Late Saxon Shelly Ware' found in London. This pottery may have been made in Oxfordshire and transported down the Thames. (Museum of London)

and tail-race of the abbey mill are known to have been cut by abbot Æthelwold (c. 955-63),[168] and this is unlikely to be a unique case. By 1086 mills were widespread, many of them on quite small streams though with concentrations along the Thames, Cherwell, Windrush and Evenlode.[169] The 956 bounds of Tadmarton begin at *Eadwardes mylne*, and the name of Beard Mill on the Windrush records a *bord-myln*, 'mill made of boards'.[170] Higher up the Windrush, the 'mill-weir which belongs to Ducklington' appears in the 1044 charter-bounds of Witney.[171]

The braided side-streams along the Thames and around its confluence with the Cherwell were excellent sites for fish-weirs, and here fisheries abounded by 1086.[172] The typical weir consisted of wattle barriers, set in V-shaped formation to funnel the fish into a small central opening where they would be trapped in a wicker basket (Figs. 6, 72–3). In 1005 Shifford had two weirs on the Thames, 'one above the *lade* and the other below it', and the slightly later bounds of Sandford-on-Thames begin at *stubbucwere*, the 'little tree-stump weir'.[173] The most valuable Domesday fisheries (33s.), listed under Bampton, can almost certainly be located at Chimney (Fig. 5),

72 Model of a typical late Anglo-Saxon fish-weir mounted with a wicker trap. (Canal Museum, Nottingham; photograph by C.R. Salisbury)

where a fishing community is recorded in thirteenth-century sources.[174] The traps would have been set with their openings up-stream to catch full-grown eels moving seawards in the autumn migration, or down-stream for salmon swimming to the head-waters in spring.[175] In 1086 several mills and fisheries paid their rents in eels,[176] and eel pie was staple working-class food on the Upper Thames as late as Victoria's reign. This trade must have been very considerable: in the 1060s the monks of Abingdon took a yearly custom of 100 eels from each Oxford boat using their new canal between 2 February and Easter.[177]

A WELL-MANAGED LANDSCAPE

By 1086 the face of Oxfordshire had assumed a form which, in broad outline, it kept until the great enclosures of the eighteenth century. Domesday Book (Fig. 74) suggests a pattern of regional variation which later sources confirm: developed agriculture in much of northern and western Oxfordshire and along the Clay Vale, contrasting with the wood-pasture economies of Wychwood, the Oxford Heights and the Chilterns.[178] This definition of specialised land-use had much to do with economic growth since the mid-

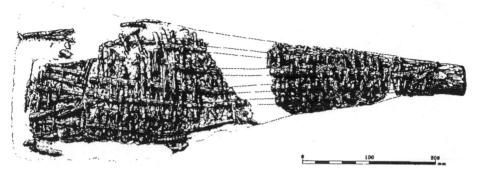

73 Late Anglo-Saxon wicker fish-trap from a side-stream of the Kennet. (Trust for Wessex Archaeology; Butterworth & Lobb 1992, Fig. 43)

ninth century. Scholars working on surrounding regions, above all Della Hooke, have stressed the emergence of self-sufficient late Anglo-Saxon estates based on well-balanced and well-exploited assets. Hooke writes of the Berkshire Downs and the Avon Valley:

> Boundaries seem to have been drawn up deliberately to include all three types of land within each estate: valley land suitable for cattle; arable on the better-drained soils where they were not too steep; and open downland, particularly suitable for sheep, with . . . occasional woodland providing additional summer pasture. The estates, therefore, show a close relationship to the nature of the land as it was in the Anglo-Saxon period . . . Their demarcation may have coincided with the allocation of estates to Anglo-Saxon landholders. This is unlikely to have occurred in the earliest stage of the Anglo-Saxon settlement, but seems to represent a later stage, when a hierarchy had become firmly established within Anglo-Saxon society that included a lordly element below the level of the aristocracy. The delineation of the roughly parallel units seems to indicate deliberate planning at some stage and there is some evidence to suggest that the southern side of the Vale of the White Horse, incorporating the scarp face of the north Berkshire Downs, may initially have been appendant to the royal vill of Wantage.[179]

An equally clear specialisation of land-use is evident in most Oxfordshire farming communities when manorial records appear in the thirteenth and fourteenth centuries. Our evidence for the late Anglo-Saxon landscape is fragmentary, but greater than is widely thought, and from it we can start to piece together a picture. There are two great linguistic sources: place-names (which are prolific but not easily dated), and the boundary descriptions normally included in tenth- and early eleventh-century charters (Fig. 75). Although charter-boundaries are hard to interpret, and by definition describe the peripheries rather than the hearts of land-units, they can give a marvellously detailed snapshot of a walk through the late Anglo-Saxon countryside. Here, for instance, are the bounds of Crowmarsh and Newnham Murren in 966:[180]

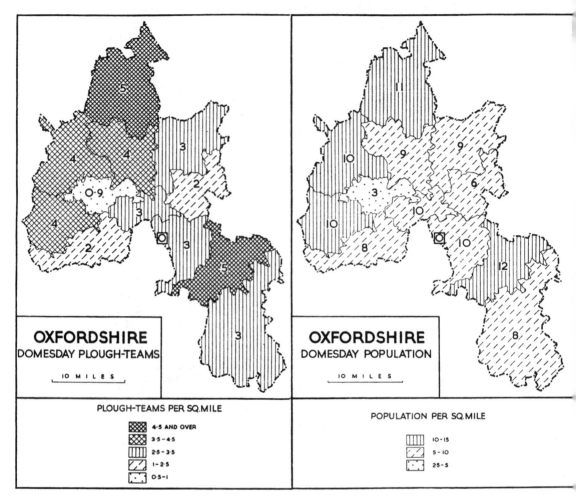

74 Distribution of plough-teams and population in 1086, according to the Domesday Book data. (*Dom. Geog. S.-E.*, Figs. 65 and 67; H.C. Darby.)

From the heathen burials up along the ditch to the boundary way; up along the boundary way to the watch-hill where the crucifix stood; thence up to the red slough as far as the old fort; from the red slough to the quarry outside which the park (*haga*) lies; from the quarry to the middle slade; along the middle slade to the grey stone; from the grey stone along harp-dene to the calves' wood-pasture (*leah*); downwards from the calves' wood-pasture always by the park and the old way to the beck; thence along the beck to the Thames; along-stream to Catta's island.

By the thirteenth century, Oxfordshire north of the Chilterns was classic open-field country: most of the arable lay in dispersed and intermixed strips, grouped usually into two large 'fields' which alternated from year to year between cultivation and fallow.[181] The recent work on alluviation in the Thames floodplain suggests that arable farming

75 Edward the Confessor's charter of 1059 giving Taynton and its appendages to the abbey of Saint-Denis (S.1028; Archives Nationales, Paris, and S.D. Keynes). Although it is uncertain whether this manuscript is original or a near-contemporary copy, it illustrates a typical late Anglo-Saxon royal charter. The central section, in English, describes the boundaries of Taynton itself, of its meadowland at Northmoor (þam more) and of its woodland in Wychwood (þam wuda).

intensified once more during the ninth to eleventh centuries,[182] and it seems likely that open fields were a product of this intensification. Della Hooke has shown that in the adjoining regions of the West Midlands and the Vale of the White Horse, at least some of the later open fields existed by the mid- to late tenth century.[183] The Oxfordshire evidence, inferior though it is, points to the same conclusion. Six hides at Brighthampton, Aston Bampton and Lew were said in 984 to be 'divided in the common land' (*in communi tellure diremtis*), and four hides at Sandford-on-Thames granted in 1050 were likewise 'in the common land' (*on þam gemannan lande*); in 1086 a hide of the demesne (*inland*) of Garsington lay 'dispersed among the king's land' (*iacet inter terram regis particulatim*).[184] Charter-boundaries are rarely helpful, for the obvious reason that open fields were normally at the centres of estates, not their margins, but can be revealing when they describe divided land-units: in 904 the boundary of Water Eaton ran *þwyres ofer þ' furlang*, 'diagonally over the furlong', and in 1002 that between the two Haseley townships went *on ðæra æcera heafada*, 'on the headland of the acres'.[185] In 1004 the Cowley boundary went partly through open-field land where it rose above the Cherwell floodplain: eastwards to *ofranfurlange*, and then northwards to the 'wheat-furlong's head' (*hwet furlanges heafde*).[186] Clearly some land in late Anglo-Saxon Oxfordshire was farmed in strips and furlongs. None the less, it would be wrong to assume that the 'Midland System' of common fields existed in all its complexity. The arrangements described in thirteenth-century sources were the result of a long and complex evolution, which was under way by 950 but certainly very far from complete.

By the tenth century, as arable farming spread and intensified, the resources of the woods and wastes would have been coming under greater pressure. Pasture zones were valuable assets in their own right, closely defined and apportioned. Some late Anglo-Saxon charters describe, in addition to the main estates, the outlying enclaves of woodland and 'moor' which provided vital support for cattle, sheep and swine (Fig. 75). Beryl Schumer's important study of eleventh-century Wychwood emphasises that it 'was not an indeterminate trackless wilderness, but rather an organized area of wood and wood-pasture with definite and fairly stable boundaries, and clearly defined routes through it'. Most manors within three miles of its fringes, and some much further away, had rights of grazing animals, cutting timber and hunting game, so that much of Wychwood was carved up into a complex patchwork of manorial outliers.[187] The Chilterns, in contrast to the rest of Oxfordshire, supported a mixed economy in which open fields were relatively unimportant.[188] Long, narrow townships resembling those on the Berkshire Downs rose up the dip-slope and the scarp from the more developed zones on either side (Fig. 62). The charter-bounds of Pyrton illustrate one of these straggling entities (Figs. 3–4), in which the main estate was linked end-to-end with its upland pasture comprising a mixture of woodland with *feld* on the open plateau.[189]

The wet-lands of Otmoor and the floodplain were still more valuable, and had a distinctive economy of their own. The near-circular bowl of Otmoor (Fig. 76) was ringed by small communities, some identified in Domesday Book, which lived partly by farming and partly by the resources of the marsh: sheep and cattle pasture, fishing, fowling, and industries using osiers and willows.[190] In the Thames floodplain, small land-units consisted of alluvium interspersed with gravel islands, mostly bounded by the sluggish, meandering streams known in local dialect as 'lakes' from Old English *lacu*.[191] Thus the bounds of Sandford ran from a weir along a branch of the Thames to

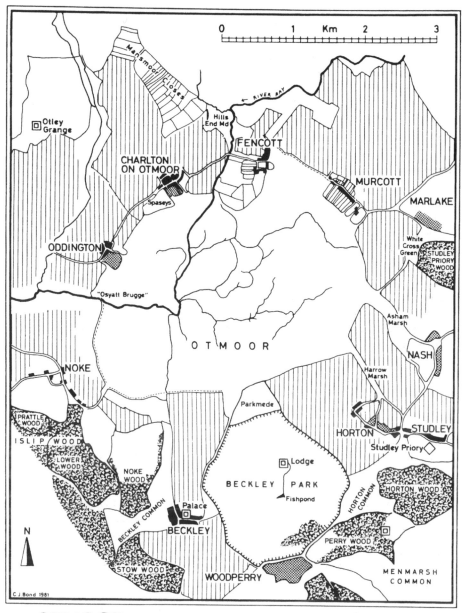

OTMOOR AT THE END OF THE MIDDLE AGES

- Medieval villages
- Moated site
- Approximate extent of late medieval open-field cultivation
- Areas of settlement desertion or contraction
- Monastic house
- Park pale
- Woodland

76 Otmoor in the later Middle Ages, showing the ring of small communities around the edge of the marshy bowl which were probably developing during the eleventh century. (Bond 1981, Fig. 4)

Sandfordes lace, and then 'up through the moor'; those of Chimney went along *Ceoman lace* and the Thames to a confluence, along the 'northern stream' to 'a *lace* between Berhtwulf's island and rush island', and thence back to the start along the 'north stream'.[192] Like woodlands, many of these small riverine holdings began as 'moorland' dependencies of larger manors, but were developing as free-standing entities by around the time of the Conquest. Northmoor, bounded by the Thames, the Windrush and the *dic-lace*, first occurs as *þam more* in the Taynton charter of 1059 (Fig. 75).[193]

Mōr is a general word for marsh or waste, though in this context it may usually mean 'grassland' (above, p. xxiii); 'meadow' (*mæd*, literally 'mowed') is much more specific, indicating hay-making.[194] Two Oxfordshire charters make this explicit: in bounds ascribed to 887 (though possibly later), Brightwell Baldwin had detached *mæd-lond* between two fords, and the Witney boundary of 1044 passed 'the *mæd-ham* that belongs to Shilton'.[195] The original name of Madley Brook at Cogges, first recorded in 969, seems to have been *mæd-sæge*, 'slow-moving stream by a meadow'.[196] These references support palaeo-botanical evidence that more floodplain grassland was developed as hay-meadow as the economy grew in the late Anglo-Saxon period. In the words of Lambrick and Robinson:

> The later Saxon and early medieval integration of settlement with land use and the development of communal systems of management seem to parallel the Iron Age response to pressure on land. . . . Hay making may never have ceased since the Roman period, but its development on a very large scale may have helped underpin early medieval agrarian and urban economic growth. The spread of minor settlements onto the floodplain again repeats the Iron Age pattern.[197]

Where several sets of charter-boundaries survive for one small area, it is possible to get an extremely good idea of the landscape and its variations. In the lower Windrush valley (Fig. 77), for instance, we have the contiguous or near-contiguous boundaries of Witney, Eynsham, Ducklington, Bampton, Shifford, Chimney and Northmoor.[198] The contrasting geographical and land-use zones stand out clearly in the distribution of terms. To the south-east, the floodplain was dissected by streams, ditches and 'lakes'. The marshy area south of Witney itself (Witta's island') was known as 'Witta's moor'; the Witney and Ducklington estates both had long tongues projecting south-eastwards between the two branches of the Windrush to take in as much as possible of the precious water-land. By contrast, the north-western part of the area rises up into Wychwood Forest, on the clay-lands and towards the edge of the Cotswolds, and here woodland terms abound: the 'wood-street', the 'hunter's way', a *wyrtwala* ('root-wall' or wood-bank) and several *leahs*. *Spon leage* and *spon weg*, the 'wood-chipping clearing' and 'wood-chipping way', suggest a logging area from which timber was presumably carried down the 'way' to the Windrush. Around Ducklington was another wooded area: 'Beorna's *leah*' and 'east *leah*' (now Barley Park and Cokethorpe), a *haga* (enclosure, probably of a park-like character), and another *wyrtwala*. For the south-western zone, mostly open-field land in the later Middle Ages, the charters are more equivocal. North of Claywell, a tortuous stretch of the Ducklington boundary includes *andlang fura*, 'along the furrow'; on the other hand, the 955-7 (?) bounds of Bampton[199] cut across the future open fields of Aston without a hint of their existence.

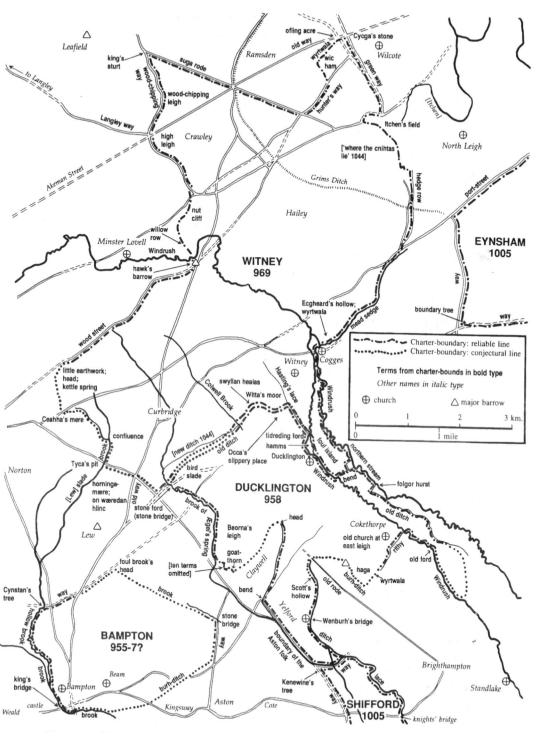

77 A group of charter-boundaries in the lower Windrush Valley.

78 '*Andlang hege-rewe on met sinc*'. The boundary between Witney and North Leigh is still marked with a 'hedge-row' as described in the Witney charter of 969 (S.771), here seen running down-hill to meet *met sinc* (Madley Brook), the 'slow-moving stream by a meadow'. (Bailey 1989)

Much in these tenth-century texts would have been familiar to a late- or post-medieval inhabitant of the area: the open fields, the carefully apportioned moor, the managed woodland of Wychwood, the park-like terrain around Cokethorpe. But it was not an unchanging landscape. The open fields were probably expanding, and it seems likely that the floodplain was being ditched, managed and exploited ever more intensively. It is scarcely coincidence that 'kettle acres', the 'new ditch', the Shilton *mæd-ham*, the Ducklington mill-weir and the 'wain-moor' (moor traversed by hay-wains?) all appear in the Witney bounds of 1044, but not in those of 969. If we had similar detail from two centuries earlier, we would probably see a landscape painted with a broader brush: similar in its basic geographical contrasts, but less precisely demarcated.

MANORS, LORDS AND PEASANTS

A concomitant of this tighter definition and exploitation was that much of the land was administered in smaller units: the 'classic manor', containing one or two village communities rather than many, became normal during the two centuries after 850. We have far more charters from the tenth century than from any earlier period, and they grant land in smaller numbers of hides to lesser people. The detailed boundary descriptions which they now contain speak of a society of small proprietors, ready to quarrel over rights which earlier landlords had been content to leave vague.

It would be wrong to assume that there were no small manors in Oxfordshire in the poorly-documented period before 900. Estates of ten hides or less were sometimes acquired by religious corporations as early as the mid-ninth century (above, p. 78), and the '887' charter-bounds of Brightwell Baldwin define the surrounding land-units in terms of ownership and local communities: 'Ceolwulf's tree', 'Æthelheah's boundary', 'Ecgfrith's boundary', 'the boundary of the Cuxham folk', 'the boundary of the Ingham folk'.[200] But there are three good reasons for thinking that the fragmentation of large land-units into self-contained, cellular manors was happening after 850 on a wholly new scale.

First, the dismemberment of some specific complexes is well-attested. The fragmentation of the 300-hide Eynsham estate during the ninth and tenth centuries has already been noted (p. 68). The eastern sector of the large royal territory centred on Bampton was systematically dismembered and given away between the 950s and 980s: Chimney in 955–7, possibly Curbridge before 957, Ducklington in 958, Shifford sometime in Eadgar's reign, land at Brighthampton, Aston and Lew in 984.[201] What we seem to see here is the endowing of royal servants with land-units which had now for the first time become viable in their own right, and which were deliberately 'zoned for development'. Secondly, the layout of estates was, as we have seen, closely related to late Anglo-Saxon patterns of land-use. The characteristic 'strip-townships' formed by progressive linear subdivision, such as those on the Oxfordshire Chilterns, have been studied in detail on the Berkshire and Surrey Downs and are widely agreed to be of tenth- to eleventh-century date.[202] Thirdly (though north Berkshire illustrates this better than Oxfordshire), place-name scholars have come to recognise a distinct 'layer' of names, dating from the ninth century and after, which define land-units by reference to the names of their lords: Woolstone (*'Wulfric's tūn'*) in the Vale of the White Horse is so called because in 960 King Eadgar gave it to his thegn Wulfric.[203]

Despite the tendency towards scaling-down, the multi-vill estate was certainly not an obsolete form. The thirty hides of Witney, comprising the townships of Curbridge, Hailey and Crawley (Fig. 77), were probably assembled so that King Eadgar could give them to his thegn Ælfhelm in 969.[204] The inferred fifty-hide comital manor of Langford-Broadwell (above, p. 111), and the twenty-six-hide manor of Stanton Harcourt,[205] may be further examples of big estates formed late in the Anglo-Saxon period. Elsewhere some very small manors were added to the scattered holdings of very great men, as when Ealdorman Byrhtnoth acquired the three hides of Shifford, or Earl Godwine the four hides of Sandford-on-Thames.[206] But we can also see the genuinely humble thegns for whom these grants may have made all the difference between man-at-arms and landed proprietor: Ælfstan with his five hides at Cuxham (995), for instance, or the brothers Eadric, Eadwig and Ealdred with a meagre two hides between them in Benson (996).[207] The Worcester archive, the classic demonstration of how small manors could be formed by leasing from a great ecclesiastical estate, includes two Oxfordshire cases: five hides at Brightwell Baldwin to Byrhtric in 973, and five at Pyrton to Leofward in 987.[208]

We are witnessing here the creation of the English country gentry: a new class of small resident proprietors for whom manorial fragmentation provided an economic base.[209] Like the emergence of common fields and nucleated villages, their appearance marks a crucial stage in the development of the high medieval manorial regime. With them came other familiar landmarks of the later rural scene: the manor-house (often substantial and defended) and the manorial church, centres respectively of the local economic community and the local religious community. It was as private chapels that the great majority of our parish churches were founded, and until the twelfth century they remained the property of their lords. Hence that most characteristic of English rural scenes: manor-house and church side-by-side, squire and parson living and working as neighbours.[210]

No Anglo-Saxon manor-house in Oxfordshire has been excavated fully, but a few sites have produced fragmentary evidence. At Cogges, where we know that the

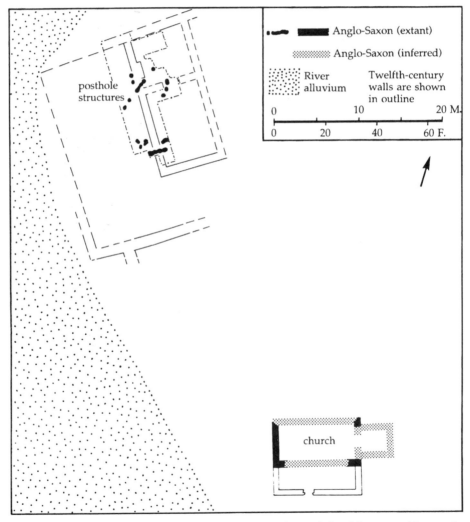

79 Late Anglo-Saxon Cogges, showing the relationship between the post-holes of the presumed house and the earliest standing parts of the parish church. A classic grouping of timber manor-house with small two-cell stone church.

80 Langford: the smaller late Anglo-Saxon rood. (Photo-montage, showing the pieces re-assembled in something like their original arrangement.)

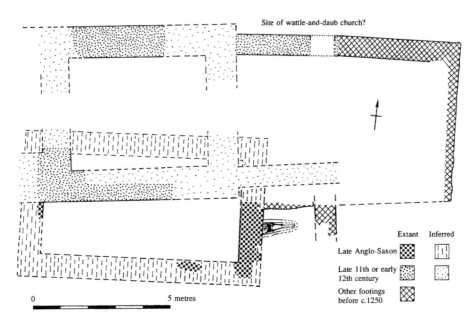

Site of wattle-and-daub church?

Extant   Inferred

Late Anglo-Saxon

Late 11th or early
12th century

Other footings
before c.1250

0   5 metres

81 Wood Eaton: the birth and growth of a local church. A timber church with a graveyard is indicated by burnt daub fragments and at least one grave. It was replaced by a small stone church, probably also late Anglo-Saxon, of which the east wall was built across the grave. After the Norman Conquest a larger stone church was built in a slightly different position, to be replaced in turn by the existing thirteenth-century church (not shown). (Oxford University Archaeological Society)

Norman lord founded a priory in about 1100 on the site of the manor-house, the priory buildings overlie the post-trenches of timber structures (Fig. 79).[211] Deddington and Middleton Stoney castles were also superimposed on late Anglo-Saxon buildings, and in the latter case the enclosing bank and ditch may be partly pre-Conquest.[212] It has recently been pointed out that Little Tew manor-house stands within a sub-circular enclosure with concentric boundary banks, and although further work is needed an Anglo-Saxon date seems distinctly possible.[213] Only small-scale archaeological work has hitherto taken place, but manorial sites were clearly widespread through the county by c. 1000, and more can be expected to come to light.

The urge to have private churches was deep-rooted in early medieval aristocratic culture, so there was a natural tendency for units of landlordship, of whatever size, to acquire them. Churches on the large, multi-vill estates of magnates would be correspondingly important, perhaps showing some of the features characteristic of minsters. Instances of this may be Hook Norton, Tackley and Witney, all of which have probable remains of late Anglo-Saxon naves,[214] or Broadwell, Stanton Harcourt and Langford where the churches were evidently of some status but no pre-Conquest fabric survives. At the last of these, however, two exceptional late Anglo-Saxon crucifixion sculptures (Fig. 80) are re-set in later walls.[215] The suggestion that Langford was a comital estate (above, p. 111) raises the interesting possibility that these could have been commissioned by that notable patron, Earl Leofric of Mercia.

82 Caversfield church: 'double-splayed' window formed of rubble around a pierced slab set half-way through the wall. A good illustration of the simple style characteristic of small manorial churches in the late tenth and eleventh centuries.

There are scattered fragments of evidence, written and physical, for a few other churches. Whitchurch clearly had one by the time of the first reference to it (as *Hwitecyrcan*) in 990–2;[216] so did Great Tew, called 'Church Tew' (*Cirictiwan*) in 1050–2 (below, p. 138). An odd and exceptional case is the small and otherwise uninteresting church of Cokethorpe, which the Ducklington charter of 958 calls 'the old church'.[217] Of buildings conventionally thought to be Anglo-Saxon on architectural grounds, Langford, North Leigh and Waterperry have post-Conquest Romanesque features and must be ruled out (below, pp. 179–80). This leaves just Caversfield (Fig. 82) and Swalcliffe to represent ordinary rural churches;[218] Cogges (Fig. 79) and Cottisford may be others, though neither case is conclusive.[219] Occasionally Anglo-Saxon foundations come to light beneath the floors of later churches, as at Westcot Barton where excavation has disclosed three phases preceding the standing mid-twelfth-century nave,[220] or Wood Eaton where recent drainage works unexpectedly revealed a complex sequence (Fig. 81).

When most of these local churches were founded remains unclear, especially since Oxfordshire is one of those counties where Domesday Book ignores them. The great majority of Oxfordshire parish churches are not mentioned in written sources before the mid-twelfth century, and architectural features popularly called 'Norman' are also in most cases post-1150. Whether three-quarters, a half, or a quarter or less of the

83 Personal piety in the mid-eleventh century: a reliquary for suspension around the neck, found at Sandford-on-Thames. The front bears a figure of Christ in Majesty; the edge inscription may be translated 'May that which lies within/ Guard us from all sin'. Actual size. (Ashmolean Museum; Hinton 1974, No. 30)

churches standing in the county in 1200 had existed in 1066 is at present completely imponderable. Nor do we really know how far the late Anglo-Saxon private churches remained under the authority of their parent minsters (above, p. 116).[221] It is safe to say only that in Oxfordshire, as elsewhere, there was a shift at some time between the mid-tenth and mid-twelfth centuries from a system of pastoral care based on central minsters to one based on churches dispersed through the countryside, and that this must have brought the Church's sacramental message closer to ordinary people.

A good illustration of these various trends is a small area of north Oxfordshire, west of the Cherwell and including the valleys of the Glyme and Dorn (Fig. 84).[222] The modern settlement pattern consists of farms, hamlets and rather dispersed villages, many of them grouped along the river-valleys. A similar pattern much earlier is suggested by the number of settlements with 'surnames': Great, Little and Duns Tew; North, Middle and Steeple Aston; Westcot, Middle and Steeple Barton; Nether and Over Worton. The Tews, in particular, look like fragments of a large land-unit which must have also included Sandford and the Wortons.[223] Amid these scattered communities, a few relatively important and central estate churches evidently existed by 1066. Great Tew was called 'Church Tew' in the 1050s, and 'Church Enstone' had a valuable church serving a large estate of Winchcombe Abbey. 'Steeple Barton' and 'Steeple Aston' are not recorded as such until long after the Conquest, but it may be significant that their names follow a similar pattern.

A little window on to the manorial society of this region is the lease of 'Church Tew' by St. Albans' Abbey to Tova, widow of Wihtric, in 1050-2.[224] The manor which she acquired was evidently a large one – sixteen hides according to Domesday

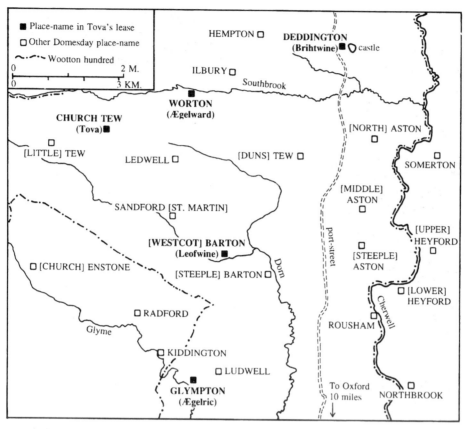

84 The local witnesses of Tova's lease.

Book.[225] The village (Fig. 85) has an unplanned appearance and may be of pre-Conquest origin (below, p. 144); south-eastwards lies the church, and beside it until *c.* 1800 was the manor-house, perhaps much where it stood in Tova's day. Of the thirteen thegns' names in the witness-list, five are linked by the preposition *æt* to Oxfordshire place-names: *Æglric æt Glimtune, Brihtwine æt Dædintune, Leofwine æt Bertune, Ælfwine æt Ingham* and *Ægelward æt Ortune.* Ingham is in south Oxfordshire, but Glympton, Deddington, Barton and Worton are all in the northern half of Wootton hundred (Fig. 84). Leofwine can be identified in Domesday Book, which shows that he held an estate at Westcot Barton, Little Tew, Duns Tew and Dunthrop totalling fourteen hides.[226] These were a group of local gentleman-farmers: Tova's friends and neighbours. As it happens, some of them can be associated with sites already mentioned. The domestic remains under Deddington Castle may have been Brihtwine's house; the first church at Westcot Barton presumably belonged to Leofwine; and some other neighbour of Tova's would have lived in the ditched enclosure at Little Tew. We cannot know if these people normally used toponymic surnames, but their names as stated in the lease are strikingly like those adopted by

minor manorial lords in the twelfth and thirteenth centuries.[227] The impression is of a
gentry firmly rooted in the land.

They were not rooted immovably: there are hints of significant and possibly traumatic
tenurial change during the two decades before 1066. In Oxfordshire as elsewhere, the
rise of Godwineson power boded ill for owners of land coveted by Godwineson
clients.[228] Of the people named in the Church Tew lease, only Leofwine of Barton can
be identified in Domesday Book. Great Tew itself had passed by 1066 from both St.
Albans and Tova to the wealthy Æthelnoth of Kent – an ally of Godwine – who also
held the twenty-six-hide manor of Stanton Harcourt.[229] Meanwhile the great thegn
Wulfweard White, a dependent of Godwine's daughter Queen Edith, had acquired
Ægelric's land at Glympton as part of a seven-manor estate totalling sixty-eight hides.[230]
Domesday Book mentions two men who had been 'commended' to Earl Tostig, Saegeat
at Ledwell and Edward at Caversfield.[231] Another major figure in the immediately pre-
(and indeed post-) Conquest years was Wigod of Wallingford, a kinsman of Edward the
Confessor who may have amassed a large estate in Oxfordshire (below, pp. 174–5). If the
aristocratic land-grabbing which followed 1066 was on a totally new scale, the gentry of
Oxfordshire may not have been unfamiliar with the principle.

The expansion which enabled so many manorial lords to maintain aristocratic life-
styles must have profoundly altered the lives of ordinary peasants. The old tribute and
food-render regimes were designed to feed large, mainly itinerating households on an
episodic basis. In a world in which hundreds of landowners, great and small, needed
regular supplies of goods to consume and to sell, something more systematic – and
oppressive – had to develop. For the growth of commerce, as Pauline Stafford
observes, 'the fragmentation of estates . . . may be important, especially if it located
individual landlords in villages, efficiently exploiting their local demesnes and creating
surpluses':[232] small manors were more productive than great ones, and were better
managed. This was bound to intensify exploitation of lords' directly-managed land,
and hence the demands on their dependents' labour. But only part of the rural
population was caught up in this seigneurial nexus. It consisted of dependent peasant
groups who inhabited what would later be termed the 'demesnes' or 'home-farms' of
the manors, but what in their very different, late Anglo-Saxon forms are best defined
(in the language of the time) as *inland*, contrasted with *outland*.[233]

The Anglo-Saxons had always been a slave-owning society, and the core of the
labour needed for working the 'inland', the lord's own land, had from the earliest
stages of land-management been provided by slaves. The grant to Worcester in 887 of
land at Brightwell Baldwin and Watlington includes the transfer of six 'men' from the
royal vill at Benson with all their families. Presumably these were slaves, and the list of
their names – Alhmund, Tidulf, Tidheh, Lull, Lull and Eadwulf – is a rare record of
the very humble.[234] Slaves must have carried out much of the tenth- and eleventh-
century agrarian expansion, and the distribution of slaves in Domesday Book suggests,
not surprisingly, that they comprised a higher proportion of the population in open-
field than in wood-pasture terrain; there were more of them in north and west
Oxfordshire than in the Chiltern region, for instance.[235] But alongside broad
geographical patterns were marked contrasts between estates. In Worcestershire,
Warwickshire and Gloucestershire the demesnes of lay tenants-in-chief and subtenants
were not only better stocked and more heavily manned than royal and ecclesiastical

demesnes, but also contained a higher proportion of slaves.[236] The most enthusiastic slave-users were the minor gentry resident on their estates.

Here the term 'slave' needs definition. These were not single workers living in barracks: the Benson men of 887 had families (*cum omni prole et stirpe eorum*), and there are strong grounds for thinking that the *servi* enumerated in Domesday Book were mostly married, with their own dwellings.[237] The 'hutting' of slaves, the giving to them of smallholdings which made them self-supporting though still economically dependent, was good management policy. Thus slaves were the forerunners and progenitors of a range of 'demesne-oriented people'[238] with tenancies on the inland, distinguished from other smallholders by their low status and heavy, often specialised labour services.

Oxfordshire sources contribute little to the general picture of these semi-servile peasants. The categories of Domesday Book are crude,[239] and its blanket term *villani*, 'vill-dwellers', must cover a variety of different people, perhaps including both inland and outland tenants. *Gebur* ('boor') is the standard late Anglo-Saxon term for a low-status inland peasant, and in some counties Domesday uses it as equivalent to *colibertus* or 'freed-man'; in the Oxfordshire folios these only occur at Bampton, where there were 17 *buri* as well as 40 *villani* and 13 *bordarii*.[240] In 1086 most Oxfordshire manors had *bordarii*, 'bordars', a French term which well describes a class of Englishmen whose function was to supply their lord's 'board' or table. 'It is probable', Rosamond Faith writes, 'that Domesday classes as bordars a very heterogeneous group of freed slaves and other inland workers, distinguishing them simply by their small-holdings near the *curia*, their inferior housing, their work on the inland and their dependent status'.[241] Doubtless these bordars would have included *cotsetlas* or cottagers, inhabitants of what seems to have been a distinct type of settlement, normally formed on the inland, which place-names distinguish as a *cot*. Names incorporating this element, often associated with personal names (e.g. Alvescot, Kencott), concentrate in the area where Oxfordshire, Berkshire and Wiltshire meet, and *cot-stōw* and *cot-steall* are common throughout Oxfordshire.[242]

Not everyone was a 'demesne-oriented person'. Peasants of a freer and more substantial kind are so poorly recorded that it is easy to forget them, but they were very numerous and important; indeed, they formed the backbone of the shire community. If the traditional picture of early England as a classless society of free *ceorls* farming their hides needs severe qualification (above, p. 80), there can be no doubt that families living on a hide or so were very common in the tenth or eleventh century. We can see traces of them in Domesday Book, such as the one-hide holdings of Ælfwine and Ælfgar at Combe, Siward at Sandford or Ketel at Somerton.[243] Ought we to call these men lords or peasants? And were the twenty-six 'free men' (*liberi homines*) recorded in 1086 at Aston Rowant, Pyrton, Enstone and Goring closer to the kinds of people who might have received royal charters, or to *villani*? There was no simple contrast between exploiters and exploited: we must envisage a multi-layered society, to which such seemingly anachronistic terms as 'gentleman', 'yeoman' or 'farmer' are in fact often appropriate.

Some holdings of this scale, as the above cases show, were manors in their own right which might be recorded as such in charters or Domesday Book,[244] but many more formed part of the 'outland' of larger manors.[245] Unlike the inland people with their heavy manual duties, the tenants of these were *gafolgeldas*, 'rent-payers' whose

obligations to their lords were of a financial, or at any rate non-servile, kind. Another
fundamental difference is that their land was assessed in hides subject to the public
burdens of military service and tax, for which they were responsible in their own
right. These were free men, entitled and obliged to bear arms and participate in public
life, even though the land that they held belonged to the estates of greater men. Two
or three centuries later much of this land, split into quarter-hides or 'yardlands' and
redistributed in the common fields, would be held by unfree 'villeins', who must often
have been their descendants but who had come down in the world.

These formed the bulk of the men who attended the hundred courts and manned
the local levies. Often they would have been of long-standing local descent, their lands
inherited in accordance with customary practices which usually involved partition
between heirs. They would have been a traditional element in society, maintaining
values and customs, such as violent vendetta, not always welcomed in the increasingly
centralised tenth-century state. This world of traditional kin-structures, loyalties and
feuds is illustrated by the sad story of the three brothers of Ardley, who held five hides
there in the 990s:[246]

> There were three brothers sharing a certain establishment (*in quodam residentes
> convivio*), one of whose men, by name Leofric, stole a bridle at the instigation of
> the devil; and when it was discovered in his bosom, those who had lost the
> bridle, and the three brothers, the masters of the aforesaid thief, rose up hurredly
> and made war on one another. Two of the brothers, namely Ælfnoth and Ælfric,
> were killed in the fight, and the third, Æthelwine, barely escaped along with the
> aforesaid robber, entering the church of St. Helen.

How did a society of relatively free smallholders turn into the dependent peasantry
of the medieval manorial regime? Part of the answer to this question is that later
medieval peasants were far from universally dependent: the conventional picture tends
to ignore the widespread survival of free tenements, and the formal definition of free
tenure during the twelfth and thirteenth centuries. Wood-pasture regions, such as
Kent or the Chilterns, never developed tightly-integrated agrarian communities. What
seems clear is that the growth of seigneurial demands on the outland peasants was
intimately connected with the growth of agrarian inter-dependence and communal
integration, seen in formal nucleated villages, common field-systems and equally-sized
smallholdings. These institutions developed against the background of older, looser
and less structured ways of life, and even in a predominantly open-field region like
non-Chiltern Oxfordshire they never became universal.[247]

Nor had they necessarily reached their fullest development by 1066. That elusive
entity, the 'village community' as a social unit over and above the identity provided by
lordship or shared resources, is hard to grasp until we reach the late twelfth and
thirteenth centuries. It seems possible that it was coming into focus during the tenth
and eleventh centuries. One hint that this may be so is provided by what
F.W. Maitland termed 'the surnames of villages': the tendency, which we have already
noted at the Tews, Astons, Bartons and Wortons, for groups of settlements to share a
single name with qualifiers such as 'Great' and 'Little', 'Upper' and 'Lower' or 'West'
and 'East'. Although fragmentation of this kind can be ancient, it seems especially

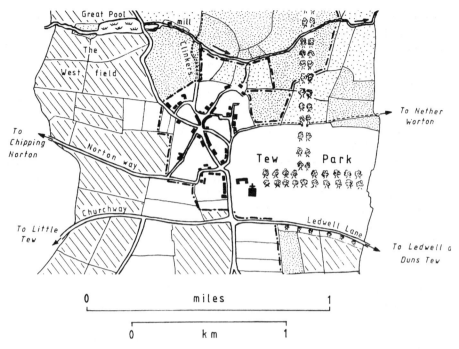

85 Great Tew in the late eighteenth century. This sprawling, loosely integrated village shows little sign of planning, and may have evolved from a series of distinct settlement foci. (*VCH Oxon.* xi, 226)

characteristic of the late tenth and eleventh centuries, and is occasionally caught by Domesday Book at a half-way stage.[248] Fission of estates does not necessarily mean fission of communities, but the terminology does suggest that the fragmented units were conceived in community terms, and may have had focal settlements: thus a charter for Little Haseley in 1002 calls it 'Haseley at the lower *tūn* (*Hæseleia æt þan nyðeran tune*)'.[249] Place-names of this sort abound in Oxfordshire, and may speak of critical changes in how local society was organised during the last Anglo-Saxon century.

It is impossible to know how soon the open fields mentioned in charter-bounds developed into true common field-systems, in which the choice of individual cultivators was restricted by decisions taken at a township level. A parallel development, settlement nucleation, ought to be more tangible. Local studies from many parts of England have now shown that just as the farming landscape and the land-management structure were transformed, so was rural settlement: from a pattern of shifting farms and hamlets to one of larger, more regular and more settled villages. Whether this change resulted from lordly or from peasant initiative is still debated, but it is fairly clear that it coincided with the emergence of a more intensive and exploitative seigneurial regime.[250] Dating it is therefore important.

Village nucleation came sooner to some regions than others: in parts of northern England it may not have got under way until the twelfth century, whereas at Raunds

(Northants.) it has been identified in the tenth.[251] Oxfordshire borders on Northamptonshire, and belongs to the same highly-developed Midland belt, yet hard evidence for nucleated or planned settlements in the Anglo-Saxon period is so far entirely lacking. Excavations of Oxfordshire villages have sometimes proved that their regular plans were laid out in the twelfth or thirteenth century, but have in no case shown significant continuous occupation from an earlier date.[252] What this means, unfortunately, is that we have only a rather vague idea of how the ordinary people of late Anglo-Saxon Oxfordshire lived. It is in vain that some writers refer to this or that Oxfordshire village being 'mentioned in Domesday Book':[253] Domesday Book describes estates, not villages, and its entries tell us nothing whatever about the forms of actual settlements. Archaeology takes us little further: there are several isolated finds of features or pottery scatters from the tenth and eleventh centuries, but they provide no coherent picture beyond an impression of rather small, dispersed settlements.[254]

Medieval Oxfordshire was not, however, a region of exclusively village settlement but also contained farms and hamlets, many of which can be traced back to the thirteenth century in written sources.[255] It is these less developed or centralised forms, not overlain by systematic planning, that are likely to give a better idea of late Anglo-Saxon patterns. In cases where Domesday Book records a single very small manor, and later medieval sources point consistently to a single farmstead or hamlet, it is fair to assume that this perpetuates the eleventh-century site. There are also many clusters of the kind that Christopher Taylor has termed 'polyfocal', which might typically comprise a hamlet, a church, a manor-house and a penumbra of farms.[256]

Occasional villages can be pinned down more precisely. The grouping of nucleated settlements along rivers and spring-lines, such a clear feature of later Oxfordshire villages,[257] had probably begun by the tenth century. Some seem to have occupied their later sites, if not in their later forms, when charter-boundaries were written: it is notable how many of the perambulations start at the point on the boundary which lies closest to the later medieval village. The opening phrase in a description of 958 is 'First from Ducklington to the Windrush (*Ærest of Duclingtune on We[n]ric*)';[258] it can be shown that the perambulation begins where Ducklington village now stands, so this *tūn* has remained on one site since the 950s. In 995, the charter-bounds of Ardley (five hides in *villa quae . . . vocatur Eardulfes lea*) pass the site of the modern village with the phrase 'from the ford to *Eardulfes lea*, from the *lea* to the great ditch'.[259] This looks like a village in the making: developed enough to have become the estate centre, but still conceived as a *leah* or wood-pasture.

If the chronology and the details still leave many problems, the general tendency towards a more integrated pattern of rural life is clear enough. Exploitation of the inland peasantry clearly was intensifying during the tenth and eleventh centuries, and it seems likely that the transition from groups of free hide-holders and rent-payers on the outland to the manorialised society of medieval Oxfordshire was under way during the same period. The simple fact is that as population and the incentive to produce surpluses grew, resources came under greater and greater pressure and needed tighter and tighter supervision.[260] Thus in an important sense the price of growth was freedom, and its end-product the classic manorial regime described in so many thirteenth- and fourteenth-century estate records.

CHAPTER FOUR

OXFORD 900–1066: FROM FRONTIER FORTRESS TO COMMERCIAL CITY

The expansion surveyed in the last chapter transformed Oxford too, turning it into something worth the name 'town' by late medieval or early modern standards. Both the original *burh* and its development over two centuries have been gradually elucidated by a series of devoted scholars, and this chapter harvests the fruits of their labours.[1] Before getting down to details, though, it may be useful to evoke the contrasting townscapes of tenth- and eleventh-century Oxford as seen by two imaginary Mercian herdsmen, one in the year 950 and the other a century later, driving their cattle southwards through the town to the 'oxen-ford'.

Tramping down the Banbury Road to the place where the Martyrs' Memorial now stands, the herdsman of 950 would see a rampart of coursed rubble walling, topped by a parapet and fronted by a ditch. Once through the central North Gate, he would find ahead of him a broad roadway of compacted limestone cobbles and gravel, running on over the central crossroads at Carfax and dipping down towards the river. The walls and street-surfaces might seem novel, but little else would. Across roadside fences he would see open farmyards containing timber-built halls, chambers, byres and storehouses, with sheep and cattle in their pens and swine and poultry rooting. Individually, these premises would resemble manor-houses which he had passed on his journey through the South Midlands; the odd thing about Oxford would be that so many of them were gathered together. As he drove his herd through the South Gate and down onto the cobbled ford, the church and houses of the priests at St. Frideswide's, over on his left, would seem to dwarf all other buildings in their scale and density.

If our herdsman could have returned in 1050, he would probably have been most struck by the great increase in people both inside and outside the walls. There may already have been a sprinkling of suburban cottages along the two roads that converged on the North Gate. Beside the gate a new walled enclosure jutted out into the ditch, and rising from it a tall tower of gleaming yellow stone with twin belfry openings. This tower served the priests of St. Michael's church, but the gate-keeper would have access to its ground floor through a doorway just inside the gate. The wide road ahead may have been cluttered with stalls of market traders. The frontages on either side would have been a dense, almost unbroken huddle of small timber buildings: shops selling clothes, shoes and other consumer goods, butchers and victuallers stalls, workshops of weavers, smiths and brasiers. Cellar-pits stacked with bulk goods might be glimpsed through open doorways. Throughout the town, and especially at gates and street-corners, small churches would be starting to poke their bell-cotes above the domestic roofs. If the herdsman happened to come between 10 and 16 July, he would have to steer his flock through the crowds converging on the annual fair. Beyond the South Gate, even the boggy ground along the approach to the ford would already be lined with suburban dwellings.

THE ORIGINAL TOWN

The burghal towns of King Alfred's time were built by expert surveyors and engineers, who developed techniques for setting out the streets, laying down metalling and building the defences.[2] Oxford (Fig. 86) shows clear evidence for these techniques, and was undoubtedly built in a deliberate, planned campaign, probably in the late 890s by the Mercian rulers Æthelred and Æthelflæd (above, p. 101). It is, however, less regular than some other burghal towns such as Wallingford or Cricklade, as well as being simpler. An important point here is that Oxford was not built on a completely 'green-field' site: it had to be fitted around existing topographical and perhaps tenurial constraints.

The most obvious of these constraints were the old roads coming from the north towards the ford, and the Trill Mill Stream which marked the south edge of the gravel terrace and of the St. Frideswide's precinct (above, p. 63). The Woodstock Road dictated the axis of the new town, and although the original line of the Banbury Road was diverted to funnel traffic into the North Gate, its old course was retained as the eastern intra-mural street. The trapezoidal shape of the south half of the town is therefore a reflection of the fact that these roads were neither straight nor parallel, and did not run at right-angles to the terrace-edge. Where the surveyors were unhampered they managed to set out their lines on an accurate grid, notably in the north-western quarter of the town (Fig. 91). Similarly, the west–east axis of Queen Street and High Street, which probably does not follow any older route, was set out at right-angles to Cornmarket and St. Aldate's; the discrepancy between this axis and Magdalen Bridge, the natural crossing-point of the Cherwell, explains the sharp southwards curve of High Street east of the original East Gate. The water-locked site meant that Oxford could never be a major crossroads: the eastward routes to Headington and London may have existed from an early date, but most significant long-distance traffic came from the north or the south.

Less visible to us are the influences of property rights or agriculture. The southernmost third or so of the town probably swallowed up the monastic precinct of St. Frideswide's, perhaps already including the three churches of St. Mary (later the

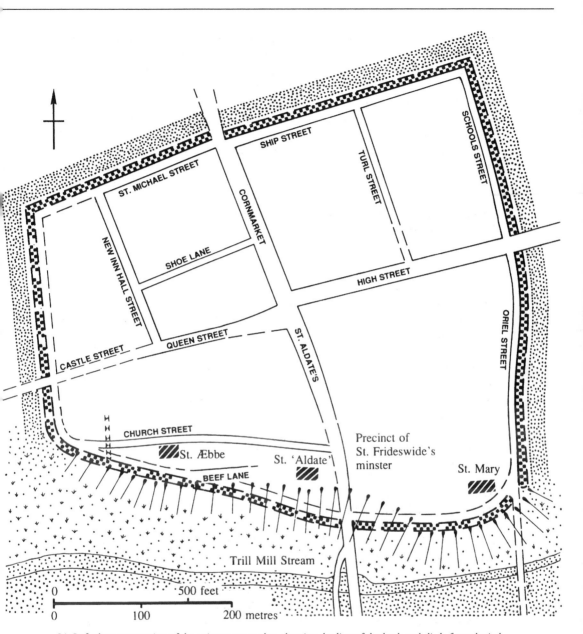

86 Oxford: reconstruction of the primary town plan, showing the line of the bank and ditch (hypothetical on the west and south), and streets certain or strongly likely to be original. (This is a minimal interpretation; other roads which existed in the later Middle Ages could also be primary.)

priory and cathedral), St. Aldate and St. Ebbe (above, p. 63). The axial alignment of these churches, conforming to the terrace-edge, was followed by Church Street and Pembroke Street, new streets of the burghal period.[3] Memories of a former monastic precinct may be preserved in the various twelfth-century references to 'land of St. Frideswide's altar', comprising scattered tenements in the south-eastern corner of the town.[4] Oxford had of course been founded on a royal estate, and the rest of the walled area must have taken in land attached to Headington. Its original character is recalled by the phrase used in Domesday Book and later texts for urban tenements which owed royal dues: 'the king's eight yardlands (*ehteard*)'.[5]

The gravel terrace had always been prime agricultural land, and the site of Oxford was probably a developed farming landscape. Excavations in St. Michael's Street have suggested that the north rampart coincided with a headland along the edge of arable fields, itself covering the ploughed-out hump of a Bronze Age ring-ditch.[6] As long ago as 1936, H.E. Salter argued that streets on the north side of High Street follow the boundaries of open-field furlongs.[7] In the light of more recent work on the chronology of open-field-systems (above, pp. 126–8), it is doubtful if the arable of ninth-century Headington would have been cultivated in strips and furlongs. It is in any case a question whether professional surveyors laying out a new town would feel themselves constrained by such things, though they could have used major linear features as base-lines. This is a problem which requires further metrical analysis and excavation.

A prime concern of the builders of Oxford was to fortify it, especially on the vulnerable north side. Thanks to Brian Durham's excavations in St. Michael's Street and near the North Gate, we now have a very good idea of how the northern defences were constructed (Fig. 87).[8] A ditch (at present of unknown width) was dug, and its spoil moved back for re-use in the rampart. Timber posts were then driven into the ground some five feet apart, forming a line set back about thirteen feet from the edge of the ditch. Planks were trapped behind the uprights, to retain the dumped spoil which in turn held them in position. The spoil, forming a bank some twenty feet thick, was mainly gravel and loam from the ditch, though alluvial clay brought in from the floodplain was packed behind the timber shuttering to improve stability; turf seems to have been used for this purpose at other points on the circuit. As the spoil piled up it would have put pressure on the shuttering, so lacing, consisting of long timbers running back from the posts, was incorporated into the bank. These techniques can be paralleled, with small differences, at other burghal towns such as Hereford, Cricklade and Wallingford, Hereford providing the best parallel for the timber shuttering: they are the stock-in-trade of the engineers employed by King Alfred's family.

The first rampart had the obvious weakness that settlement of the bank material would tend, despite the lacing, to force the timber breastwork outwards. A revetment, faced with regular ragstone blocks bedded in clayey mortar, was therefore built along the front of the bank. This seems to have happened quite early in the tenth century, before the timber shuttering had had time to collapse very far. Thereafter Oxford had the external appearance of a stone-walled city, awesome and unfamiliar; no inhabitant of the Upper Thames would have seen anything like it since the decay of Dorchester and Alchester.

We still know much less about the other three sides of the town. On topographical

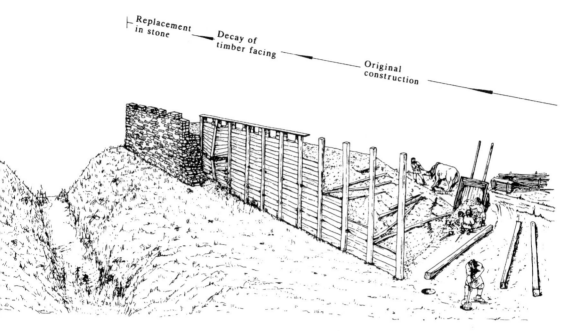

87 The original northern defences of Oxford: reconstruction, based on the excavations in St. Michael's Street, showing the successive timber and stone revetments of the bank. (Oxford Archaeological Unit)

grounds it can be reliably inferred that the eastern bank and ditch ran just outside the intra-mural street line formed by Schools Street and Oriel Street. It has never been found, but excavations near the Bodleian Library in 1899 appear to have encountered the original north-east corner of the *burh*, with a revetment resembling that on the St. Michael's Street site.[9] The western defence remains rather a puzzle. The north end of its ditch seems to have been found on a site between St. Peter's College and George Street, but its course further south was not located in the extensive excavations in the St. Ebbe's area, where it certainly did not coincide with the later town wall;[10] it must, by elimination, have run more-or-less as shown on Fig. 86. On the south side the broad floodplain and the Trill Mill Stream obviated the need for a ditch. Traces of a turf bank have been found north of Brewer Street, and although we still have no firm evidence for the rest of its line it seems most likely to have hugged the irregular contour of the terrace-edge.[11] There was at all events a southern wall by the 1120s, when the canons of St. Frideswide's were allowed to build across it.[12]

Within the walled circuit, the surveyors laid out the main roads and some side-streets. The first metalling has now been recognised in several places, and its distinctive, uniform character points very strongly to a co-ordinated operation (Fig. 88). The life of the first town has left its mark on these surfaces in the form of heavy wear and scattered domestic debris, including a penny of Edward the Elder.[13] Partly from this evidence and partly through topographical deduction, some original streets can be identified. The four main axial streets clearly existed from the start, but have not remained completely unaltered. In Cornmarket the eleventh-century buildings projected beyond the modern frontage on the west side but were set well back from it on the east side, implying a wider road set very slightly further east.[14] At the east end of Queen Street, limited excavations on the south corner have identified primary metalling well behind the present frontage, suggesting that the street originally broadened in a funnel towards Carfax.[15] In the tenth century as later, Carfax was probably the focus of a market-place extending into the adjoining streets.[16] On at least the north, east and south sides of the town[17] there was an intra-mural street running along the back of the rampart, and primary metalling has also been found on two minor streets, New Inn Hall Street and Turl Street. It has become equally clear, however, that several of the streets existing in the later Middle Ages are not original, and it looks as though the interior was initially split up into large, rather unequal blocks by a relatively small number of roadways.

These blocks were not divided into the narrow tenement-plots of the developed medieval town. Excavation has consistently suggested that frontages were not built up until well into the tenth century, and that tenement boundaries developed later still:[18] the Oxford of *c.* 900 contained big open spaces. Since we have no written evidence

88 An original Oxford street surface. The first layer of Church Street, composed of small limestone cobbles, pebbles and coarse gravel, presumably laid down by workmen of the Mercian rulers around 900. The surface is heavily worn and compressed, and scattered with food debris. (Oxford Archaeological Unit)

before the eleventh century, we cannot know for certain how they were used. However, the testimony of rather later sources, combined with the analogy of better-recorded Winchester, suggests that they contained the houses of important men, proprietors of large rural estates in Oxford's hinterland.

The detailed surveys of eleventh- and twelfth-century Winchester show a fragmenting pattern of very large tenements, typically comprising a main house, a group of dependent houses and sometimes even a church, over which the owners might exercise private jurisdictional rights; in short, they were manors in miniature. Often they had long-standing links with rural estates, soon to dissolve but recorded in a range of sources including Domesday Book. Martin Biddle has suggested that blocks of burghal land demarcated by streets were apportioned to landowners from the start, to be administered as part of their rural holdings. Such tenements 'could provide the lord of the estate with access for his produce to the largest market in the region, together with the town house that was necessary for the maintenance of his social position; or they could ensure a regular source of income from houses and other properties in the town'. However, the distribution of linked estates was 'probably based on more than simple economic or commercial factors. Perhaps the link between some of these manors and their urban tenements may initially have been the means by which the inhabitants of the county were guaranteed accommodation within the defences of Winchester in times of trouble'.[19]

In eleventh- and twelfth-century Oxford there still survived some tenements which were either well above average size or lay in groups owing rents to the same landlord,[20] and three of these can plausibly be identified as early medieval 'urban manors'. The first is the block of houses in the south-west corner of the *burh* on either side of Church Street, including St. Ebbe's church. Notes from a lost Eynsham Abbey register record that the founder, Ealdorman Æthelmær, gave to Eynsham 'his court (*curia*) in Oxford in which St. Ebbe's church was situated, with certain other rents pertaining to that court'. This is clearly the abbot of Eynsham's 'church and thirteen houses' listed in Domesday Book, and Eynsham was still receiving rents from the area in the thirteenth century.[21] Secondly, a charter of Cnut dated 1032 gives Lyford (Berks.) to Abingdon Abbey together with 'a certain little minster (*monasteriolum*) consecrated in honour of St. Martin the Bishop, with the adjoining little estate (*praediolum*), in the town called by the famous name of Oxford'; there is an additional note that Æthelwine (perhaps the abbot of Abingdon of that name who died in 1030) bequeathed this estate to Abingdon with the tenement in Oxford where he himself dwelt (*þone hagan on Oxnaforda þe he sylf onsæt*)'. St. Martin's church at Carfax remained Abingdon Abbey property, and it is clear that Æthelwine's *praediolum* or *haga* was the adjoining block of land, between Queen Street and Shoe Lane (Fig. 91), where Abingdon retained a large tenement into the late Middle Ages.[22] The third case is the large block of land immediately north of Æthelwine's house, bounded by Shoe Lane, St. Michael's Street, New Inn Hall Street and Cornmarket (Fig. 91). The western half contained a Norman stone house (now Frewin Hall) standing in open grounds, occupied probably by the mid-twelfth-century sheriff Henry of Oxford and possibly by Henry I's chamberlain Geoffrey de Clinton; the eastern half was split into burgage-plots, many of which owed rents to the owners of Frewin Hall.[23]

These properties recall the Winchester pattern in their large size, their fragmentation into groups of linked tenements, and their association with important late Anglo-Saxon and Anglo-Norman figures. Two of them had churches; the third shows a very clear division into 'demesne' and 'tenant holdings', evidently controlled in the twelfth century by some kind of manorial court held there by the owner's bailiff in the presence of townsmen.[24] Given the archaeological evidence for low-density occupation, it seems a reasonable conclusion that Oxford, like Winchester, was originally divided up into large blocks for magnates to occupy and develop. The links between town houses and rural estates are more problematic. Post-Conquest Oxford provides abundant evidence for such links, but there are strong grounds for thinking that they have more to do with the economic circumstances of the mid-eleventh century than the defensive ones of the late ninth (above, p. 117 and below, p. 158). We are in no position to reconstruct Oxford's original catchment area.

What really matters, though, is that Oxford always had tenurial and economic links with a hinterland around it. Town houses enabled magnates to meet on official business, but it is perhaps more important that they provided a base for marketing the produce of a developing countryside, and dependent plots where traders and craftsmen could set up shop. To lay out a town was one thing, but to populate it another: apart from the old settlement around St. Frideswide's and the ford, it is unclear whether Oxford in 900 would have had a stable community at all. The building-up of an urban population must have taken some years, and in the long run rural wealth was probably a more important stimulus than official incentives.

THE URBAN COMMUNITY

For Oxford the tenth century was an age of almost undocumented growth. We have no means of tracing how it was influenced by the commercial and industrial tide creeping in from northern and eastern England;[25] we can only say that when it re-appears in written sources shortly after 1000, it was a developing urban centre already very different from the Alfred-period *burh*.

One tiny trickle of evidence is the series of moneyers' signatures on coins (Fig. 89), which provide at least the names of some important tenth-century citizens, and show that every king between Alfred and William the Conqueror had a mint at Oxford.[26] The coins of Æthelstan (924-39) offer rather unexpected evidence of Oxford's importance, perhaps because of its location on what was still a frontier between West Saxons and Mercians.[27] After the mints called *civitates* (all within Roman walls), only four places, 'Darent', Lewes, Oxford and Southampton, are given the title 'town' (*urbs*). Christopher Blunt has written:

> The peculiar position of Oxford as a former Mercian borough lately taken into Wessex is reflected in Æthelstan's coinage there which shows a combination of Wessex and Mercian features not found elsewhere. Equally, with its eight moneyers (no doubt not all working together) it ranks numerically after London and equally with Winchester in the southern group. There can be no doubt that it was a place of far more importance than the documentary evidence might suggest.

89 Examples of silver pennies minted in Oxford. *A*: Æthelstan (924–39), moneyer Mæthelweald at OX URB. *B*: Eadgar (959–75), moneyer Æthelwine at OXNA. *C*: Æthelred II (979-1016), at OX; halfpenny produced by cutting a penny in half. *D*: Edward the Confessor (1042–66), moneyer Ægelwig at OXNEF. Actual size. (Ashmolean Museum)

It is unclear how far this administrative or strategic importance implies urban importance. The transformation from fortress to town probably followed lines similar to those which have been established for Winchester: the build-up of population, the development of marketing areas for rural produce, the localisation of urban trades.[28] Weaving and leatherworking were Oxford's main industries in the early twelfth century,[29] and may have been so since the early tenth: shoes were being made near the ford well before 900 (above, p. 91), and spindle-whorls, loom-weights and thread-pickers have been found on sites in the town.[30] Metalworking and bone-working are attested by crucibles, slag and horn-cores.[31] What we cannot see archaeologically, except indirectly in the cellar-pits where they were stored, are the bulk goods such as cloth, wool and corn on which the wealth of the richer citizens would have been founded.

The townsfolk would have formed a hierarchically-organised community, capable of bargaining with royal officials and with a sense of collective identity embodied in gilds and other social activities; but it is anachronistic to think of them as a community in any more formal or 'constitutional' sense.[32] The dues and services which they owed were included, from the point of view of those above them, in the general profits of the shire, and were controlled by the sheriff.[33] In Edward the Confessor's time the borough farm ('for toll and gable and all other customs') was divided, as usual, between the king and the Mercian earl in a proportion of two to one (£20 and six sesters of honey to the king, £10 to the earl); the king also received £20 yearly from the mint.[34] Most tenements paid geld when the king levied it on rural property, as well as the urban tax called 'gable'.[35] When military service was exacted the town sent twenty burgesses,[36] which suggests that it was considered equivalent to a hundred (i.e. twenty five-hide units) for taxation purposes.

A major responsibility, the maintenance of the town wall, fell on the individual holders of those tenements which Domesday Book terms 'mural mansions' (*mansiones murales*). This was clearly very different from the Alfredian system, which seems to have imposed this duty on estates making up the required total of hides, but it is probably wrong to envisage a radical shift of the burden from the shoulders of rural landlords to those of townsmen.[37] The 'mural mansions' were special tenements in the hands of people above burgess status, all or most of whom also held rural property (below, pp. 157–8). The wall, then, remained the responsibility of the seigneurial interests which continued to pervade the town, and was in no sense a common burden on the urban community.

Like most substantial towns, Oxford was generally known as a 'port' and its citizens as 'portmen'. At least three of the main roads leading to it were called 'portway' or 'portstreet', and Port Meadow (formerly *Portmanneyt*, 'the meadow of the portmen') is still the name of the 'pasture outside the walls' which 'all the burgesses of Oxford' held in common in 1086.[38] A town court (*portmanmoot*) existed by the 1130s, and by 1172 was meeting in St. Martin's churchyard at Carfax.[39] Whether this reflects older practice is unknown, but the portmen are given a collective identity (under the alternative name of *burhwaru*) in the Great Tew lease of 1050–2, where the last witnesses are 'Godwine the portreeve of Oxford, and Wulfwine the earl's reeve, and all the townsmen' (*Godwine portgerefa on Oxnaforda, 7 Wulfwine þæs eorles gerefa, 7 eall seo burhwaru*).[40] The occasion was probably a meeting of the shire court (above, p. 107), not a borough assembly,[41] and the two officials named were unequivocally seigneurial rather than communal: the portreeve governing the town on the king's behalf, the

90 Ivory seal-matrix of *c*. 1040 found in Wallingford, inscribed 'The seal of Godwine the *minister*'. He holds a sword point-upright, probably a sign of delegated royal power; the carved handle illustrates the theme of royal power delegated from God (Psalm 110). Godwine 'portreeve of Oxford' must often have visited Wallingford; could he have lost his seal there? Actual size. (British Museum)

earl's reeve ensuring that Earl Leofric obtained his third-share and other perquisites. Given that the portreeves of London at this date were probably also moneyers,[42] it seems significant that a Godwine and a Wulfwine both struck coins in Oxford under Cnut and Edward the Confessor. The seal-matrix of one 'Godwine the *minister*' found in Wallingford (Fig. 90) raises fascinating possibilities, for the bust is probably modelled on coins of Harthacnut or Edward.[43] The duties of Godwine and Wulfwine need not have been confined strictly to the town,[44] and their presence at the shire court, a delegation of citizens in tow, emphasises the extent to which Oxford was still part of Oxfordshire.

It is likely that by the end of the tenth century an urban patriciate would have emerged, including pre-eminently the moneyers. The analogy of other towns suggests very strongly that the names preserved on Oxford's silver pennies are those of leading burgesses, with extensive property interests in the town and perhaps also outside it.[45] The sources are otherwise too fragmentary, but thanks to the Anglo-Saxon habit of repeating name-elements within families we can just possibly glimpse one leading burgess dynasty. Names beginning *Sae-* are common, but eleventh-century Oxford seems to have had more than its share of them. Saewine struck Oxford pennies under Cnut; Domesday Book lists Oxford householders called Saegrim (two or three), Saewig and Saewold, as well as one 'Saewulf of Oxford' who had a house in Wallingford.[46] 'Sewy' (Saewig) remained a prominent Oxford surname into the thirteenth century, now commemorated by Shoe (i.e. Sewy's) Lane off Cornmarket (Fig. 91). Saewold can perhaps be identified as the last Anglo-Saxon sheriff of Oxfordshire, an English survivor of possibly urban origin with interests in both town and country (below, p. 175).

It is of course Domesday Book that offers the best view of the developed late Anglo-Saxon town.[47] The Oxford entry contains an ostensibly complete list of houses in the town and its suburbs, describing the situation in 1086 but probably drawing data from pre-Conquest rentals or surveys.[48] Understanding this is not straightforward, but becomes possible once the presence of some internal inconsistencies is acknowledged. The list falls into three sections, which will be described here as A, B and C:

A: A statement that 'within and without the wall' there are 243 geld-paying houses, plus another 478 houses which are so wasted and destroyed that they are unable to pay. The forty-two geld-paying and eight waste houses 'within and without the wall' which a separate entry ascribes to Robert d'Oilly[49] are assumed to be duplications, leaving the total as 721 houses.

B: A list of 217 houses held by the king, bishops, abbeys and important Norman lords. The entry for the royal houses terms them 'mural mansions', explaining that this is because they are obliged to repair the town wall if the need arises and the king commands it. At the end of the list are further notes that 'all the above hold these same mansions free on account of repairing the wall', and that 'all the mansions called "mural" in King Edward's time were free of all custom except military service and repairing the wall'. In eight cases, houses are said to belong to named rural manors, but the selection of these links for specific reference seems arbitrary. Apparently of like kind (because of the rural-urban links) are a further fourteen houses attached to the Berkshire manors of Steventon and

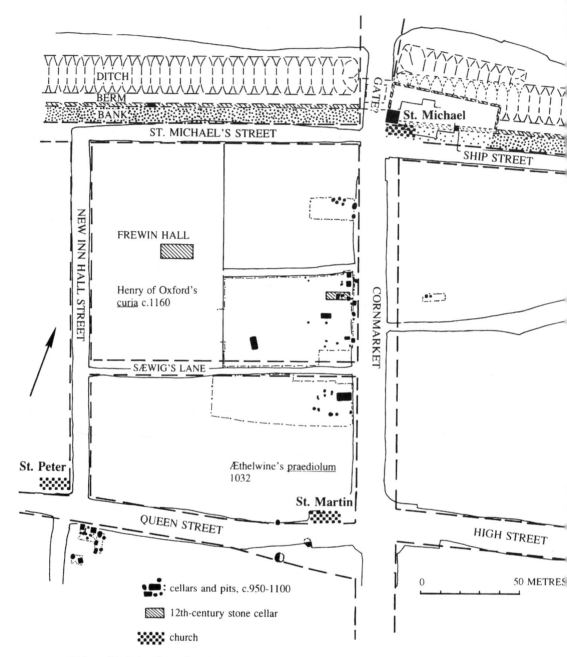

91 Part of Oxford in the tenth and eleventh centuries, showing the regular layout of the block to the west of Cornmarket, and the intensification of frontage development during the eleventh century as revealed in various excavations. Note the cellar-pits cutting primary road-surfaces at the east end of Queen Street, probably encroaching on a funnel-shaped market area. The North Gate enclosure is shown as built *c.* 1050.

Streatley, listed not in the Oxford entry but in the Berkshire folios under their respective manors; addition of these brings the total to 231 houses.

C: A list of eighty houses, held by the priests of St. Michael's (2), the canons of St. Frideswide's (15), one man with a Norman name and thirty-nine people with English names. Since several of these names are repeated some individuals may occur more than once, though there are only two (rather half-hearted) attempts to distinguish between them: 'Sægrim', 'another Sægrim' and 'Sægrim', and 'Swætmann the moneyer', 'Swætmann' and 'another Swætmann'. Six houses are said, in a variety of phrases, to be mural mansions or to repair the wall, some are 'free' and some owe specified rents; the list ends with a note that 'if the wall is not repaired when there is need by he who must do it, he shall either pay the king 40s. or lose his house'. The chaotic appearance of this list suggests that it may be an abridgement of earlier documents.

The arrangement of the Domesday entry seems intended to distinguish between (A) ordinary houses owing geld; (B) the important houses of important landowners, not owing geld but obliged to maintain the wall; and (C) miscellaneous houses of prominent townsfolk, held by a variety of services including wall-duty and rent but apparently geld-free. There is a very clear contrast between the landowners of list B and the townsfolk of list C, and it is striking that everyone in list B also occurs in the Oxfordshire folios as tenant of one or more manors. It may be, in fact, that every one of the 'B' tenements was formally attached to a rural manor, and that this is what makes them a distinct group. If so, we can probably infer such links in cases where proprietors of houses in Oxford are recorded separately as lords of manors; in turn, the 1066 lords of the same manors (where recorded) can be suggested as the former proprietors of the town houses. The following is an attempt, using all available external sources, to re-cast list B as it might have appeared in King Edward's time, omitting the eighty-one unassignable houses held by Norman lords with several manors apiece:[50]

Tenant TRE	Number of houses	Head manor
King Edward	1	Shipton-under-Wychwood
King Edward	1	Bloxham
Earl Ælfgar	20	[some to Broadwell?]
[Earl Harold]	13	Steventon (Berks.)[51]
[Earl Harold]	1	Princes Risborough (Bucks.)[52]
[Countess Godgifu]	2	Twyford (Bucks.)[53]
[Bishop of Dorchester]	30	?[54]
Archbishop of Canterbury	7	[Newington?]
Bishop of Winchester [include Bishop of Worcester]	9	[Witney and/or Adderbury?]
	7	[include Pyrton][55]
[Bishop of Exeter?]	3	[Bampton church manor?][56]
Abingdon Abbey	14 [+ St. Martin's church]	[include Tadmarton and Lyford (Berks.)][57]

Tenant TRE	Number of houses	Head manor
Eynsham Abbey	13 + [St. Ebbe's] church	[Æthelmær's manors?][58]
[St. Frideswide's?]	1	Whitehill[59]
[Saint-Denis Abbey]	1	Taynton[60]
[Ælfwig the sheriff?]	1	Bletchingdon[61]
[Bondig the staller?]	2	?[62]
[Azur?]	2 + St. Mary's church	Iffley[63]
Asgar	1	Streatley[64]
[Toki?]	10	[Horley?][65]
[Ælfwine?]	4	[Crowell and/or Emmington?][66]
[one of 5 thegns?]	1	Hampton[67]
?	1	Burford[68]
?	2	[North Aston and/or Hempton?][69]
?	1	[Milton-under-Wychwood?][70]
?	2	[Wroxton?][71]

The primary cause of these links must have been the need for important landlords to have town houses, but by 1086 the tenements were often farmed out to townsmen.[72] Links recorded after 1100 are few and residual, and it is clear that by then the system was in decay. None the less, there are three good reasons for thinking that it was alive and expanding until very close to the Conquest. The first is the distribution of attached manors, which extend well outside Oxfordshire and suggest a commercial catchment area rather than administrative planning (above, pp. 117–19). The second is the location of 'mural mansions' within Oxford: it has recently been shown that many, perhaps most of them, lay east of Catte Street, within the eastwards extension to the walled area which is unlikely to have been created before the eleventh century.[73] The third is Domesday's statement that one of Walter Giffard's 'mural mansions' was given to his predecessor by King Edward out of the royal 'eight yardlands'. No link with a manor is stated, but the use of the phrase *antecessor Walterii* suggests that the house was considered to pass with manors which Walter had inherited *en bloc*. This could therefore be a new link formed under Edward the Confessor, involving a house which was exempted from geld but made subject to wall-duty. The natural conclusion is that some of the associations were old, some new: the Domesday list does not reflect the needs of any one generation, but records an evolving system.

These links emphasise the aristocratic as against the mercantile element in late Anglo-Saxon urban life. The list shows that King Edward, Earls Ælfgar and Harold, and several bishops, abbots and royal thegns had houses in Oxford, some at least of which they would have maintained as residences. There may have been a royal house in the town as early as 924, when Ælfweard, King Edward's son, died at Oxford.[74] A late source describes how Edmund Ironside was horribly murdered in his lodgings at Oxford in 1016,[75] and King Harold I died in 1040 having transacted some business while he was 'in Oxford very ill, so that he lay in despair of his life'.[76] In their turn, great men such as Earl Ælfgar would exercise jurisdiction over a host of followers in the dependent tenements of their manors, and it was 'in his bower' in Oxford that Eadric Streona betrayed and murdered the chief thegns of the Seven Boroughs in 1015.[77] Wigod of Wallingford, that shadowy but evidently important local magnate, would surely have had a substantial interest in the town.[78] If Oxford was an urban community by the 1050s, it was still firmly gripped by the tentacles of rural landlord dominance.

If the Domesday lists have been interpreted correctly, they indicate a total of 1,032 houses in the city and suburbs before the post-1066 decay. Using the normal rural multipliers this would suggest a population of between 4,000 and 5,000, but there is little reason to think that the normal multipliers are relevant:[79] many tenements may not have supported whole families, while others could have housed extra workmen and servants. Rather than attempting dubious statistics, it seems more useful to consider Oxford's relative position in the hierarchy of towns as measured by similar evidence. Assessments of late tenth-century mint output put Oxford in the third rank: below London and the provincial centres of York, Lincoln, Winchester, Stamford, Chester, Thetford and Exeter, and on a level with such shire towns as Canterbury, Norwich, Shrewsbury, Wallingford or Bedford.[80] The counting of Domesday tenements, on the other hand, puts Oxford well below York and Norwich, slightly below Winchester and Lincoln, but distinctly above the next rank of towns starting with Thetford.[81] This discrepancy makes sense in the light of Oxford's conspicuous growth between 1000 and 1050, which set it on course, despite the setbacks of the Conquest, to become one of the leading provincial towns of twelfth-century England.

This growth is probably the main reason for Oxford's rather sudden rise to prominence during the crises of Æthelred II's last years, but two further reasons can be suggested. The first is Æthelred's development of London as his main strategic base, in the context of determined Viking attacks on the Thames Valley.[82] The second is the practical and symbolic convenience, in an age when provincial borders once again mattered, of a town on the upper reaches of that ancient frontier, the Thames, which was within range of Mercia, Wessex and the Danelaw. Oxford has had a natural tendency to become important during civil wars, as the 1140s and 1640s were to show. Here various councils met to debate the future of the kingdom: in 1015, probably an abortive attempt to reunite England after Swein's invasion; in 1018, when Cnut established peace with the English and re-affirmed the laws of Eadgar; in 1035, when the succession was disputed between West Saxon and Mercian nobles; and in 1065, when Earl Tostig was banished.[83] All these councils involved conflicts of interest between Wessex and its northern provinces, and 'it may be that Oxford was chosen for the meetings because of its neutral position, having ties with both Wessex and Mercia but being identified with neither'.[84]

THE EXPANDING CITY

The physical effects of growth were a dramatic intensification inside the walled area, and the formation of suburbs around it.[85] Domesday Book mentions houses outside the walls, and suburbs existed by 1002 when the Danish community defended itself

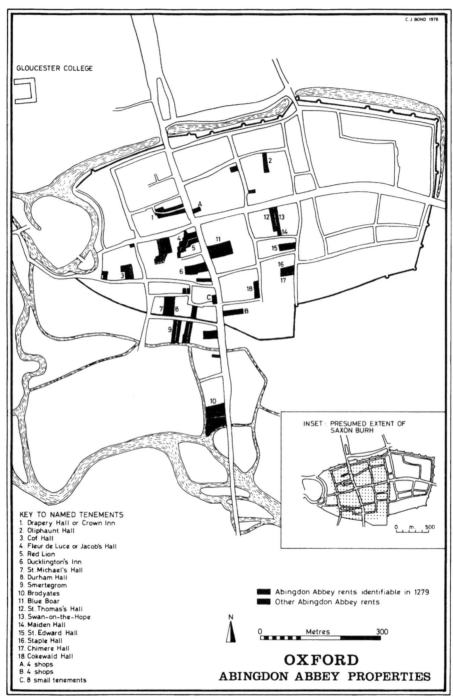

C.J. BOND 1978

GLOUCESTER COLLEGE

INSET : PRESUMED EXTENT OF
SAXON BURH

0   m   500

KEY TO NAMED TENEMENTS
1. Drapery Hall or Crown Inn
2. Oliphaunt Hall
3. Cof Hall
4. Fleur de Luce or Jacob's Hall
5. Red Lion
6. Ducklington's Inn
7. St. Michael's Hall
8. Durham Hall
9. Smertegrom
10. Brodyates
11. Blue Boar
12. St. Thomas's Hall
13. Swan-on-the-Hope
14. Maiden Hall
15. St. Edward Hall
16. Staple Hall
17. Chimere Hall
18. Cokewald Hall
A. 4 shops
B. 4 shops
C. 8 small tenements

■ Abingdon Abbey rents identifiable in 1279
■ Other Abingdon Abbey rents

N

0   Metres   300

OXFORD
ABINGDON ABBEY PROPERTIES

92 The developed city, showing the eastern extension (early eleventh-century) enclosed by the later town wall, and, on the extreme west, the Norman castle built over a late Anglo-Saxon suburb. Note how Abingdon Abbey's properties are entirely within the original *burh* or along the line of the ford. (Bond 1979, Fig. 7)

contra urbanos et suburbanos (below, pp. 167–8). The expansion of the city must have had its impact on the countryside around: the need to produce, collect and process food would have created opportunities and encouraged specialisation.[86] St. Peter-in-the-East was the focus of a suburban community in Holywell where twenty-three 'men with little gardens' (*homines hortulos habentes*) lived in 1086, their produce presumably feeding the town.[87] By the mid-eleventh century there were at least five mills at Oxford, most of them probably on its south side near Grandpont and on the Trill Mill Stream.[88]

The suburb outside the South Gate, along the line of the 'oxen-ford', was in a special category, for here the pre-Viking settlement had developed. The pulling-power of St. Frideswide's must still have been important in the tenth and eleventh centuries, especially since the minster controlled the main town fair.[89] We now know, thanks to recent excavations, that the erection of timber buildings along the sides of the ford began during the tenth century;[90] a considerable 'ribbon development' flanking the road had built up by about 1200, and perhaps much earlier.

By *c*. 1000 there were apparently also suburbs on the other three sides of the town. Probably the first of these lay eastwards, between Catte Street and East Gate. This was within the later medieval walled city, but discontinuities in the lines of the north and south walls mark it out as an addition to the original plan (Fig. 92). Within this area, material dating from *c*. 1000–70 seems almost as abundant as inside the original *burh*,[91] and there is no reason why development could not have begun well before 1000. The extension of the wall, encapsulating both this suburb and the former 'sub-minster' of St. Peter-in-the-East, must have happened by the Conquest, for a high proportion of the 'mural mansions' lay in this part of the town.[92] Further east, the bridge over the Cherwell (now Magdalen Bridge) existed by 1004; beyond it was a little settlement along St. Clement's known as the *brycg-gesett* ('bridge-settlement').[93]

The area outside the North Gate, now St. Giles, was certainly developing in the twelfth century, and the possibility of an earlier suburb is strengthened by tenth-century deposits observed under St. John's College.[94] Settlement outside the West Gate, along a westwards continuation of Queen Street, is much more clearly attested, by pits and structures starting in the mid- to late tenth century and overlain by the Norman castle.[95] The pottery assemblages found in this suburb differ from those on town-centre sites, and emphasise the distinct, probably immigrant character of its occupants (below, p. 167).

Inside the original walls, the large blocks of land were gradually broken up into tenement plots and their frontages developed. It is also possible that new streets were laid out, though many of the non-original streets seem to date from re-planning during the Norman period.[96] The chronology of tenemental division remains very uncertain, especially since excavation has tended to suggest that minor property boundaries recorded on the earliest maps are mainly post-Conquest. As a market in property developed, the interests of existing major landlords would presumably have diversified. One sign that this may have started relatively early, before the development of the eastern suburb, is the distribution of Abingdon Abbey properties recorded in the later Middle Ages (Fig. 92): virtually all of them lay either within the original *burh* or along the ford to its south.[97]

Most striking archaeologically is the sudden appearance of domestic sites and finds:

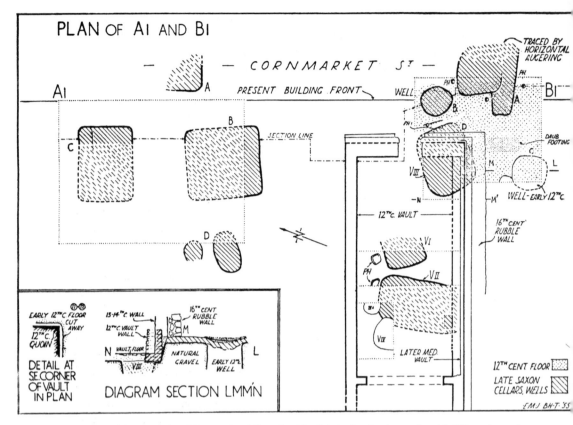

93 Part of the west side of Cornmarket (Clarendon Hotel site), showing how cellared buildings clustered against the frontage in the first half of the eleventh century. (Jope 1958, Fig. 3)

as a high-density settlement, Oxford only becomes visible at the end of the tenth century.[98] Growth is most conspicuous on the main market frontages, especially on the west side of Cornmarket where redevelopment between the 1950s and 1970s exposed large areas of the eleventh-century ground-surface (Figs. 91, 93).[99] Cellars, surrounded by rubbish-pits, clustered in a band running some seventy feet back from the street. Although the buildings were detached, the density of occupation would have produced a visual effect close to that of a continuously built-up frontage.

It is possible to identify three main types of cellared building (Fig. 94),[100] in addition to the presumed range of ground-level buildings of which all trace has been destroyed by later development. Simplest is the straightforward sunken hut, descended from the fifth-century *Grubenhaus*, consisting of a shallow, flat-bottomed pit with one or two pairs of postholes supporting the roof. Examples have been found in Cornmarket, Queen Street and the western suburb,[101] all of them apparently of the later tenth rather than eleventh century. A more specialised urban type is the square or near-square cellar-pit (Fig. 93), usually some six by eight feet in plan and about six feet deep. The vertical sides are occasionally shored, but more frequently are daubed with alluvial clay to stabilise the exposed gravel. These must have been enclosed within ground-level buildings, and probably served as cold-stores for perishable goods. The grandest form – in Oxford an eleventh-century innovation – is the large rectangular cellared building, the timber walls of its semi-basement rising to support one or more upper storeys. The example at 55-8 Cornmarket 'had near-vertical sides, with a collapsed timber wall or lining surviving as impressions both *in situ* and leaning out in all directions'; the fill contained burnt daub and other debris, pottery, a lamp, a coin of 979-85, a spindle-whorl and four iron knives.[102] This type, which foreshadows the Norman stone chamber-block with its barrel-vaulted basement, is characteristic of major late Anglo-Saxon towns such as London, Thetford and York (Coppergate); it epitomises Oxford's boom period under Cnut and Edward the Confessor.

The town contained several churches by 1066.[103] Three of them, aligned along the edge of the gravel terrace, may have been survivals from the ancient monastic complex (above, p. 63), but if so their ownership had fragmented by the eleventh century. Only the main church of St. Frideswide's remained in the canons' hands; St. Aldate's, first mentioned *c.* 1140 as a 'minster' (*monasterium*), was controlled by clergy of the town,[104] and we have already seen that St. Ebbe's belonged to Ealdorman Æthelmær's urban estate. Apart from St. Peter's-in-the-East there is no hint that any other churches existed before the eleventh century, and all those with likely Anglo-Saxon origins belonged to urban manors. St. Martin's at Carfax was part of Æthelwine's *praediolum* in 1032, while St. Mary the Virgin's seems to have belonged to a pair of houses attached to Iffley (above, pp. 151, 158). Another church on an urban manor may have been St. Peter-le-Bailey: in 1203 the bishop of Exeter claimed it as a chapel of Bampton, and three houses belonging to Bampton are probably concealed in Domesday's list of mural mansions.[105] We should not, however, multiply pre-Conquest churches too enthusiastically:[106] the excavations in All Saints' show that it was founded after the Conquest on the site of an eleventh-century house.[107] The boom in urban churches is likely to have synchronised with the boom in rural ones, between the late tenth and mid-twelfth centuries, or if anything to have lagged somewhat behind it: it may have been an essentially eleventh-century phenomenon, little affected by the Conquest.

This leaves one very special case: St. Michael's-at-the-North Gate. It was a church of status, for in 1086 the *presbiteri Sancti Michaelis* had two houses in the town, and its tower is the most impressive Anglo-Saxon building remaining in Oxfordshire. A recent detailed survey (Fig. 96) has improved understanding of the tower's function and context.[108] It is of five stages, with a west-facing doorway on the ground floor, a south-facing one on the first stage and a north-facing one on the second stage. The top two stages have twin belfry openings with baluster-shafts. A particularly odd feature is the pair of porthole windows at the top of the north elevation. Although both are original, only one of them is pierced right through the wall: the other is a mock-up to create an external appearance of symmetry.

These puzzling features start to make sense in context. The tower stands on the west side of a rectangular enclosure (Fig. 91), defined by the medieval city wall, which has been pushed out northwards across the Alfred-period bank and ditch.[109] The date of this extension to the walled area is still not wholly clear, but the tower makes no sense in defensive terms unless the enclosure already existed when it was built. The

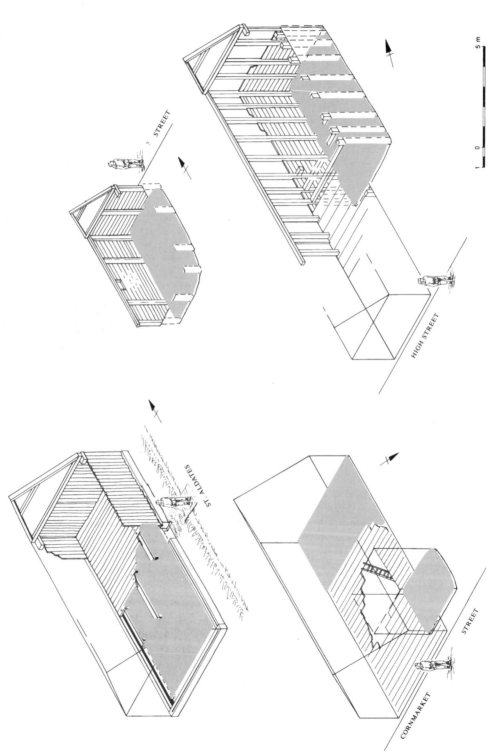

94 Four cellared buildings in late Anglo-Saxon Oxford: perspective views of the archaeological evidence with reconstructed detail. *Top left*: 89 St. Aldate's. *Top right*: underlying Oxford Castle. *Bottom right*: underlying All Saints' church, High Street. *Bottom left*: Clarendon Hotel, Cornmarket (as in Fig. 93). (Oxford Archaeological Unit)

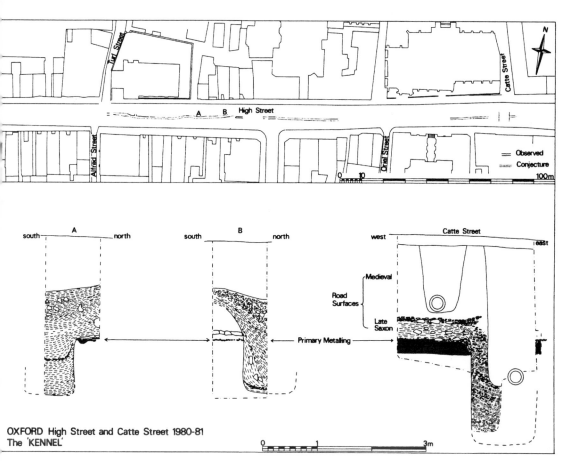

95 Public drainage in Anglo-Saxon Oxford: the 'kennel' or open drain, presumably timber-lined, which ran down the centre of the High Street. This was an original feature of the *burh*, continued along the High Street when the eastwards extension was created. (Oxford Archaeological Unit)

north-facing ground-floor window is large and cannot have been left unprotected, while the doorway two floors up on the same side is at about the right level to have led out on to a wall-walk. The single porthole window high above commands a good view of the roadway approaching the gate, and is probably a look-out. The ground-floor doorway on the west suggests that the well-lit base of the tower was used by guards or officials at the gate. The position of the original church is unknown, but the first-floor doorway, which could have provided access to the upper levels of the tower via a west gallery, suggests that it lay to the south. As Brian Durham writes, 'it is reasonable to suppose that the town watch should have the opportunity of getting to the top of the tower without infringing the privacy and security of the church . . . The tower could have been designed as a package to be used independently on different levels, by the keeper of the gate, by the church and by the town watch, each with their separate access.'

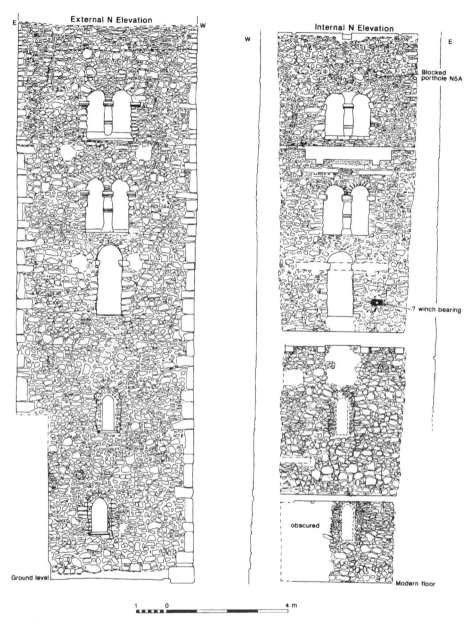

96 The mid-eleventh-century tower of St. Michael-at-the-North Gate: drawings of the outer and inner faces of the north wall. (Oxford Archaeological Unit; drawings by Tim Morgan)

These structures, abutting the principal town gate, amount to an ecclesiastical/ official complex of a most unusual kind. If, as seems likely, they were contemporaneous, the enclosure is dated by the architectural features of the tower, around the second quarter of the eleventh century.[110] It looks as though the church and enclosure belonged to whoever controlled the gate and the town defences. Among gate-churches in late Anglo-Saxon towns, St. Michael's is anomalous both in the scale and complexity of its structures and in the fact that it had an independent community of clergy. One possible context is the eleventh-century fashion, in both England and Normandy, for collegiate churches at fortified aristocratic residences; St. George's College in Oxford castle is a local example of a few decades later.[111] Could there have been some kind of official residence at the North Gate, perhaps even the town house of the earl of Mercia or his reeve?

'COCKLE AMONGST THE WHEAT': THE DANISH COMMUNITY IN OXFORD

One sign of Oxford's prosperity in the late tenth and eleventh centuries is that it contained a Danish community. Given the effect of the Vikings on English political life, this seems a paradox. Yet the men who came as plunderers were also some of the most successful merchants and traders of the age. The Danes' commercial contacts extended from Ireland to the Caspian Sea, and by 1000 they were established in all the great international ports of north-west Europe.[112] Excavations in York and Dublin have dramatically revealed the extent and intensity of Viking urban settlement. The evidence from Oxford is thin by comparison, yet there is enough to show the presence of Danish townsfolk, and probably of Danish soldiers and rulers, in the years on either side of 1000.

Oxfordshire lay only just outside the East Midland zone that was regarded by Cnut's time as culturally Danish (above, pp. 104–5). Although some of the Oxford 'Danes' may have been merchants fresh from Scandinavia, many of them were probably a long-naturalised, perhaps mixed population percolating in through Cambridgeshire, Bedfordshire and Buckinghamshire. Archaeology is now suggesting that they may have retained a preference for Danelaw-produced pottery. It has already been noted (above, pp. 121–2) that the shelly fabrics known as 'St. Neot's Ware' were exported south-westwards from Huntingdonshire down the Clay Vale in the late tenth and eleventh centuries, Oxford lying near the furthest fringe of their distribution. Maureen Mellor's work on assemblages from the city has revealed an interesting pattern.[113] Although 'St. Neot's Ware' occurs throughout the town, late tenth-century groups in which it predominates come from peripheral sites: in the south-west corner of the *burh* (Church Street), in the eastern extension (Logic Lane) and in the western suburb (the Castle). It starts to look as though the fringe areas were being developed by people who chose to buy East Midland pottery rather than the local hand-made Shelly Wares.

As Viking raids intensified during the 990s, Danish settlers in the Midlands were easy targets for racial hatred. The Oxford Danes are the best-known victims of the synchronised massacres ordered by Æthelred II on St Brice's Day (13 November)

1002. The charter which Æthelred issued for St. Frideswide's minster two years later tells the story:[114]

> Since a decree was sent out by me with the counsel of my leading men and magnates, to the effect that all the Danes who had sprung up in this island, sprouting like cockle amongst the wheat, were to be destroyed by a most just extermination, and this decree was to be put into effect even as far as death, those Danes who dwelt in the afore-mentioned town [i.e. Oxford], striving to escape death, entered this sanctuary of Christ [i.e. St. Frideswide's], having broken by force the doors and bolts, and resolved to make a refuge and defence for themselves therein against the people of the town and the suburbs; but when all the people in pursuit strove, forced by necessity, to drive them out, and could not, they set fire to the planks and burnt, as it seems, this church with its ornaments and its books.

This atrocity was visited on the citizens seven years later, when Swein's Danish army burnt Oxford.[115] The Vikings harried the Thames Valley during Æthelred's last years, and in 1013 Swein 'turned to Oxford and the citizens at once submitted and gave hostages'.[116] With Cnut's conquest in 1016, the immigrants who had been persecuted as traders returned as masters. It is highly likely that Oxford would have had a garrison of Danish troops, and 'all the earl's housecarls' attended the shire court in the early 1050s (above, pp. 106, 107). Perhaps it was a member of this Danish patriciate who was buried in a stone coffin at the east end of St. Aldate's church, wearing a splendid Viking-style ring of plaited gold rods (Fig. 97).[117]

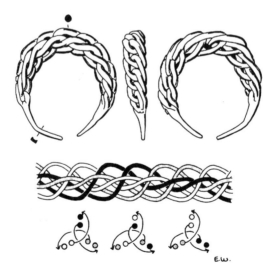

97 Early eleventh-century gold ring from a burial by St. Aldate's church, perhaps the grave of a high-status Dane based in Oxford under Cnut. Actual size. (British Museum; drawing by Eva Wilson)

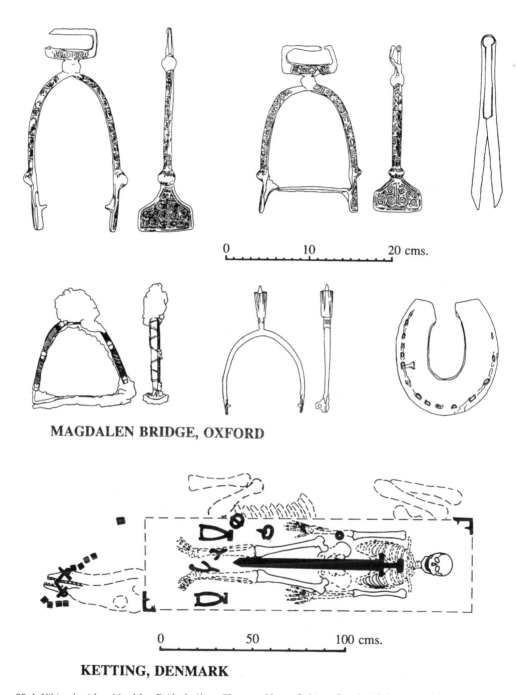

0   10   20 cms.

MAGDALEN BRIDGE, OXFORD

0   50   100 cms.

KETTING, DENMARK

98 A Viking burial at Magdalen Bridge? *Above*: The assemblage of objects found with human and horse bones in 1884 (after Seaby 1950). *Below*: Tenth-century burial of a man over his horse at Ketting, Denmark (after Brøndsted 1936, Fig. 37, reconstructed), to illustrate one possible form of the Magdalen Bridge grave.

The devastation of 1009, serious enough to disrupt the output of the Oxford and Wallingford mints for several months,[118] was none the less quickly followed by remarkable growth: the great cellar-pits are probably all post-1009, for instance, the one at All Saints' church being actually cut into fire debris ascribed to that year.[119] Furthermore, the pottery patterns change: after the early years of the century 'the settlers with a preference for St. Neot's-type pots are to be found in more central sites along the market frontages, living alongside others who still used locally made pots'.[120] A Danish infiltration of the prime sites after 1016 seems distinctly possible.

Two pieces of evidence suggest that the *brycg-gesett* of St. Clement's (above, p. 161), across Magdalen Bridge, was a settlement of Danish troops. The first is the presence there, by at least the 1120s, of a surburban church dedicated to St. Clement.[121] The cult of this early pope was concentrated in Denmark, where it was closely associated with seafarers and merchant-traders from the late tenth century.[122] As Barbara Crawford has recently shown, most English churches dedicated to St. Clement lie in the eastern half of the country, and nearly all the others are coastal, estuarine, or in the major late Anglo-Saxon towns. St. Clement Danes in London was probably a garrison church,[123] and the churches with this dedication in Norwich, Cambridge, Rochester and Worcester were each at the end of the main bridge. These parallels create a circumstantial case that St. Clement's in Oxford may have been the focus of a Danish garrison at some point between Cnut's conquest and the 1050s.

In 1884, an assemblage of artefacts (Fig. 98) was found with 'horse skulls and other bones' and 'men's thigh-bones' to the south of the westernmost arch of Magdalen Bridge, on an eyot between the branches of the Cherwell.[124] The group consists of two sumptuous brass-inlaid stirrups (matching though not an exact pair), a simpler stirrup, a spur, an iron shears and a horseshoe. The inlaid stirrups belong to a well-known Viking type, and are probably Anglo-Scandinavian work of the early eleventh century or very late tenth;[125] all the other items (except the horseshoe) are consistent with this date. It is unlikely in the extreme that these objects, found with human and horse bones, were casual losses, and still more so that a well-dressed warrior was shot down with his horse as he crossed the Cherwell and left to lie. It looks as though this deposit was an elaborate late-Viking burial, of a man whose grave-goods included stirrups and a spur and who was buried with his horse (cf. p. 99 above). Many such graves, mostly of the tenth century, have been found in Denmark; stirrups and spurs are standard, horses common, and shears recorded at least twice.[126] If the lower end of the complete burial shown in Fig. 98 had been disturbed casually, the finds would have resembled those from Oxford.

With Christianisation, furnished burials were becoming increasingly rare in Denmark by the end of the tenth century. This resilient pagan is most likely to have been a member of the immigrant Danish community from the 980s onwards, or, at the latest, a casualty of Swein's army in 1009 or 1013. The proximity of this find to St. Clement's church is striking, and suggests that Cnut's soldiers could have established their base near the grave (possibly marked by a barrow) of one of their former leaders.

THE ENGLISH IN A NORMAN OXFORDSHIRE

It would be foolish to pretend that 1066 was anything other than disasterous for the people of Oxfordshire. The English did not want to be ruled by Normans, and few Normans had much interest in England or the English beyond their opportunities for exploiting them. Domesday Book, in 1086, records twenty years of disruption: the old aristocracy destroyed, manors transferred in a bigger land-grabbing exercise than would ever occur again, Oxford itself over-taxed and seemingly half in ruins. If English government, law and culture survived, it was in spite rather than because of the invaders who had battened on a society more complex than their own.

Yet a good deal *did* survive. We still call ourselves 'English', and speak the English language. And compared with the rest of Europe, the continuity of early medieval institutions is remarkable. Hundreds and hundred courts remained important through the Middle Ages; shires are still with us (though mangled in 1974); and, even if his role is now largely ceremonial, a sheriff of Oxfordshire is still elected yearly. It cuts the Norman Conquest down to size to remember two periods of much more fundamental change: the seventh century, when political and religious structures acquired a stable, physical form in the landscape; and the tenth, when towns and the rural economy burgeoned and village communities started to take shape. Rural roads and hedges are still where the Anglo-Saxons put them, and manor-houses and churches occupy the sites chosen by tenth- and eleventh-century thegns. Lines drawn before the Conquest often mark where one parish council's authority ends and the next begins, and it is because a Bicester, a Charlbury or a Bampton was a 'minster-place' that it seems a town rather than a village today.

Nor was continuity just at this basic level. Our sources (notably Domesday Book), concentrating as they do on the greatest men and on the formal tenurial relationships, make the obliteration of the thegnly class look more total than it really was. A few substantial families, and many lesser ones, did manage to retain status in the new world, to intermarry with Normans and to pass property down to their descendants. We cannot know how many Englishmen remained as sub-tenants or lessees of manors which Domesday Book ascribes to Norman lords, nor how many of them felt it prudent to call their sons by Norman names. Many a twelfth-century deed shows that some landowning Robert, William or Geoffrey had an Ælfric, a Leofnoth or an Eadwine for his grandfather. England by 1150 had a peasant and urban population that was still almost wholly English or Anglo-Scandinavian, a broad middle class of freeholders who can best be described as lightly Normanised English, and an upper class of heavily Anglicised Normans. No wonder that so many aspects of English life and culture which 1066 cut off at their roots were blossoming again by the 1120s.

Oxfordshire was peripheral to the Conquest process. It was too far from the south-east to be directly affected by the campaigns of 1066, though William crossed the Thames at Wallingford during his circuit of London, and received there the first submissions of the English leaders. Nor did it suffer anything like the punitive devastation of the north in 1069. It lay on the fringe of the less disrupted western counties, where great religious centres such as Worcester, Evesham and Malmesbury preserved records and memories of the Anglo-Saxon past. In a sense, Oxford was left to retreat from the political limelight into obscurity. It saw no more great national councils, William I may never have come there,[1] and the Norman barony centred on Oxford was a minor one. The old royal manors naturally continued to provide William with revenue, but they were farmed out by 1086 and it can have been rarely if ever that they saw the life of the court. In 1072 the shire even lost its episcopal seat, when the cathedral was tranferred from the mere 'village' of Dorchester-on-Thames to the city of Lincoln, at the further end of its huge diocese.[2] After 1100 Oxfordshire once again contained a hub of political life, but not in Oxford: Henry I held court amid his beloved hunting-grounds of Woodstock as Æthelred II had done a century earlier.

In Oxfordshire as elsewhere, the estates which best survived the changes were the ecclesiastical ones, notably the great complex which belonged to the bishops of Dorchester/Lincoln (above, p. 79) and the individually valuable manors of the sees of Canterbury, Winchester and Salisbury. There was no major religious institution within the shire itself (Eynsham Abbey being in temporary eclipse), but on its Thames boundary the great tenth-century monastery of Abingdon was still a force to be reckoned with. Under the English abbot Ealdred (1066-71) and his Norman successors Adelelm (1071-83) and Rainald, the monks weathered the storm laboriously but in the end relatively well. The twelfth-century Abingdon Chronicle recounts their adventures in often lively detail, opening a window on the world of Normans and English in the Upper Thames.[3] Norman wolves were snapping all around, and survival required astute management, well-chosen contacts and the judicious purchase of good-will. One story illustrates the fate of many Anglo-Saxon church treasures:

> Losses penetrated even to the ornaments inside the very sanctuary. Indeed, by order of the queen, she instructed that the most precious of these should be brought to her. When the abbot discussed with the brethren what ought to be done in regard to these, they decided to send some of the choicer ornaments to the queen. When these were shown to her, she scorned them and requested more splendid ones. The clergy, oppressed on all sides by fear of what was foreign and their new rulers, brought out into the open, at the wishes of the imperious

queen, what they ought to have preserved more carefully, that is, a chasuble with an orphrey marvellously sewn all over it, a truly splendid choir-cope, a white stole, and a manuscript of the Gospels, all of them covered with gold and gems in magnificent workmanship.[4]

The monks' problems mainly involved land. It was a worrying time for any proprietor who had leased property to dead, expropriated or fugitive Englishmen: forfeitures were liable to be taken indiscriminately. Thus the priest Blachmann had held Abingdon manors, including Sandford-on-Thames; when he fled the country 'all his property was handed over to the king on the grounds that it belonged to a deserter', and it was 'by great effort that the abbot won from the king the restitution of the same lands'.[5] Even the support of great Normans could be a mixed blessing. When the English thegn Leofwine sold Nuneham Courtenay to the abbey for 'a very large chalice of marvellous workmanship in silver and gold', Abbot Adelelm had the transaction ratified by Odo, bishop of Bayeux, King William's half-brother. But then Odo was disgraced, and those who had enlisted his help 'won the censure rather than the favour of the king. Hence, when he knew that the transaction mentioned had been carried out with the permission of that bishop, he was so angry about the incident that he took this land away from the abbot and gave it to another'.[6] A formidable neighbour and one-time adversary was Robert d'Oilly, the castellan of Oxford, who appropriated the monks' revenues at Tadmarton and a meadow just outside Oxford. On that occasion, however, the English abbey was a match for the Norman baron: Robert was tried for his crime by the Virgin Mary herself:

Robert fell victim to a severe illness, in which he suffered for many days without repentance, until one night it seemed to him that he was standing in the palace of some great king. On one side and the other a multitude of important men were standing by; in the midst of them a certain glorious figure was sitting on a throne, in female clothing and extremely beautiful. Before her were standing two brethren from the number of the aforesaid community, whose names he knew. And when these two had seen him entering the palace, they genuflected before that Lady, saying, with a deep sigh, 'Behold, Lady, that is he who is usurping for himself the possessions of your church and has recently taken from your monastery the meadow, which is the reason for our outcry.' She, incensed against Robert, ordered him to be thrown out of doors, taken to the meadow which he had stolen from the monastery, and there tortured. At her bidding two young men arose from the bystanders, took him to that meadow, and there made him sit down. And immediately most rascally boys gathered there, carrying hay from that very meadow on their shoulders, laughing and saying to each other, 'Look! There's our dearest friend. Let's play with him.' Then they took the bundles off their shoulders, urinated on them, and thrusting a firebrand beneath, thus fumigated him. Some of them made twists of that hay and threw them into his face. Others set fire to his beard. Robert indeed, finding himself in such straits, began to cry out, though still fast asleep, 'Holy Mary, take pity on me! Any moment I shall die.' . . . A few days afterwards, at the instigation of his wife, he had himself rowed to Abingdon and there, before the altar, in the presence of

Abbot Rainald and with all the congregation of the brethren and his friends standing around him, he fully restored the revenue of £10 from Tadmarton . . . For, just as before that vision he was a plunderer of churches and of the poor, so, afterwards, he became a repairer of churches and a restorer of the poor and an accomplisher of many good works.[7]

In contrast to the relative stability of these large ecclesiastical estates was the collapse of noble and gentry fortunes, as the dispossession of major political figures was followed by rampant extortion from their poorer neighbours. Shortcomings in the Oxfordshire section of Domesday Book make it impossible to trace the tenurial revolution in detail, but the general pattern was clearly much as elsewhere.[8] Great lords – Odo of Bayeux, Robert d'Oilly, Miles Crispin, Roger d'Ivry, William fitz Osbern – had eaten up the lands of whole groups of predecessors, great and small. Odo's estate, for instance, included the manors of Æthelnoth of Canterbury at Great Tew and Stanton Harcourt, and at Deddington he built a large castle as his local headquarters on the site of a former manor-house.[9] Lesser proprietors sometimes acquired a single estate *en bloc*; thus the bishop of Lisieux's manors had all been held by Leofwine of Barton, William Peverel's by Ælfwine, and Countess Judith's by Hakon.

Straightforward, predecessor-based transfers seem to have been a feature of the earlier stages of the Norman settlement, up to the mid-1070s; thereafter few wealthy English remained to be expropriated, and lordships had to be formed by scraping together the lands of humble proprietors through piecemeal and often illegal spoliation.[10] Twenty-one of Miles Crispin's thirty-one Oxfordshire manors have evidence for their pre-Conquest tenure: three of these had been held by Wigod of Wallingford, one by Queen Edith, and the remaining seventeen by a total of fifteen Englishmen. Like other powerful Normans, Miles seems to have pressurised English neighbours into accepting lordship in return for protection. Toli's small estate in Cowley had been free before the Conquest, but by 1086 he held it from Miles; of Berrick Salome and Gangsdown the Domesday jurors observed that 'these two lands, which Ordgar holds from Miles, he ought to hold from the king, for he and his father and his uncle held them freely in King Edward's day'.[11] Men like Toli and Ordgar could have counted themselves lucky to strike deals which would save them from the general wreck.

But occasionally, Englishmen of status not merely survived the Conquest but did well out of it. Nearly all of these belong to a special category, which can best be examined by taking four examples: one man who integrated himself almost immediately into Norman aristocratic society; two who not merely kept their lands but increased them; and the lesser 'king's thegns' as defined by Domesday Book.

Wigod of Wallingford was a kinsman and official of Edward the Confessor, holding property in at least seven shires. Despite his name, most of his lands were not in Berkshire; his Oxfordshire estate, which cannot be exactly quantified, is likely to have been large.[12] By 1086 he was dead and most of his lands were divided between Robert d'Oilly and Miles Crispin, but this estate had descended by marriage, not confiscation. Within a year of the Conquest Wigod's daughter Ealdgyth was married to Robert, and seventeen years later their own daughter married Miles.[13] Wigod's son Toki had meanwhile died, in surprising circumstances: he was shot in 1079 defending King

William's life at the siege of Gerberoi.[14] Domesday Book also has an entry for 'Alfred nephew of Wigod', who had acquired the Oxfordshire manors of one Wulfred.[15] It looks as though Wigod kept both his lands and his status undiminished until his heirs inherited them in the natural course of events. For reasons that now escape us (had he supported William's claim in 1066?), this Englishman was accepted by the Normans from the outset and identified himself and his family with Norman interests.

In 1067 King William addressed an Oxfordshire writ to two English officials, Bondig the staller and Saewold the sheriff.[16] The latter, the last Anglo-Saxon sheriff, was still alive in 1086, when he held an Oxfordshire estate comprising eighteen hides in five places (mainly in the Thame area), nine houses in Oxford, and two mills near the town wall 'which the king gave to him with his wife'.[17] A man of this name had lost two very small rural properties since 1086,[18] but the acquisition of manors at Waterstock and Tiddington which had belonged to one Ælfwig were more than compensation. Whether or not Saewold belonged to a family of Oxford citizens (above, p. 155), he was evidently an official of Edward the Confessor whom William chose to support. He seems, however, to have been in some trouble by 1086, for much of his property had been pledged to Robert d'Oilly.

The third example, Ælfsige of Faringdon, was an Englishman to whom the Conquest offered a chance of bettering himself very considerably. His only recorded lands in King Edward's day were a mere two hides at Littleworth in Great Faringdon (Berks.),[19] but by 1086 he had amassed a substantial estate in the upper reaches of the Thames where Oxfordshire, Berkshire and Gloucestershire meet (Fig. 99). Most of it had been Earl Harold's: in Oxfordshire Langford (fifteen hides), Shipton-under-Wychwood (eight hides plus two hides) and Rycote (two hides),[20] in Berkshire Barcote (five hides) and a further holding in Great Faringdon (four hides),[21] and in Gloucestershire Great Barrington (four hides) which had been held by Harold's housecarl Tovi.[22] Ælfsige had also augmented his Great Barrington holding with seven hides in nearby Windrush, half acquired from three freemen and the rest held under Winchcombe Abbey, and had obtained a freeman's half-hide in Wantage hundred.[23] His son Ælfwig had a house in Wallingford and a hide in Milton-under-Wychwood,[24] and we happen to know that the second of these passed to Ælfwig's grandson Robert of Astrop: a perfect example of a twelfth-century country squire descended from a late Anglo-Saxon thegn.[25] Clearly Ælfsige was a trusted servant of King William, who had farmed Great Barrington, Langford and Shipton to him and had donated the Barcote and Wallingford properties. This being the case, it is striking that at Littleworth he had already held his two hides 'formerly of the villans' (*quae fuit villanorum*) under Harold. It rather looks as though Ælfsige had been engrossing peasant land under Earl Harold's patronage before graduating to acquire very much larger holdings under King William's.

The Oxfordshire folios of Domesday Book contain a final section devoted to the holdings, mostly modest, of the 'king's thegns' (*ministri regis*) as existing in 1086. The thirty-eight entries itemise the lands of ten men with Norman names, and of between eleven and thirteen men with non-Norman, mainly English names.[26] Some of them had kept their own pre-Conquest lands, and one had acquired his lands by marriage; overall, the turnover had been very much less drastic than usual. These men were 'thegns' in the sense of being royal servants and retainers, not in the sense of being

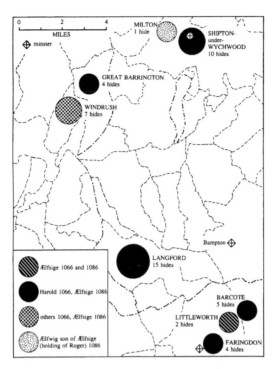

99 The 1086 lands of Ælfsige of Faringdon and his son in Oxfordshire, Berkshire and Gloucestershire. (Not shown: two hides in Rycote, half a hide in Wantage hundred and a house in Wallingford.)

aristocrats: as well as Saewold and Ælfsige, both of whom appear in this company, the list includes Richard the 'engineer' (*ingania*), Reynold the archer, Theodoric the king's goldsmith, Siward the hunter, Hervey who can be identified as a king's messenger, and Aretius and Saeric whose descendants owed serjeanty services to Bampton royal manor (cf. above, pp. 110–11).[27] Here we glimpse men in the bottom tier of the administration, who kept it going from day to day in the royal manors and hundredal centres.

What these cases illustrate is the very strong advantage, if one wished to keep or augment one's lands, of having been a royal official under the old regime. Superficially this might seem a striking *dis*advantage, and doubtless there were similar figures of a different temperament, or with a different past record, who vanished from the scene. But the Normans must have had a very poor idea of how England was run at a local level, and if the men who were running it already were prepared to collaborate it made sense to buy their support. It is an interesting question in what sense Wigod and Ælfsige were 'of' Wallingford and Faringdon. Little of Wigod's land was in Berkshire, and only six of Ælfsige's forty-nine-and-a-half hides were in Great Faringdon parish; the toponyms may be official rather than tenurial. It has been observed before how many notable Anglo-Saxon survivors were said to be 'of' somewhere: Edward 'of' Salisbury', Colswein 'of' Lincoln', Thorkil 'of' Warwick'.[28] These were leading reeves and administrators who operated from locally important political and economic centres and knew how they worked; it was surely thanks to Ælfsige's early links with Harold that he found himself running some of Harold's former manors. To use a term that may be less anachronistic than it sounds, Wigod and Ælfsige could have been the castellans of Wallingford and Faringdon.

The major economic centre of the region did not escape the convulsions which rocked its hinterland. Oxford has one of the worst records of urban decline in the whole of Domesday Book. Between 1066 and 1086 the town's tax burden had been doubled to £60, whereas 583 houses – probably over half the total – were 'waste'.[29] At least part of this decay can be blamed on the ruthless implantation of Robert d'Oilly's castle, where excavation has found late Anglo-Saxon houses obliterated during the 1070s to make way for it.[30] It is all the more striking that Oxford's slump was of very short duration, and that the same Norman lord who built the castle made the single biggest capital investment in the growth of the town. Among the 'many good works' performed after his nightmare, d'Oilly built a massive stone causeway ('Grandpont') to carry traffic across the Thames floodplain on the line of the ancient 'oxen-ford': 700 metres long, with seventeen flood-arches, it is probably the oldest post-Roman bridge built entirely of stone in western Europe.[31] In the late eleventh and twelfth centuries new streets were laid out and new suburbs founded,[32] and by the 1130s Oxford had emerged as one of England's leading towns. This growth put it in the front rank of towns seeking political liberties, finally declaring itself a commune in 1191.[33]

Throughout this period the townsfolk, including the urban aristocracy, were basically English. All but one of the forty householders listed in 1086 had Anglo-Saxon names (above, p. 157), as did all of the ten moneyers who struck coins in Oxford during the reigns of William I and William II.[34] Even in a rental of the 1130s nearly half the names are English or Scandinavian,[35] which is remarkable given the general adoption of Norman nomenclature. One figure whose Norman name certainly hid an English past was the great Henry of Oxford, the Empress Matilda's local henchman and sheriff of Oxfordshire and Berkshire in the 1150s. A charter of Henry II reveals that he had a grandfather called Godwine and a father called Eilwi. If the latter was the *Ailwinus prepositus* mentioned in 1139, it seems possible that descent from a family of town reeves contributed to Henry's local standing. At all events the career of Henry, whose great stone house still partly survives under Frewin Hall (Fig. 91), shows how well an English townsman could make his way in a Norman world.[36]

The fall and rise of Oxford illustrates two stages in the Norman impact on English society. An exploitative first generation, brought up in Normandy and retaining their personal ties there, was succeeded by second and third generations which were assimilated more and more to the people and culture which they found, and came with remarkable speed to consider themselves English. By the 1130s, English and Norman gentry families co-existed in a countryside where they were equally well-rooted; the distinction is often invisible to us, and even for them it was fading. One straw in the wind is that Normans were starting to take toponymic surnames from their English manors. Geoffrey, Henry I's chamberlain and one of the classic *nouveaux-riches* of the early twelfth century, is known to history as Geoffrey of Glympton (*Clinton*):[37] he took his name from the same manor in the Glyme Valley where *Ægelric æt Glimtune* had lived seventy years previously (above, p. 139). The community of the shire, disrupted after 1066, was re-forming; it would remain for many centuries a fundamental part of English political life.

In the countryside the economy continued to grow and society continued to

100 The late eleventh-century tower of Langford church, an 'overlap' building combining Anglo-Saxon pilaster strips and double-splayed windows (cf. Fig. 82) with round mouldings derived from Norman Romanesque. Set in the south face of the tower is a sundial, carried on the shoulders of figures resembling those in the Bayeux Tapestry. The patron of this fine building was almost certainly Ælfsige of Faringdon.

develop, as they would have done if no Conquest had happened. Norman rule obviously had its impact, both positive and negative, but it is doubtful if it changed much decisively. The imposition of forest law is notorious, but the king's forests in Oxfordshire had existed before the Conquest in fact if not in name (above, p. 110). Communities which already existed within them were allowed to remain and expand, and assarting in Wychwood continued through the twelfth and thirteenth centuries, even if more-or-less strictly controlled by royal officials.[38] Conservation of woodland was in the inhabitants' interest as well as the king's, and it is unlikely that the forest regulations were a serious long-term handicap to the growth of these regions.

The Norman settlement also brought some able landlords. Ernulf de Hesdin, who confirmed a grant in his house at Chipping Norton in the presence of his wife, children and household knights, was portrayed by William of Malmesbury as an energetic estate manager and skilful agrarian improver, and this judgement is supported by the rise in the value of his manors between 1066 and 1086.[39] Subinfeudation, which involved the endowing of military followers with two or three hides apiece to support the quotas of knights required by the king,[40] gave humble, previously landless men the incentive to exploit their land for maximum profit. None of this was completely new, and a large proportion of the unrecorded farmers and reeves who were doing the real work on the ground were certainly English, but the changes must have stimulated the continued development of the landscape along lines laid down during the tenth and eleventh centuries. The main impact on the peasantry came gradually, as 'inlands' were enlarged and reorganised as demesnes to support a more opulent style of seigneurial life, and 'outland' peasants were transformed into the tenant smallholders of the classic manorial regime. This was probably the great age of planned villages, which during the twelfth and early thirteenth centuries were augmented by some new planned towns such as Burford, Witney and Woodstock.

Woodstock was a magnet for the great of Henry I's England. Notable among these were the bishops, some of whom had inherited Oxfordshire manors from their English predecessors. Contemporary needs and older practices merged: their attitudes to ancient churches on their lands could be much like those of the circle of clerics at Edward the Confessor's court, and included a predeliction for using them as desirable residences. The Benedictine monastery of Eynsham, for instance, had a chequered and much disrupted history during the Anglo-Norman period, and excavations on the site suggest that the cloister of the later medieval abbey was not built until well into the twelfth century.[41] It rather looks as though Henry I's bishop of Lincoln maintained a house there, just as the contemporary bishops of Salisbury and Exeter may have done with the old minsters of Oxford and Bampton, and as the bishop of Winchester did beside Witney church.[42] Although this cluster of major episcopal residences near Woodstock reflects early twelfth-century conditions, they were founded on resources inherited from the Anglo-Saxon past.

The building of village churches likewise continued on its mid-eleventh-century course, although the Conquest gave new stimuli. Architectural historians are now recognising a large category of late eleventh-century churches which show a mixture of English and Norman style and technology, the work of an 'overlap' generation of Anglo-Saxon masons who were picking up traits from the new Romanesque abbeys and cathedrals.[43] Thus the Oxfordshire churches of Langford, North Leigh and

Waterperry, traditionally classified as 'Anglo-Saxon',[44] must all have been built in the decades following 1066. Langford (Fig. 100) is a superb monument to the Anglo-Norman fusion, and it can be no coincidence that in 1086 this manor belonged to that hardy survivor, Ælfsige of Faringdon. At Tackley a Norman-derived moulding is worked, with considerable technical skill, on a doorhead made from one piece of stone in the English fashion.[45] By about 1100 the Anglo-Saxon technology had finally given way to the small, squared blocks and single-splayed windows of the Norman Romanesque, but the mid-twelfth century saw a remarkable flowering of architectural ornament which owed much to the Anglo-Saxon past. The decorative forms used to such dramatic effect in some otherwise humble Oxfordshire churches of the period c. 1140-70 (Fig. 101) are partly derived from English and Anglo-Scandinavian decoration of the tenth and early eleventh centuries.

These small but sumptuous parish churches show that the Anglo-Norman gentry had become willing to plough back some of their profits into religious and artistic projects near their own homes. At a higher level, changing attitudes to monastic

101 Barford St. Michael, doorway of *c.* 1160. Built a century after the Conquest, this doorway derives much of its decoration from the repertoire of Anglo-Saxon art: interlace on the tympanum, acanthus foliage on the capitals, biting heads around the arch.

patronage reveal the same putting-down of roots. When the Norman lord of Cogges, Manasses Arsic, decided in about 1100 to found a priory near his manor-house, he entrusted it to the Benedictine monks of Fécamp in his native Normandy.[46] Very soon, this would seem old-fashioned behaviour: early twelfth-century magnates and gentry preferred to found abbeys or priories on the English estates with which they were coming increasingly to identify. Many of these foundations were for the benefit of a new religious order, the canons regular of St. Augustine. Some were completely new – the d'Oillys' great abbey of Oseney on the outskirts of Oxford is an outstanding example – but others were founded in decayed Anglo-Saxon minsters. Thus in about 1120 Henry I's justiciar, Roger of Salisbury, replaced the minster-priests of St. Frideswide's with Augustinians, a course which was to be followed *c.* 1140 by the bishop of Lincoln at Dorchester, and towards the end of the century by Gilbert Bassett at St. Eadburh's, Bicester.[47]

It is no accident that the re-foundation of so many old minsters took this particular course.[48] The Augustinian canons were ordained priests, capable of administering the sacraments to the laity, but they lived a common life under a monastic-type rule. Thus they were the acceptable face of the tradition which English minsters had represented for three or four centuries, and highly appropriate successors to unreformed clerical communities. Such continuity suited a world in which traditions were being valued again. The great flowering of historical scholarship in twelfth-century England, which owed so much to awakened consciousness of the Anglo-Saxon past, had its local dimension: a new interest in the past glories of ancient monasteries (the Abingdon Chronicle is a notable product of this), and in the shadowy seventh- and eighth-century founder-saints whose bones they still housed.[49] The lives and doings of these saints were legendary and unwritten, the stuff of folklore; as the historian William of Malmesbury lamented in the 1120s, all too many of them were 'bare names'. This deficiency the literate twelfth-century clerks and canons could not tolerate. Hence the burgeoning hagiography of these years, in which tradition and local history were seasoned with large doses of bizarre nonsense (cf. above, pp. 73–6).

One of these legends, which in its twelfth-century form has lived on to the present day, makes a fitting conclusion for this book. During the 1120s the story of St. Frideswide of Oxford was recounted briefly by William of Malmesbury, and at greater length ('Life A') by a rather incompetent hagiographer working for the first Augustinian community (above, pp. 52–4). By the 1160s the pretensions of the community were growing, and their prior, Master Robert of Cricklade, was a noted scholar. The rough-hewn 'Life A' would no longer do: Master Robert re-wrote it in more luxuriant prose ('Life B'), perhaps at much the same time as he was rebuilding the priory church in a sophisticated late Romanesque style.[50] The saint's Life was the literary equivalent of her church or her jewelled shrine: it needed embellishment to do her due honour.

Hagiography served the needs of the present, emphasising the status and rights of those whom the saint especially favoured and protected. Such may be the story of the punishment of King Algar, blinded at the gates of Oxford while in hot pursuit of Frideswide. Both Malmesbury and 'Life A' add the curious comment that kings of England have ever since been afraid to enter Oxford. This story can scarcely have been tenable before the Conquest (above, p. 158). But there is, as it happens, no evidence

102 An eighth-century princess as the 1180s saw her: the seal of the Augustinian canons of St. Frideswide's, Oxford. Actual size. (Heslop 1988)

that the Anglo-Norman kings *did* enter Oxford (their palace of Beaumont was outside the walls), and the legend seems to have been taken seriously by Henry II in 1180 and by Edward I in 1275.[51] At all events, Master Robert re-worked the story to make full use of its dramatic possibilities:

> Meanwhile the wicked king reached Oxford, and tried to discover from the inhabitants by threats, entreaties and promises of bribes where Frideswide had gone. But it was known to God alone: it had been done without the knowledge of any of them, and they could say nothing about it. Thereupon the enraged and distracted king was driven to an unbearable fury, and gazing ferociously on the city he vowed to destroy it. But when he approached the gate which defended it on the north side, intent to carry out the promptings of his madness, he instantly lost the light of his eyes. Thus he learnt how vain are the labours of human perversity when divine power stands against them. Terrified at the swift revenge of divine power against him, but not forsaking his wicked stubbornness, the fool carried home the heart of Pharaoh who perceived the plagues of Egypt but continued in deserved blindness. Never forsaking the pride of his insolence, he lacked the consolation of his lost eyes all the days of his life. On account of the most just punishment of this cruel tyrant, kings of England have an instinctive terror, so that in truth not a single one of his successors has dared to enter the city of Oxford.[52]

This version adds a new twist: now it is Oxford itself, not merely Frideswide, which is miraculously saved from Algar's wrath. The story has been transmuted into a civic salvation myth (Godiva's legendary ride through Coventry is a compelling if contrasting parallel), and Frideswide into a tutelary power, protecting Oxford through the divine favour extended to her. Probably for the same reason, Master Robert greatly expands and dramatises a passage in which Frideswide kisses and heals a leper in a crowd of townsfolk: 'The city overflowed with gladness; everyone exulted, everyone gave thanks, and at the coming of such a patron they could not contain themselves for joy.'[53] Just as Frideswide's monastery had given birth to a great city, so her patronage had spread beyond the cloister to encompass the whole civic body.

Soon it would spread further. The re-enshrinement of her bones in 1180 was followed by miraculous healings of visitors from far and wide;[54] for a time the cult seemed set to assume national importance. In the event its main constituency was to be local, and of rather a different kind. Oxford was becoming noted as a home of scholars (including Master Robert himself), and the 1180s provide the first clear references to an organised academic community. The senior religious house of Oxford must have had a special place in this new world of learned clerks, and its saint seems to have been quickly modified for her new role. The Priory seal made in the 1180s shows Frideswide enthroned under a canopy, an open book in her left hand (Fig. 102). This unusual attribute recalls contemporary personifications of the Liberal Arts, and its obvious association is with learning.[55] More than a century after Duke William had destroyed the Anglo-Saxon state, the eighth-century princess was making her presence felt: first barring Norman kings from Oxford, and now re-cast as the patron of its incipient University.

NOTES

INTRODUCTION

1   This paragraph is based on *P-N Oxon.* i,
    xi–xiv; Emery 1974, 25–30; *Dom. Geog. S-E.*
    233–7.
2   In *P-N Oxon.* i, xi.
3   Bond 1981.
4   Robinson 1981, 251–3, for what follows.
5   Robinson 1981; Robinson & Lambrick 1984;
    Lambrick & Robinson 1988; Robinson 1992.
6   Marshall 1943, 203–6.
7   Davis 1973 is the main contribution here.
8   See below, pp. 14, 87, 122.
9   Lecture by Richard Bradley, Oxford, 1993.
10 Lambrick & Robinson 1988, 56.
11 Ibid. 55; Robinson 1992, 200.
12 Bradley 1986, 46–7.
13 Miles 1986, 50–1, 52–5.
14 Ibid. 54.
15 Robinson & Lambrick 1984, 813; Robinson
    1992, 200–1.
16 Miles 1986, 51–2; Young 1986, 58–9.
17 Benson & Miles 1974a, 84–7.
18 A recent and spectacular discovery: see T.
    Allen in *SMA* xxi (1991), 97–9.
19 Cook & Rowley (eds.) 1985, 16–20.
20 Miles 1986, 55–6.
21 Sellwood 1984; Hooke 1985, 4–8.
22 Tim Allen, pers. comm.
23 Miles 1986, 56.
24 Young 1986 for what follows.
25 Ibid. 62; D. Miles pers. comm.
26 Copeland 1988, 288; cf. Miles 1986, 56.
27 Lambrick & Robinson 1988, 58–60.
28 Robinson 1981, 274; Robinson & Lambrick
    1984, 813; Robinson 1992, 200–2.
29 This takes a more traditional line than
    Higham 1992, which I believe to go too far in
    the opposite direction.
30 Gelling 1984, 6, criticising F.M. Stenton
    quoted ibid. 5. Cf. Gelling 1988, 70–1.
31 Gelling 1984, 85, and map of Chiltern terms
    on p. 122.

32 Cole 1982; cf. Gelling 1984, 89–99.
33 Emery 1974, 75; Gelling 1984, 142, 149–51.
34 *P-N Oxon.* ii, 460, 353–4; Gelling 1984,
    179–80.
35 Rackham 1986, 77–8.
36 Higham 1992, 77–80. For local evidence see
    Miles (ed.) 1986, 23 (Barton Court Farm) and
    Day 1989 (a pollen core from Shotover).
37 Gelling 1984, 222–4. Burford, on the edge of
    the Cotswolds, is *Burford upon the Wold* in
    1449 (*P-N Oxon.* ii, 311).
38 *P-N Oxon.* ii, 305, 312; Gelling 1984, 226.
39 Baines 1981. The term *on clænan dune* (ibid.
    16) suggests the same usage of *clæne*, as distinct
    from woodland and scrub, that occurs in
    Clanfield. Cf. Gelling 1984, 235–6, and *P-N
    Berks.* iii, 836, 926–7.
40 *P-N Oxon.* ii, 486.
41 Lambrick & Robinson 1988, 60.
42 *P-N Oxon.* ii, 454; *P-N Berks.* iii, 819, 931–2;
    Gelling 1984, 34–40.
43 Gelling 1988, 71, 73. These are the single
    most common group among names recorded
    before 730, whereas the element is not
    common in late or minor names.
44 *P-N Oxon.* ii, 466–7, 475; Benson & Miles
    1974, maps 21–2.
45 *P-N Oxon.* ii, 431.
46 S.883, S.771 (*P-N Oxon.* ii, 483, 489–90).
47 S.361 (*P-N Oxon.* ii, 489, 421). The villa at
    Fawler has been found: T.G. Allen in *Oxo.* liii
    (1988), 293–315.
48 *SMA* xx (1990), 82–3.
49 Bradley 1987.

CHAPTER ONE

1   I have made no attempt here to survey the
    luxuriant growths of literature on post-
    Roman Britain and the *Adventus*. Recent

1 general surveys are Esmonde Cleary 1989 and Higham 1992; Campbell (ed.) 1982, chs. I–II, remains a masterpiece of inspired compression.

2 The latest and fullest statement of the 'federate' hypothesis is Hawkes 1986, 64–77.

3 This is well argued by Esmonde Cleary 1989, ch. IV.

4 Frere 1962, 121–3; Miles (ed.) 1986, 14; Brodribb et al. 1968, 16, 26–7; Brodribb et al. 1972, 140–2. These dates depend on estimates of how long after 410 copper coins would have continued to circulate, which is open to debate. On the other hand, as David Miles points out to me, the very late peaks in the histograms of coins from Dorchester, Frilford and Barton Court suggest something slightly odd in the very last days of Roman rule: possibly the payment of troops to guard the Thames corridor?

5 Watts 1991, 88, 216–17, notes no Christian features in the late Roman burials at Dorchester, and comments on the puzzling absence of evidence for Christianity in a big area stretching from the Cotswolds to the Chilterns. This is now, however, modified by the discovery at Caversham of a lead tank with a *Chi-Rho* symbol (ibid. 217, 224–5).

6 At Abingdon the rampart ditch was back-filled in the late Roman period (above, p. 185 note 18), but the fact that its line survives in the modern town plan shows that it survived as a conspicuous topographical feature.

7 Doggett 1986, 53–7.

8 PRNs 1982, 5783, 8013, 12528, 12956, 13190, 13586; *Oxo.* xix (1954), 117; *SMA* ix (1979), 126, x (1980), 174, xiii (1983), 126.

9 Chambers 1987, 58.

10 Meaney 1964, 207; Dickinson 1976, corpus No. 50; Hawkes 1986, 69–70; Welch 1992, 100–2.

11 Esmonde Cleary 1989, 55–6, 191, who suggests a parallel with the graves at Lankhills, Winchester, which have Bavarian and Hungarian analogies. See also the generally sceptical views of Hills 1979, 305–8.

12 Welch 1992, 101 (no source stated).

13 S.C. Hawkes in Brodribb et al. 1968, 96–101, and Brodribb et al. 1972, 74–7; but see criticisms by Brown 1972, Alcock 1973 and Hills 1979, 304–5.

14 Meaney 1964, 207–8; Dickinson 1976, i, 401–4, ii, corpus Nos. 50–1; Hawkes 1986, 73–4.

15 Frere 1984, 163–5; Hawkes 1986, 88.

16 Bede, *HE*, I.15 (James Campbell's translation).

17 Dickinson 1976; Hawkes 1986. The general subject can now be approached through Welch 1992, chs. V–VII.

18 Dickinson 1976, i, 29–31, 113–14; Hawkes 1986, 77–8.

19 Dickinson 1976, i, 415–17.

20 *P-N Oxon.* i, xviii–xix.

21 Dickinson 1976, i, 418–19, 6–7.

22 The following is based on Dickinson 1976, i, 256–63, and Hawkes 1986, 78–80.

23 Hawkes 1986, 78.

24 Ibid. loc. cit.; the stoup is illustrated in Campbell (ed.) 1982, 37.

25 Dickinson 1976, i, 401–7, 422–5.

26 For a detailed view of this area see Miles 1974.

27 Esmonde Cleary 1989, ch. V, and Gelling 1992, ch. IV, are good recent syntheses of this problem on respectively a general and a local scale.

28 Note 13 above for Shakenoak. In Brodribb et al. 1978, 205–10, the excavators counter the criticisms of Brown and Alcock, successfully to the extent that the presence of Germanic fifth-century pottery and a brooch seems not in doubt. Miles (ed.) 1986, 16–19 for Barton Court, where a small fifth-century settlement of normal Anglo-Saxon type overlay the outer enclosures of the villa.

29 For one example see Bassett 1985b; others are summarised by Higham 1992, 128–33.

30 Cf. *P-N Oxon.* i, xvi–xvii; *P-N Berks.* iii, 800–12.

31 Gelling 1978, 67–74, 203. She also discusses the Wilcote example in Brodribb et al. 1972, 134–40.

32 Compare the recently excavated cemetery at Wasperton (Warw.), discussed by Esmonde Cleary 1989, 201 as an instance of continuity masked by acculturation, and more negatively by Welch 1992, 104–7.

33 Meaney 1964, 46–7; Dickinson 1976, i, 401–2, ii, corpus No. 69. Out of a minimum of 212 burials, only twelve are certainly Roman and twenty-eight certainly Anglo-Saxon.

34 Meaney 1964, 205–6; Dickinson 1976, corpus No. 33; *Oxo.* xv (1950), 104–6 and Pl. VIIIc. For parallels for the bone plaques see *Antiq. Jnl.* xvii (1937), 448 and Pl. XCVII.

35 See below, p. 72, for the general problem of unfurnished, orientated burials. In the absence of knives they could be any date between the fourth and tenth centuries: much more radiocarbon work is needed.

36 Dickinson 1976, i, 198–202, 399–402.

37 Ibid. i, 118–41 (a derivation which has since been challenged).

38 Ibid. i, 331–2; Hawkes 1986, 79.

39 Thesis in progress, University of Durham. I am most grateful to him for allowing me to cite his provisional conclusions.

40 Again this is Christopher Loveluck's point. The issue was debated at a conference held in Oxford in April 1993.

41 The *beneficiarius consularis* inscription suggests that Roman Dorchester was a collection point for agrarian produce, and perhaps a customs post on the Thames (Young 1986, 60; Dickinson 1976, i, 385; D. Miles pers. comm.). David Miles also points out to me that the distribution of Roman pottery made in Oxfordshire parallels that of 'Late Saxon Shelly Ware' (below, p. 122).

42 This paragraph is essentially based on Dickinson 1976, i, 425–30.

43 Now also see Butterworth & Lobb 1992.

44 Scull 1993, 264–8, is the most recent consideration of the cemeteries in the Vale of the White Horse.

45 The argument of Rutherford Davis 1982. This book has been much criticised, but it seems to me that the central case for a late-surviving British state in Hertfordshire and the Chilterns is convincingly made.

46 Hawkes 1986, 81–2.

47 For the latest over-view, using unpublished cemetery evidence, see Gelling 1992, 30–48.

48 Heighway 1987, 20–5; Bassett 1992, 15–16.

49 Dickinson 1976, i, 113–14, 428–30, for what follows. I am grateful to Tania Dickinson for her latest (and more cautious) thoughts on saucer-brooches (to appear in a paper in the forthcoming *Anglo-Saxon Studies in Archaeology and History*, vi), and I have tried to modify this paragraph accordingly.

50 See also Gelling 1992, 34.

51 *P-N Oxon.* i, 198, 238. Note, however, the comment of Sims-Williams 1983, 29–30.

52 *P-N Oxon.* i, 141.

53 Ibid. i, 92, ii, 328. Why should *geseldas* and *cnihtas* be particularly associated with bridges?

54 This suggestion, with references to the *cnihtas* of Shakenoak, was made to me by Patrick Wormald, and I am very grateful to him for allowing me to use it.

55 S.1001 (*P-N Oxon.* ii, 490).

56 M. Gelling in Brodribb et al. 1972, 136; Gelling 1978, 203–4. The burials are described in Brodribb et al. 1973, 32–5, 172–83.

57 The broad date-range is suggested by the fact that these are unaccompanied and orientated burials (was this therefore a Christian community?), and the parallel with the other villa burials discussed below. The possibility that the *cnihtas* were executed criminals seems to be discounted by the orderly layout of the cemetery, and the stone linings in some of the graves.

58 Davidson 1989. The Shakenoak men, though, seem from their bones to have been mostly in their thirties, so the model of adolescent trainee warriors is not quite appropriate.

59 Gelling 1992, 92–3, summarises her work on this topic.

60 *P-N Oxon.* i, xix–xx. These are, however, dubious cases which involve etymological problems.

61 Ibid. i, 195.

62 Ibid. ii, 454, 462 (and add Pug Pit in Bampton). For the general context see Gelling 1978, 150.

63 *P-N Oxon.* ii, 250.

64 Ibid. i, 211.

65 Dickinson 1976, i, 237f.

66 Boyle et al. (forthcoming); Miles & Palmer n.d., 16–19.

67 The best account currently available (though unpublished) is Berisford 1973, summarised by Hawkes 1986, 83–5. The reports on Barrow Hills, Worton Rectory Farm and Eynsham Abbey are eagerly awaited. The general subject can now be approached through Hamerow 1991, Hamerow 1992, and Welch 1992, chs. II–IV.

68 Berisford 1973, 50–63; Clayton 1973; Chambers & McAdam (forthcoming).

69 Hamerow 1991.

70 *SMA* xxi (1991), 86–92; report by G. Hey in preparation.

71 Berisford 1973, 90–2; Brodribb et al. 1972, 30, 129–30; Miles (ed.) 1986, 37.

72 Brodribb et al. 1972, 30, 118–29; Berisford 1973, ch. VII.

73 Boyle et al. (forthcoming); Miles & Palmer n.d., 16–17, 20–1.

74 This conclusion is supported by Hamerow 1992, 40–1. However, Scull 1992, 264–8, argues that regional retrieval bias has been very serious in the Vale of the White Horse.

75 Hamerow 1992, 41.

76 Robinson 1981, 269; Miles (ed.) 1986, 36. There was a slight rise in tree and shrub pollen, and in contrast to the Roman phases the only cereal found was *Hordeum vulgare*.

77 Robinson & Lambrick 1984, 813; Robinson 1992, 200–1.
78 Gelling 1988, 69–70.
79 Some of the evidence presented by Sturdy 1963 looks convincing, though the disposition of the St. Frideswide's estate is surely tenurial; and cf. the critique of Emery 1974, 55–6. For Wychwood see Schumer 1984, ch. IV. There is no evidence that Oxfordshire ever had transhumance on the scale of, for instance, the Weald or the Forest of Arden; cf. Gelling 1992, 13.
80 *P-N Oxon.* i, 1–2.
81 As Scull 1993, 266–7, suggests in relation to the Vale of the White Horse.
82 Hamerow 1991, 13–14, stresses the difficulty of dating the ends of 'early' Thames Valley settlements.
83 Hamerow 1991, 10.
84 Allen & Dalwood 1983; Yeoman 1986.
85 *SMA* xxi (1991), 102–6; xxii (1992), 46.
86 PRNs 4449, 4493, 8042–3, 9980, 9989, 9952.
87 This can best be appreciated from Briggs, Cook & Rowley (eds.) 1986, map 11. Miles 1974 maps the Abingdon and Dorchester areas in more detail.
88 See Charles-Edwards 1972.
89 Dickinson 1976, i, 428–9.
90 Boyle et al. (forthcoming); Miles & Palmer n.d., 13–14.
91 The following remarks owe much to lectures given by Christopher Scull on the Lechlade cemetery in 1992–3. Cf. Scull 1992.
92 Boyle et al. (forthcoming); Miles & Palmer n.d., 13.
93 Hawkes 1986, 82–3.
94 Hawkes 1986, 89 and Pl. 8a.
95 Dickinson 1976, i, 364–5. New finds will be discussed by Boyle et al. (forthcoming) (Lechlade and Watchfield) and by Boyle & Mudd (forthcoming) (Didcot area, formerly thought Roman).
96 Scull 1990.
97 See B. Odenstedt and R. Page in Scull 1993, 246–51, and Ibid. 267–8.
98 Stewart 1978, 148–9. Of the six known specimens, the only two with recorded provenances were found at Dorchester on Thames and Eastleach Turville (Glos.)
99 The case for Merovingian lordship over Kent is made by Wood 1983; cf. Kirby 1991, 34–5. Hawkes 1986, 85, emphasises Æthelberht's lordship over other English kingdoms, but this is severely compromised by the new chronology for his reign (Kirby 1991, 31–4).

100 For the general context see Welch 1992, ch. VII.
101 Dickinson 1974.
102 Benson & Miles 1974b; Hawkes 1986, 88–9.
103 Hawkes 1986, 89.
104 Dickinson 1976, i, 411, stresses the traditional rather than the novel character of this practice. The fact remains, though, that coherent groups of graves re-using earlier barrows are overwhelmingly late, especially those (notably Stanton Harcourt) with elements of orderly layout.
105 This follows the reinterpretation by Brown 1972 of the data presented in Brodribb et al. 1972.
106 Miles 1986, 16–19.
107 *Oxo.* xxxi (1966), 153–4 (PRN 2337); *Oxo.* iv (1939), 7 (Fig. 3), 37–9.
108 Cf. Bradley 1987, 4, 10.
109 Gelling 1992, 53 et seq.
110 Sims-Williams 1990, 75–83; Bassett 1992.
111 I am grateful to Elizabeth O'Brien, who is currently working on this topic, for discussing it with me. The papers in Edwards & Lane (eds.) 1992 contain much that is relevant.
112 James, Marshall & Millett 1984, 205–6.
113 Coates 1989–90, 3–7. The case for Ceawlin is rather less certain than that for Cerdic.
114 The starting-point is now Bassett 1989 and the collection of essays which it introduces; the review by Patrick Wormald in *Oxo.* liv (1989), 420–2, gives an excellent over-view of the issues.
115 Bassett 1989, 24–6; Blair 1989, 98–103.
116 Hooke 1985, 74–106; Hooke 1986; Bassett 1989, 18–23; Gelling 1992, 140.
117 *P-N Oxon.* i, xviii; Blair 1989, 98–103.
118 Baines 1981, 8; *P-N Oxon.* i, 94–5 (though there Gelling favours a derivation from a lost personal name 'Wæcel'), ii, 316; S.217, S.771.
119 A. Howkins, *Reshaping Rural England: a Social History 1850–1925* (1991), 30. I am grateful to Rosamond Faith for this reference.
120 Charles-Edwards 1972.
121 For recent and contrasting views of the Tribal Hidage see Yorke 1990, 9–13 and Kirby 1991, 11. I am inclined to see it as a relatively late, probably antiquarian compilation, though certainly including seventh-century material.
122 The phrase of Scull 1992, 16–17; this paper argues powerfully that 'we are not dealing with the long-term evolution of sophisticated hierarchical societies, but with a much shorter-term transformation and subsequent

123 The following paragraphs rely heavily on: Dumville 1985; Yorke 1990, 130–48; Kirby 1991, 48–60; Hawkes 1986, 85–7; Yorke 1989, 94–6; Sims-Williams 1983.

124 Coates 1989–90, 1–3.

125 *ASC* 12–14.

126 Sims-Williams 1983 tends towards this position.

127 Dumville 1985, 51.

128 Kirby 1991, 54. For the second suggestion I am grateful to Barbara Yorke.

129 Yorke 1990, 142–8, drawing useful analogies from later West Saxon practice; Kirby 1991, 49, 53–5.

130 Dickinson 1974, 32–4; Hawkes 1986, 89–90. Cf. the caveat on the 'Cuth-' names in Sims-Williams 1983, 28 n. 20.

131 Cam & Crawford 1935.

132 Bede, *HE*, II.5, II.9.

133 See pp. 191 note 72 below, which casts strong doubt on the suggestion of Hawkes 1986, 88, that 'the whole complex might well represent a palatial establishment in the town before the arrival of Birinus'.

134 May 1977. It is important to note that this site was later episcopal.

135 Dickinson 1974, 25–30.

136 Ibid. loc. cit.

137 For reasons for revising the traditional date of 635 see Kirby 1991, 49–50.

138 Bede, *HE*, III.7.

139 Barbara Yorke points out (pers. comm.) that the exiled Cenwealh of the Gewisse fled to Anna of the East Angles (Bede, *HE* III.7), which might suggest links between the Gewisse and earlier East Anglian kings such as Rædwald.

140 Cf. Blair 1992a, 245–6.

CHAPTER TWO

1 Brooks 1989, 160–3.

2 Ibid. 165–6, 169–70, and, for a slightly different dating of Penda's reign, Kirby 1991, 82.

3 Bede, *HE*, II.20, III.1; Kirby 1991, 81–2 for chronology.

4 Bassett 1989, 6; Kirby 1991, 82–3.

5 *ASC* 17; Kirby 1991, 57, 82, for the context of this event, which he dates slightly later.

6 Brooks 1989, 166–7, *contra* Kirby 1991, 91.

7 Brooks 1989, 167; Yorke 1990, 136.

8 *ASC* 21; Kirby 1991, 59, 114–16.

9 Bede, *HE*, III.7.

10 Yorke 1990, 136; Kirby 1991, 58–9.

11 Yorke 1989 for what follows.

12 Cf. Kirby 1991, 114: Wulfhere's marriage to a Kentish princess was 'probably intended to bring the Mercians more closely into association with the Anglo-Frankish world of the Kentish court'.

13 Dickinson & Speake 1992, 115–16, and 97 Fig. 14.

14 Dickinson & Speake 1992 for the rest of this paragraph.

15 Dickinson 1976, i, 445–6.

16 Meaney 1964, 212–13, 208, 213, 214; Dickinson 1973; Dickinson 1976, corpus Nos. 132, 56, 44, 135–6, 168.

17 Hawkes 1986, 93–4.

18 Dickinson 1973; Dickinson 1976, i, 446.

19 Dickinson & Speake 1992, 123.

20 PRN 1599, Dickinson 1976, corpus No. 168; Boyle & Mudd (forthcoming).

21 What follows is based on Dickinson 1976, i, 437–47, and Hawkes 1986, 91–3.

22 Dickinson 1976, i, 202–13, 227–32, for these categories of object. For the exceptional Standlake grave see Speake 1989, 72–4 and Figs. 65, 68.

23 Meaney 1964, 49; Dickinson 1976, corpus No. 100.

24 Webster & Backhouse (eds.) 1991, 21–31, 47–60; for a good over-view of some of the Midland evidence see Stafford 1985, 152–6.

25 Campbell 1986, 91.

26 Bassett 1989, and the essays which it introduces, for this and what follows.

27 A brief survey of a very complex and controversial topic; for fuller accounts see Campbell 1986, 85–98, Charles-Edwards 1989 and Wormald 1983.

28 Foard 1985, 198–9.

29 *P-N Oxon.* i, xix.

30 The first reference is in a charter of 841 (S.196), which shows that Wychwood was then regarded as extending further north to include Spelsbury (and so presumably Charlbury), though this part of it was already hidated land.

31 As Barbara Yorke points out to me, the Gloucestershire–Wiltshire border causes similar problems: the shire and diocesan boundary was established by the ninth century, but earlier indications suggest something significantly different and certainly less tidy.

32 *ASC* 19.

33 For the individual Middle Anglian tribes see Foard 1985, 193–203.

34 Dumville 1989, 130–2, 140; Yorke 1990, 64–5. One voice dissenting from the 'artificial' view of the Middle Angles and the Hwicce is D.P. Kirby's: Kirby 1991, 8.

35 Bede, *HE*, III.21.

36 Foard 1985, 198–9 for Northants.; Morley Davies 1947–52 a–b for Bucks.

37 Note 30 above.

38 Dumville 1989, 133–4.

39 For the extent of the *Cilternsæte* see Morley Davies 1947–52 b.

40 Blair 1989, 105–7.

41 This entire section is based on Blair 1987 and Blair 1988a.

42 *Pipe Roll 22 Henry II*, 28–9, and subsequent years.

43 *P-N Oxon.* ii, 256; Bede, *HE*, II.16.

44 Cf. Bede, *HE*, III.21: 'filio Pendan regis', 'frater Uttan presbyteri'.

45 Edwards 1988, 195–6, and Kelly (forthcoming), as against Stenton 1913, 12–22. The *locus* of involvement of the sub-king Cissa, and over-king Ine, must now be identified as the Bradfield area, much further south.

46 Edwards 1988, 126–7; Yorke 1990, 136; Kirby 1991, 117, 133. I am grateful to Dr P.H. Hase for discussions on this problem.

47 Yorke 1990, 111–17; Kirby 1991, 129–36.

48 This problem is considered by Dumville 1992, 3 n. 16, citing in particular S.1786.

49 *ASC* 30; Yorke 1990, 140–1; Kirby 1991, 133–4 for a rather different view.

50 Kirby 1991, 164.

51 *ASC* 33; Yorke 1990, 141; Kirby 1991, 168–9.

52 *Chron. Ab.* i, 14; see commentary by Parker 1885, 109–11.

53 S.225.

54 Sims-Williams 1975, 8–9; Edwards 1988, 123; Yorke 1990, 141; Sims-Williams 1990, 159–60; and works cited there.

55 S.1258; Stenton 1913, 22, 24–5; Yorke 1990, 113.

56 But note the qualifications of Wormald 1983, 112–17.

57 Bassett 1985a, 84. See, however, Sims-Williams 1990, 165–7, for Offa's possible involvement with Winchcombe.

58 Bassett 1985a, 85.

59 The importance of this site is suggested by the superb quality of the late ninth-century Minster Lovell jewel (below, p.100). The

other St. Kenelm dedication in Oxfordshire, at Church Enstone, shouldbe discounted, for this manor belonged to Winchcombe Abbey.

60 *The Itinerary of John Leland*, ed. L. Toulmin Smith, ii (1908), 151–2, citing a lost source. *Cherrenhul* can only be the hill on which Cherbury Camp (*Cerenburhg*, *P-N Berks.* ii, 390) stands, even though it is not exactly 'between Abingdon and Oxford'.

61 *ASC* 40.

62 *ASC* 40.

63 This retracts the suggestions in Blair 1990, where I proposed on insufficient evidence that the Thames was a frontier 'for considerable periods between the reigns of Penda and Offa'.

64 Sims-Williams 1983, 32–3.

65 For a recent summary of the issues relating to Faringdon–Langford on the one hand and Sonning-Dunsden on the other, see Hooper 1988, 3, 11; the first is considered more fully in *P-N Berks.* ii, 366. I am sceptical about both cases, especially the Faringdon–Langford link which surely results from late tenurial connections, especially involving Ælfsige of Faringdon.

66 I am grateful to Barbara Yorke for this point.

67 Campbell 1986, 218–19.

68 Sims-Williams 1990 is now the best exposition of this evidence.

69 For the general context see Foot 1992, Blair (ed.) 1988, Blair 1992a.

70 Bede, *HE*, IV.23 (and Plummer's commentary, ibid. ii, pp. 245–6).

71 Rowley & Brown 1981. I am grateful to Christopher Loveluck for discussing with me his view that the timber phase was in fact sub-Roman. After careful thought I still prefer the excavators' seventh-century date, for the following reasons: (i) Although the pottery assemblage is abnormal (ibid. p. 40), both the timber phase and the first stone phase produced a few grass-tempered sherds (p. 13); there is nothing surprising about most of the pottery being residual. (ii) The second stone phase was firmly dated by a coin of Burgred (852–74) found in one of its walls; it seems more reasonable to identify the timber buildings as its direct predecessors than to pull them back into a hypothetical post-Roman phase. (iii) The scale and density of the timber buildings is best paralleled on the seventh- to eighth-century monastic sites at Whitby, Hartlepool and Brandon, as (except at Brandon) is their replacement in stone (Blair 1992a, 261–4).

72   Frere 1962, 125–8; Frere 1984. Hawkes 1986, 88, suggests that this was a pre-Christian palace group, but the major building cuts across a sixth-century sunken hut, and a wall-trench belonging to one phase of the complex contained a St. Neot's Ware pot (Frere 1962, Fig. 21.19, from the 'Saxon trench' shown in Fig. 6).

73   May 1977. A description of 1146 (*The Registrum Antiquissimum of the Cathedral Church of Lincoln*, i (Lincoln Record Soc. xxvii, 1931), 247), shows that this was the site of the *ambitum grangiarum episcopalium*.

74   Bede, *HE*, III.21.

75   F. Liebermann, *Die Heiligen Englands* (Hannover, 1889); Rollason 1978, 63, 90.

76   Blair 1988c, 49, Fig. 2.3. It is worth comparing Hanbury (Worcs.), another early Irish minster built under Wulfhere's patronage on a much more dramatic hill (Sims-Williams 1990, 105–8); the Irish did not, however, have any monopoly of such sites (Blair 1992a, 227–31).

77   This is Susan Kelly's interpretation of the paraphrase S.239, long ascribed to Abingdon: see Kelly (forthcoming).

78   Eddius Stephanus, *Vita Wilfridi*, cc. 14–15.

79   S.1165; Blair 1989, 97–8.

80   *VCH Oxon*. vii, 163–5, 170–2, 199–200.

81   Rodwell (ed.) 1975, 147–53; Blair 1988c, 49, Fig. 2.3.

82   Hohler 1966, 63–4, 66; Blair 1989, 106.

83   Allen & Dalwood 1983, 2, 6–8; Yeoman 1986.

84   Hohler 1966, 63–4.

85   Blair 1985, 122, 136; Blair 1988c, 42, Fig. 2.1, 47. For Anglo-Saxon material found near Bicester church see *SMA* x (1980), 169–71.

86   S.1167; Sims-Williams 1975.

87   Blair 1988b, 226.

88   This paragraph is based on Blair 1988b.

89   Ibid. 228–31.

90   This will be fully discussed in Durham (forthcoming), Trill Mill Stream section; meanwhile see *SMA* xiii (1983), 138–40, xvi (1986), 104. The waterfront feature is F681/3.

91   These last two churches are first mentioned in the mid-twelfth and early eleventh centuries respectively: below, pp. 151, 163. The suggestion of an early line of churches is therefore entirely conjectural, though it accords with what we know about the topography of many other complexes (Blair 1992a, 246–58).

92   Blair 1988b, 233–5; Blair 1987, 89.

93   Blair 1988b, 233; Hassall 1973, 270–4; Scull 1988.

94   *Oxo*. xxxvi (1971), 5 and Pl. I; Hassall et al. 1989, 92–4.

95   *SMA* xxi (1991), 102–7, xxii (1992), 46–7.

96   *Councils and Ecclesiastical Documents*, eds. A.W. Haddan and W. Stubbs, iii (1871), 597–8; Brooks 1984, 104, 180–3.

97   S.210: 'post annum reddat XXX solidos ad Egenes homme ad illam ecclesiam aatributo [*sic*]'.

98   Blair 1984; cf. below, p. 196 note 120.

99   This section is based on the results of a long-term research project by the author, still in progress. There are interim reports in *SMA* xvi (1986), 87–92, xviii (1988), 89–93, xxii (1992), 55–62; see also *VCH Oxon* xiii (forthcoming).

100 Blair 1992a, 246–58.

101 This complex body of material, printed in *Chron. Ab.*, is fully discussed by Stenton 1913, and Biddle, Lambrick & Myres 1968. The present account, however, follows the radical re-interpretation proposed by Edwards 1988, 195–6, and Kelly (forthcoming).

102 Kelly (forthcoming).

103 Gelling 1957.

104 The important recent excavations at Abingdon were conducted by Tim Allen, and I am very grateful to him for his advice on what follows.

105 Biddle, Lambrick & Myres 1968, 27 and Pl. III; *Chron. Ab.* ii, 270.

106 Biddle, Lambrick & Myres 1968, 28.

107 Hood and Speake 1987.

108 Cf. Webster & Backhouse (eds.) 1992, 79–100, especially item 69 (i).

109 *Banbury*: *VCH Oxon*. x, 95 (mother church of large area crossing county boundary); Everitt 1974. *Cropredy*: *VCH Oxon*. x, 168 (prebendal church, chapelries of Bourton, Claydon, Mollington and Wardington). *Bloxham*: *VCH Oxon*. ix, 72 (chapelry of Milcombe, possibly another in Wychwood); *Cal. Charter Rolls 1327–41*, 332 (forged charter of William I granting Bloxham church with 1½ hides, meadow, houses, chapel and cemetery); *SMA* x (1980), 103–23 (topographical survey of Bloxham). *Adderbury*: *VCH Oxon*. ix, 30 (chapels of Milton, Bodicote and Barford St. John).

110 Blair 1992a, 234; Sims-Williams 1990, 92–3, 108–9; Stafford 1985, 150.

111 Foard 1985, 198–200. This area badly needs a detailed local study.

112 Blair 1992b.

113 Cf. Blair 1985, 133.

114 Blair 1986.

115 Cf. Blair 1985, 117–19.

116 Blair 1992a, 227–30; Blair (forthcoming) a.

117 Blair (ed.) 1988, introduction.

118 Blair 1988c, 50–5; Rattue 1990.

119 Blair 1992a, 257–8, for general context.

120 Blair 1987, 91–2, 98–9, 110.

121 Blair 1988d.

122 Blair 1992a, 257.

123 Above, p. 63, and below, p. 114.

124 S.1258.

125 There are several examples in Blair (ed.) 1988, where the general principles are discussed in the introduction.

126 For north-east Oxfordshire, which has yet to be worked on systematically, see note 109 above.

127 See for instance Blair 1988c, 52; Boddington 1990.

128 Dickinson 1976, i, 446; Hawkes 1986, 93.

129 Bede, *HE*, III.21.

130 Blair 1992a, 136n; Allen & Dalwood 1983.

131 Blair 1992b for Shipton; PRNs 2205, 2554 and 2619 for Charlbury and Marcham.

132 Blair 1992a, 136n; Allen & Dalwood 1983 for Aylesbury; Blair 1992b for Shipton; *SMA* xxii (1992), 55 for Bampton.

133 Boddington 1990, 182–7.

134 Meaney 1964, 204 (= PRN 1499), 207 (= PRN 1542), 47, 209 (= PRN 1377); PRN 5775; *Oxo.* xlii (1977), 37–9 (= PRN 12493); *Oxo.* xxxi (1966), 153–4 (= PRN 2337); Dickinson 1976, corpus Nos. 26, 44, 71, 85, 73.

135 Dickinson 1976, i, 271.

136 Meaney 1964, 206 (= PRN 1375), 211–12, 214 (= PRN 2476), 54 (= PRN 9741); Dickinson 1976, corpus Nos. 160, 164.

137 May 1977, 52–3, 68, 72; Dickinson 1976, corpus No. 53; Hinchcliffe & Thomas 1980, 33, 66–8. The dating of the Dorchester seax is on Dickinson's typology.

138 Chambers 1973; Chambers 1976; Crawford 1989.

139 J. Blair in Crawford 1989, 55–6.

140 For a similar argument based on wider evidence see Blair 1988c, 50–5. Sims-Williams 1990, 67–72, describes some West Midland cases and has judicious comments on how confidently they can be accepted as Christian.

141 This would be very consistent with the new model for 'final phase' cemeteries proposed by Boddington 1990, 196–7.

142 This is the central argument of Blair (forthcoming) b, which provides a wider context for these paragraphs.

143 Julia Smith's fascinating study of Breton cults (Smith 1990) establishes a methodology which should now be applied much more widely. For Wales cf. Pryce 1992, 60.

144 This accepts the inspired reconstruction of the story by Hohler 1966, 63–6; cf. above, p. 61.

145 *Acta Sanctorum: November*, i (1887), 685–90.

146 Edited highlights from the narrative in *Nova Legenda Anglie*, ed. C. Horstman, i (1901), 450–6. The full text is an extraordinary example of baroque medieval story-telling, and it deserves a wider audience.

147 Another link between these two stories is that Freomund's birth is foretold by a three-day-old boy. It does look as though the Rumwold and Freomund legends have sources in common, especially since Cropredy and the Rumwold sites may all have lain within the great Kings Sutton complex (note 111 above).

148 See *P-N Oxon.* ii, 423–4, and the references to the later medieval cult in F.N. Macnamara, *Memorials of the Danvers Family* (1895), 124, 251, 256–60.

149 Smith 1990, 323; Pryce 1992, 60.

150 Exeter Cathedral, Dean and Chapter archives, MS 3672 p. 33.

151 Phythian-Adams 1975, 21–5.

152 *Laws of Ine* cl. 70.1 (D. Whitelock's translation).

153 Among the extensive literature, see for instance Stafford 1985, 29–35; Hooke 1986, 87–91; Charles-Edwards 1989, 29–31; Blair 1991, 24–30; Faith (forthcoming).

154 Blair 1989, 103–5; Bassett 1989, 20.

155 Bassett (forthcoming).

156 For the earliest charters with round-figure hidages see Campbell 1986, 110–11.

157 *VCH Oxon.* i, 373–4; *Dom. Geog. S.-E.*, 197–9. More recently Leaver 1988, especially Fig. 3, has vindicated the systematic character of hidation.

158 This assumes that Domesday Yelford is part of 958 Ducklington (cf. Fig. 77).

159 S.883, S.1379, S.911, S.927.

160 Campbell 1986, 116.

161 Below, pp. 108, 111.

162 Blair 1986, 64–5. Was this originally part of the great Kings Sutton complex (above, notes 111 and 147)?

163 Dyer 1980, 28–30.

164 This question will be discussed by Faith (forthcoming).

165 DB 58c (Berks. VII.6); *P-N Oxon.* i, 31.

166 *P-N Oxon.* ii, 302.

167 Gelling 1992, 122.

168 *P-N Oxon.* ii, 434.

169 Dyer 1980, 34; Faith (forthcoming).

170 This theme is developed in Blair (forthcoming) a.

171 Metcalf 1993, 66f.

172 Metcalf 1984 is a detailed exposition of this view.

173 Metcalf 1984, 30–2; Metcalf 1993.

174 Kent 1972; Metcalf 1984, 60–1; Webster & Backhouse (eds.) 1991, No. 53.

175 Brodribb et al. 1972, 30–1.

176 Metcalf 1977, 90.

177 Metcalf (forthcoming), section on 'Series U'.

178 Ibid.

179 Metcalf 1972.

180 Above, p. 55. Metcalf (forthcoming), 309–12, runs into unnecessary difficulties by accepting Rigold's unsupported view that Æthelbald could not have controlled London before 732.

181 Metcalf (forthcoming), 312.

182 Metcalf (forthcoming), section on 'Series U'.

183 There is a good interim report on recent work in *Current Archaeology*, cxxvi (Sept./Oct. 1991), 252–5.

184 For this and what follows see Hooke 1981; Gelling 1992, 170–1.

185 Hooke 1981, 132, 140–1.

186 Ibid. 140–1. The commutation of this service is almost certainly represented by the yearly payment to Bordesley Abbey near Bromsgrove 'from the piggery of Bampton' (above, note 42). For the continuing link between Bampton and land in Droitwich see British Library, MS Cotton Vesp. E.ix, ff. 5–6 (Westwood Cartulary).

187 Above, p. 54 and below, p. 123.

188 Hooke 1981, 132–4, 138; *P-N Worcs.* 4–9, *P-N Glos.* i, 19–20, *P-N Oxon.* i, 3–4; the interpretation of the Oxfordshire references is my own.

189 *Ministers' Accounts of the Earldom of Cornwall, 1296–1297*, ed. L.M. Midgley (Camden 3rd ser. lxvi, 1942), 95; *VCH Berks.* ii, 204n. I owe the first reference to Robert Peberdy.

190 *Placitorum . . . Abbreviatio* (Rec. Comm., 1811), 85; British Library, MS Cotton Nero A.xii, f. 50v (Faringdon Cartulary).

191 Cf. Durham 1977, 171–3; Durham 1984, 59, 79, 89.

192 Durham 1977, 180; *VCH Oxon.* iv, 3–4, 284. South-west of Oxford, both roads stand out

193 *P-N Berks.* iii, 725–6, 729–30. For the possibility that 'stone ford' means a raised causeway cf. Blair & Millard 1992.

194 For the conclusive argument that the 'oxen-ford' was the southern, not the western, approach to the town see Davis 1973.

195 Blair 1988b, 223–4, 228–31.

196 Durham (forthcoming), section on British Telecom tunnel.

197 Dickinson 1976, i, 429–30.

198 Durham 1977, 91, 101–2, 175–82 (which also notes, p. 176, 'a sherd from deep in the embankment [which] is more likely to be mid-Saxon than earlier'); Durham 1984, 80–1, 85–6.

199 M. Robinson and G. Lambrick in Durham 1984, 79–80.

200 Durham 1977, 176–83, for this paragraph.

201 Ibid. 200–1 (but note the technical problems).

202 Ibid. 142–6, 152–3, 155–60, 160–2.

203 Ibid. 114.

204 Ibid. 174–5.

205 Ibid. 174–5.

206 For general context and references see Campbell (ed.) 1982, 100, 122.

207 The general hypothesis is most fully and forcefully argued by Haslam 1987; cf. Gelling 1992 ch. IX, and Shoesmith 1982, 91–3. Durham (forthcoming) will argue in favour of an Offa-period *burh* at Oxford.

208 Bassett (forthcoming) argues that West Midland hundreds were grouped in this way around such early centres as Hereford, Winchcombe and Tamworth.

CHAPTER THREE

1 S.1271; comments by Stenton 1913, 26–8.

2 S.288, S.317; Keynes & Lapidge 1983, 67.

3 Stenton 1913, 28–30; Yorke 1990, 122. It is possible that the Vale was settled on Æthelswith as part of her marriage settlement, for she granted land in her own name at Lockinge in 868 (S.1201).

4 Keynes & Lapidge 1983, 73, 78, 242.

5 Cf. *P-N Berks.* iii, 843.

6 The best short introduction is P. Wormald's in Campbell (ed.) 1982, 144–55. The campaigns can be followed through the excellent maps in Hill 1981.

7 Translation from Keynes & Lapidge 1983, 78–80 (quoted by kind permission of Simon Keynes).

8 Ibid. 81, 244; *ASC* 47; Dumville 1992, 13.

9   Dumville 1992.

10   Ibid. 7.

11   Dumville 1992, 1, boldly calls him 'Æthelred II of Mercia'. It is a problem, though, that he never calls himself king in his own charters: were they produced in scriptoria with West Saxon sympathies?

12   These uncertainties are stressed by Ibid. 7, 16 n. 79, 18 n. 85.

13   S.219.

14   ASC 52; cf. Dumville 1992, 6–7, 16–18. Forthcoming work by Simon Keynes and Mark Blackburn will suggest that Alfred's authority was recognised in London some years before 886.

15   Dumville 1992, 18 n. 85, asks this question. The annal for 872 is no obstacle to Æthelred's possession of London until 886, since he would have recovered it in 879; S.218 stands at present as a more weighty objection to the view that Æthelred was initially independent of Alfred.

16   Stafford 1989, 26.

17   S.217.

18   S.220; cf. Dumville 1992, 3, 18–19.

19   ASC 62; Wainwright 1975, 309–13; Stafford 1989, 32, for speculations on the degree of co-operation between Æthelflæd and Edward.

20   As Barbara Yorke suggests to me.

21   Hill 1981, maps 83–90; ASC 62–3; Blair 1986, 63–4.

22   Wainwright 1975, 321–4.

23   Hart 1973, 116; Williams 1982, 161–3.

24   Cf. Williams 1982, 161–2, 163 n. 97. For Æthelflæd's minster at Gloucester see below, p. 111.

25   Hart 1973, 118.

26   See for instance Hart 1973, 124–6; Williams 1982, passim. Chadwick suggested, and others have followed (e.g. Williams 1982, 165; Dumville 1992, 18 n. 87), that Oxfordshire and Buckinghamshire were united with the ealdordom of Essex in the late tenth century. This view depends on the Ardley charter (S.883), which does not in fact contain any clear evidence that the reeves of Oxford and Buckingham were under Leofsige's ealdormannic authority. I am grateful to Patrick Wormald for his advice on this point.

27   F. Liebermann, Die Gesetze der Angelsachsen, i (Halle, 1898), 216.

28   Hill 1981, map 70. A few personal names of Norse origin are compounded with Oxfordshire place-names (P-N Oxon. i, xxiv–v, ii, 481), but there is no reason to think that these belonged to first-generation Vikings.

29   Biddle & Blair 1988. For Reading as a minster see Blair (forthcoming) a.

30   Evison 1969 (where the Reading find is discussed on p. 335).

31   These figures are based on a quick count of the items listed in the Oxfordshire Sites and Monuments Record and at Reading Museum (mainly Thames Conservancy collection), but I have not attempted a full inventory. The more important items are discussed in detail by Wilson 1965 and Evison 1967. The so-called 'Shifford' sword (Reading Mus. 074–285.47) was actually found above Ten Foot Bridge, which is at Chimney; the other outlier is the seax from New Bridge, Standlake (PRN 2363, Reading Mus. 073–284.47).

32   Wilson 1965, 50–1; Hinton 1970, 1.

33   For the text, and a useful summary of the arguments about dating, see Hill 1969, and P. Wormald in Campbell (ed.) 1982, 152–3. Dumville 1992, 24–7, reaffirms the traditional date of 914.

34   Biddle 1976a, 124–37, and sources cited there.

35   Stafford 1985, 46–53; Hinton 1990, 72–94.

36   As emphasised for instance by several essays in Haslam (ed.) 1984. Haslam 1987 argues strongly for an eighth-century Mercian origin for the 'burghal system' (but cf above, p. 92).

37   Lyon 1970, 196–7; Lyon 1976, 181; M. Metcalf in Hassall 1976, 269. Durham (forthcoming) contains a new and extended discussion of the whole problem, including comments by M. Metcalf.

38   VCH Oxon. iv, 8n.

39   Cf. Lyon 1976, 181; Maddicott 1989, 17–18.

40   Durham (forthcoming), section on Shire Lake.

41   ASC 62; cf. above, p. 97.

42   Vince 1990, 20–2, 124–9.

43   Wainwright 1975, 308–9.

44   Shoesmith 1982, 74–82; ASC 62–7. Gelling 1992, 128, stresses Æthelflæd's role in West Midland shire and town formation, and recent work on Gloucester has emphasised her achievement there.

45   Durham (forthcoming) reaches the contrary conclusion that Oxford was West Saxon, and the work of Edward the Elder. The crux of the matter is whether a town plan can be labelled 'West Saxon' as against 'Mercian' on constructional and morphological grounds; I am unable to accept that it can.

46   Keynes & Lapidge 1983, 67. Cf. Taylor 1957, 18.

47 Stafford 1989, 49.

48 Taylor 1957, 23–5; Whybra 1990, 4–5, 11–12.

49 *ASC* 90–1; S.927.

50 Taylor 1957, 26–9; Whybra 1990, 7–8.

51 Hill 1969, 86 and facing table.

52 See Morris 1927, 1–39 for the West Saxon context. Whybra 1990, 13–15, thinks that 'the West Midland shire-system developed as the formal embodiment in 1007 of an informal early tenth-century arrangement of attaching districts to boroughs for military purposes'. Something of the sort had presumably happened in Wessex at an earlier date.

53 Roffe 1986, 114–16; cf. Stafford 1985, 138–42.

54 S.883.

55 *Dom. Geog. S.-E.*, 186–90; Blair 1990, 2.

56 S.567; *P-N Berks.* iii, 732, 734.

57 Here I differ from the conclusion of Durham (forthcoming), Shire Lake section.

58 *VCH Oxon.* iv, 260, 286. A meeting of the Berkshire court on Grandpont in 1335 is recorded in British Library, MS Cotton Nero A.xii ff. 75v–76v (Faringdon Cartulary).

59 For the likely context see Blair 1988b, 226.

60 *Chron. Ab.* i, 88–90; cf. *P-N Berks.* ii, 454, iii, 726, 734. The procedure has an authentic ring about it, even though it is recorded in a forged text. The dispute is said to have been with the people of Oxfordshire rather than of Oxford, and the miracle was witnessed by the *comprovinciales* of *tam Berrocensis pagi quam Oxenefordensis*, which suggests that the shire boundary was thought to be at issue.

61 Williams 1982, 163–6; Hill 1981, map 174.

62 Stafford 1978.

63 *ASC* 87–8.

64 *ASC* 90, 92.

65 S.943; Williams 1986, 1. Cf. Lawson 1993, 167–8.

66 Fleming 1991, 48–9; Lawson 1993, 176, 186.

67 *Hemingi Chartularium Ecclesiae Wigorniensis*, ed. T. Hearne, i (1733), 280; Williams 1986, 2, 6–7. Lawson 1993, 184–6, emphasises the uncertainties that surround the various Cnut-period earls mentioned in West Midland contexts; see also Ibid. 165–6.

68 DB 56b (Berks. B 1); Lawson 1993, 177–84. I am grateful to Barbara Crawford for her advice on these matters.

69 Williams 1986, 9–11.

70 Lawson 1993, 163, 164, 172.

71 Williams 1986, 15.

72 Lawson 1993, 186–7; Williams 1986, 15. For the 1050–2 reference see below, p. 107.

73 S.1105; Harmer 1952, 570.

74 Harmer 1952, 546–7.

75 DB 154a, 160b (B1, B5, LIV.1) for Ælfgar; DB 154d (I. 7a–b, 12), and 238c (Warw. I.6), for Eadwine. *Contra* E.A. Freeman, *History of the Norman Conquest of England*, ii (1868), 566–7, Eadwine clearly *was* earl of Oxfordshire. He held the large hundredal manor of Adderbury–Bloxham, and the reference in the Oxfordshire folios to 'Earl Eadwine's land in Oxfordshire and in Warwickshire' correlates with the entries under Warwickshire, where Eadwine received the earl's third penny. Freeman's proposed descent of Oxfordshire from Ælfgar direct to Gyrth (loc. cit.) therefore falls.

76 S.1139, 1147–8. Freeman's error (see last note) has misled more recent writers (Harmer 1952, 562; Nightingale 1987, 571; Fleming 1991, 56, 89–90) into thinking that Gyrth had become earl some years previously. (It follows that S.1139 can now be dated more closely, to 1065–6.)

77 Fleming 1991, ch. III, is now the best general account.

78 DB 154d, 160d (I. 8–9, LVIII. 29); cf. Fleming 1991, 89–90. For Langford as a comital estate see below, p. 111.

79 Fleming 1991, 61–3.

80 A good general guide to what follows is Loyn 1984, 138–48.

81 Morris 1927, 24–5, 37–9; Green 1990, 9–11.

82 Campbell 1987 for this aspect of the activities of reeves.

83 S.1425. This has only been known from a Latin translation, but Simon Keynes has recently rediscovered the Old English text in a seventeenth-century transcript in Brussels, Bibliothèque Royale, MS 7965–73 (3723). I am most grateful to him for allowing me to cite it.

84 For Vagn see Williams 1986, 15.

85 Williams 1989, 291.

86 The definitive exposition of this problem is now Thorn 1990, on which the present remarks are based. An earlier discussion which still has some value (especially as regards comparisons between Oxon. and Bucks.) is Morley Davies 1947–52b.

87 *P-N Oxon.*, i, 159–60, 196, ii, 335. For a recent general account of hundred mounds, some of which seem to have been created specially for the purpose, see Gelling 1992, 52, 142–5. Cf. Bassett (forthcoming) on the

Oswaldslow hundreds of *Wulfereslaw,
Cuthburgelaw* and *Winburgetreow.*

88 S.217.

89 *The Will of Æthelgifu,* eds. D. Whitelock, N.
Ker and Lord Rennell (Roxburghe Club,
1968), 42–3; *ASC* 79; S.909.

90 Blair 1986; Biddle & Blair 1988.

91 Thacker 1988, 44–5, 49. Note the eighth-
century mount from Culham and the recent
sceatta finds at nearby Sutton Courtenay (Figs.
45, 53).

92 Hinton 1974, No. 22; Webster & Backhouse
(eds.) 1991, No. 259.

93 S.675. The bounds include the core of the
estate, which must have been resumed into
royal hands again before Wootton became a
regia villa.

94 DB 154d (I.10).

95 DB 154c (I.5).

96 Day 1989.

97 S.1148, a writ by which Edward gives to
Westminster Abbey 'the estate where I was
born, Islip by name, and a half-hide at
Marston, . . . as Ælfgyfu Emma my mother
gave it to me on the day of my birth as a
first gift'.

98 DB 154d (I.12).

99 DB 157b (XV. 3); Blair & McKay 1985, 26.

100 S.853; below, p. 116, for the grant of
Bampton minster church to Leofric.

101 DB 158d, 160d (XXIX.4, LVIII.17, 26).

102 Blair 1990, 14; for the general context see
Campbell 1987, 210–11.

103 *VCH Oxon.* i, 378–9; Everitt 1974. For the
individual manors see *VCH Oxon.* ix and x.

104 *VCH Oxon.* vii, 2–3; Thorn 1990.

105 DB 154d (I.7a).

106 Held by Earl Ælfgar TRE: DB 160b (LIV.1).

107 For the trends outlined in this paragraph see
the introduction to Blair (ed.) 1988.

108 Blair 1985, esp. 118.

109 Thacker 1982, 209; Heighway & Bryant
1986; Heighway 1987, 115–19.

110 Doggett 1986, 57–60.

111 See p. 191 note 72 above (foundation-trench
dated by 'St. Neot's Ware' pot).

112 S.217; cf. Sturdy and Munby 1985, 50.

113 S.1354: 'semper possessor terrae illius reddat
tributum aecclesiasticum quod circ-sceat
dicitur to Pirigtune, et omni anno unus ager
inde aretur to Pirigtune et iterum metatur, et
suus haeres veram amicitiam habeat cum
domino aecclesiae; sin autem, sit terra in
potestate illius aecclesiae'.

114 S.909; for this and what follows, see Blair

115 Thacker 1982, 209–11; Heighway 1987,
43–4, 115–19.

116 DB 158b, 158c (XXVIII.8, 28).

117 *VCH Oxon.* iv, 271–2, 398.

118 Blair 1988b, 225, for earlier archaeological
work.

119 See above; and cf. Hereford, where St.
Guthlac's minster was just outside the original
defended circuit but enclosed by an extension
probably added by Æthelflæd (Shoesmith
1982, 74–82). A useful recent discussion of
the Mercian 'multiple minster' phenomenon
is Pearn 1988.

120 Text printed by J.B. Davidson, 'On some
Anglo-Saxon Charters at Exeter', *Jnl. of the
British Archaeol. Assocn.* xxxix (1883),
298–301; original reproduced *Facsimiles of
Anglo-Saxon Manuscripts* (part 2, Ordnance
Survey, 1881), No. XVI.

121 E.g. S.450, S.718, S.810.

122 *Chron. Ab.* i, 50; Thacker 1988, 43–6. The
severe problems of the Abingdon Chronicle
narrative of events before the 950s will be
reconsidered by Kelly (forthcoming).

123 Thacker 1988, 43, 52–7.

124 *Chron. Ab.* ii, 277–8; Biddle, Lambrick &
Myres 1968, 44–7, 60–7; Thacker 1988, 57;
Fernie 1982, 108–10. It is possible that the
pre-Æthelwold minster was divided between
the two sites, but so far there is no
archaeological evidence for this. I am grateful
to Tim Allen and Arthur MacGregor for the
information that some small metal objects
found (ex situ) in the recent excavations on
the Abbey site are tenth century.

125 Thacker 1988, 57–8, 59–64.

126 Gem 1978, 105–9.

127 S.911; *VCH Oxon.* xii, 103–4.

128 Yorke 1988, 19–20.

129 Knowles, Brooke & London 1972, 39–40;
Blair 1985, 120.

130 The Great Tew lease (S.1425, note 83 above)
is witnessed by the abbots and communities of
Abingdon and Eynsham; the final phrase states
that a copy is to be deposited at *Eowes hame,*
which must be an error for *Eogneshame.* Cf.
Knowles, Brooke & London 1972, 48–9.

131 Blair 1988b, 226–7; DB 157a (XIV 1–2).

132 The 1069 charter (above, note 120) confirms
Leofric's gift of this church to the canons of
Exeter. Given his former career in the royal
service, it seems highly probable that he had
acquired this royal minster as a gift from
Edward.

133 *VCH Oxon.* vii, 53; Blair 1985, 122, 136 for Bicester.

134 Everitt 1974 provides a useful conceptual framework for places of this kind, which he calls 'primary towns'.

135 For a previous version of this map see Jope 1956, 245. The Domesday data, both for urban characteristics and for outliers, are conveniently gathered together in the relevant volumes of the *Domesday Geography* series.

136 DB 56b (Berks. B.1); cf. Astill 1984, 63.

137 Rodwell (ed.) 1975, 103; Cook & Rowley (eds.) 1985, 38–9; below, p. 202 note 2.

138 Hill 1981, maps 213–25.

139 DB 57d (Berks. I.34), 58c (Berks. VII.6, under Barton).

140 DB 154c (I.6).

141 Rodwell (ed.) 1975; Hoskins & Jope 1954, 107–12; Briggs, Cook & Rowley (eds.) 1986, map 13; Postles 1987.

142 Cf. Postles 1987, 14–15, and Astill 1984.

143 See the relevant sections in Rodwell (ed.) 1975. Astill 1984 provides the best account of the equivalent range of places in north Berkshire.

144 Blair (forthcoming) a; Blair 1988c, 40–50.

145 Blair 1988c, 42 Fig. 2.1, 47.

146 *VCH Oxon.* xii, 106–7 for Eynsham; *VCH Oxon.* xiii (forthcoming) for Bampton; *SMA* x (1980), 103–23 for Bloxham.

147 See Blair 1988c, 40–50, for the general context. Bond 1985, 115, lists a number of Oxfordshire examples of this topographical form of which some, but not all, are known minsters. Any settlement which has developed from a sizeable enclosed precinct will, of course, take this form; observation suggests that the majority of cases are in fact ex-minsters.

148 Bampton Research Project, work in progress. The cottage tenements are listed in a rental of 1317, Exeter Cathedral, Dean and Chapter archives MS 2931. For the connection between cottagers and towns see Dyer 1985.

149 S.673, S.590 (*P-N Berks.* iii, 707, 728).

150 See Jope 1956, 250–1.

151 Blair & Millard 1992. For what may have been a similar ford nearby see *SMA* x (1980), 171.

152 Davis 1973, 263.

153 British Library, MS Cotton Nero A.xii ff. 48v–50 (Faringdon Cartulary); Exeter Cathedral, Dean and Chapter archives MS 2931 (labour services of the tenants of Chimney).

154 *Chron. Ab.* i, 480–1; ii, 282; Davis 1973, 263; Bond 1979, 69.

155 *P-N Oxon.* ii, 487. This was a *lād* rather than a *gelād*; see Gelling 1984, 23–5, 73.

156 For what follows see Hinton 1990, 82–7, 121–2; Jope 1956, 254–6; Mellor 1980, 18–21; Vince (ed.) 1991, 54; and M. Mellor's pottery reports in Durham (forthcoming).

157 The most up-to-date discussion will be M. Mellor's in Durham (forthcoming); meanwhile see Mellor 1980, 17–22, and her contributions to Durham 1977 and Durham 1984.

158 DB 156a (VII.22).

159 Mellor 1980, 19; Vince 1985, 30–4 and Fig. 6.

160 In Durham (forthcoming) Maureen Mellor expresses the view that 'if fast wheel technology had been available to Oxfordshire potters the subsequent tradition *AC* would have used it, and it seems most likely, if L[ate] S[axon] S[helly] was made on a fast wheel, it was made some way away from Oxford'.

161 Vince (ed.) 1991, 49, 53–4.

162 *P-N Oxon.* i, 90, ii, 467.

163 Jope 1956, 253.

164 DB 157a (XIII.1); Jope 1956, 251–2. Christopher Day points out to me that the unusually large population of thirty *bordarii* probably included quarry workers.

165 Jope 1964, 106–7; Durham (forthcoming), section 5.

166 Parsons 1991, 9–11, for a summary and critique of Jope's views. Many of the examples are small 'overlap' churches which could well be post-Conquest.

167 Cf. Davis 1973, 262–5.

168 *Chron. Ab.* ii, 270, 278–9; Bond 1979, 69–70.

169 *Dom. Geog. S.-E.*, 224–7.

170 S.584; *P-N Oxon.* ii, 488, 282.

171 S.1001 (*P-N Oxon.* ii, 490).

172 *Dom. Geog. S.-E.*, 221–3, which shows that the fisheries were much more concentrated on the two main rivers than were the mills. The importance of the Upper Thames is emphasised by a general regional mapping: ibid. 605. For the forms and locations of fish-weirs, Salisbury 1991 provides an excellent survey.

173 S.911, S.1025 (*P-N Oxon.* ii, 487, i, 187).

174 Exeter Cathedral, Dean and Chapter archives, MS 2931 (fishery rents in 1317); Public Record Office, JUST 1/705 m.22 (presentments for illegal fishing in 1285).

175 Salisbury 1991, 76–7.

176 *Dom. Geog. S.-E.*, 221–7.

177 *Chron. Ab.* i, 481, ii, 282.

178 The best surveys of the Domesday and later evidence are *Dom. Geog. S.-E.*, 202–21; Hoskins & Jope 1954, 103–7; Emery 1974, ch. III.

179 Hooke 1988, 139–40; cf. Hooke 1987, 133–42. However, Scull 1993, 266–7, argues that the basic patterns of exploitation already existed in the early Anglo-Saxon period; cf. above, p. 27.

180 S.738 (*P-N Oxon.* ii, 487).

181 Hoskins & Jope 1954, 106–7; Roden 1973, 345–55, 362–3.

182 Robinson & Lambrick 1984, 813; Robinson 1992, 200–1.

183 Hooke 1985, 190–201; Hooke 1987, 133–42; Hooke 1988, 124–31, 135–6. For open fields in other parts of the West Midlands see Gelling 1992, 172–7.

184 S.853, S.1022, DB 156d (IX.7). However, the Sandford land is given a continuous boundary description in the charter, and it is not really clear in what sense it was 'common'.

185 S.361, S.902 (*P-N Oxon*, ii, 489, 487).

186 S.909 (*P-N Oxon*. ii, 485).

187 Schumer 1984, 5, 32–5.

188 Roden 1973, 325–38; cf. Emery 1974, 78, which stresses the great post-Conquest expansion of Chiltern agriculture.

189 S.104, S.1568 (*P-N Oxon.* i, 86–9); Baines 1981.

190 Bond 1981, 118–24.

191 *P-N Oxon.* ii. 456; Gelling 1984, 23.

192 *P-N Oxon.* ii, 487, 483–4.

193 S.1028 (*P-N Oxon.* ii, 489).

194 Gelling 1984, 54–6, 250.

195 S.217, S.1001 (*P-N Oxon.* ii, 484–5, 490). It would be unwise to rely implicitly on the 887 date, given that this is a cartulary copy and the bounds may be added. 'Shilton Mead' at Witney remained distinct into modern times.

196 Bailey 1989.

197 Lambrick & Robinson 1988, 73.

198 All printed *P-N Oxon*, ii, 483–90. They have all recently been walked by the West Oxfordshire Charter-Boundary Group; for earlier accounts of the Witney bounds see Gelling 1967, 99–103, Gelling 1978, 202–6, and Emery 1974, 60–3. On the present map only parts of Eynsham and Shifford are shown, and Chimney and Northmoor are not shown at all.

199 Preserved in a text of 1069 (above, note 120), but there is reason to think that they are reproduced from a lost charter of Eadwig.

200 S.217 (*P-N Oxon.* ii, 484–5). But for a caveat on the date of these bounds see note 195 above.

201 Above, note 120 for Chimney; S.1292, S.678, S.911 and S.853 for the others. Curbridge became part of Witney (below, note 204).

202 Hooke 1987, 133–42; Hooke 1988, 138–41; Blair 1991, 30–4.

203 Gelling 1978, 177–84; Gelling 1988, 69–70; *P-N Berks.* iii, 822–33; Hooke 1987, 129–32; Hooke 1988, 131–4.

204 S.771. The reason for thinking this a newly-assembled estate is that Curbridge, which had presumably been a dependency of either Minster Lovell or Bampton, had been a separate entity as recently as 956–7 (S.1292).

205 DB 155d (VII.3). It is clear on topographical grounds that this was carved out of the Eynsham complex.

206 S.911, S.1022.

207 S.1379, S.887.

208 S.1328, S.1354; Dyer 1980, 30–1.

209 For the general context see for instance Blair (ed.) 1988, 7; Blair 1991, 30–4.

210 For the general context see the various essays in Blair (ed.) 1988.

211 Blair & Steane 1982, 46–7, 57–9.

212 Ivens 1984, 109–11; Rahtz & Rowley 1984, 9, 53, 156.

213 *SMA* xxi (1991), 82–3.

214 At Hook Norton long-and-short quoins on the eastern angles of the nave have recently been discovered. This church could in origin have been a minster, though perhaps moved from another site (Blair 1986). Blair & McKay 1985 for Tackley. Martin Biddle has pointed out to me that the high-level blocked windows in the nave at Witney look as though they are double-splayed.

215 Coatsworth 1988, 173–5, 190.

216 See note 227 below.

217 S.678 (*P-N Oxon.* ii, 486).

218 Taylor & Taylor 1965–78, i, 153, ii, 599–601.

219 Blair & Steane 1982, 86–7; Milnes-Walker 1978.

220 Chambers 1979.

221 For the general context and chronology of these developments, see introduction to Blair (ed.) 1988.

222 For most of the places shown see *VCH Oxon.* xi.

223 The various subdivisions existed by 1086: Domesday Book does not identify them by name, but it is possible to trace their later manorial descents.

224 See note 83 above.

225 DB 155d (VII.4).

226 DB 156d (VIII.1–4).

227 A slightly earlier example is Leofric of Whitchurch (*æt Hwitecyrcan*), who held that ten-hide manor in 990–2 but later forfeited it, and his life, for various crimes: S.1454, S.927. For 'of' names used by important Englishmen surviving the Conquest, see p. 176 below.

228 For the general context see Fleming 1991, ch. III.

229 DB 155d (VII.3–4); Fleming 1991, 73, 95.

230 DB 221a (EN 4); Hooper 1988, 19. This calculation assumes that the 'Wulfweard' who appears with four Oxfordshire manors in the Northamptonshire folios is Wulfweard White.

231 DB 154d (I.7b), 148b (Bucks. XV.2M).

232 Stafford 1985, 61–2.

233 The scheme which follows is essentially that proposed by Faith (forthcoming), and I am deeply grateful to the author for allowing me to see it in advance of publication.

234 S.217; cf. Dyer 1980, 33.

235 Moore 1989, 195, map 1.

236 Hamshere 1987, 172–7; cf. Moore 1989, 205–7.

237 Moore 1989.

238 Barbara Harvey's phrase, adopted by Faith (forthcoming).

239 For categories of people in the Oxfordshire Domesday see *Dom. Geog. S.-E.*, 204–8.

240 DB 154c (I.6).

241 Faith (forthcoming).

242 *P-N Oxon.* ii, 436–7, 473. Cf. *P-N Berks.* iii, 924–5, and Blair 1991, 75.

243 DB 155c, 156d, 159d (VII.1, IX.4, XXXV.34).

244 Cf. the remarks on Surrey holdings in this size-range in Blair 1991, 28–9.

245 Again this is the model of Faith (forthcoming). For 'free peasants' see also Stafford 1985, 158–61 – though they were by no means peculiar to the Danelaw.

246 Related in the charter of 995 (S.883, D. Whitelock's translation) by which Æthelred II re-granted the forfeited land.

247 For a similar argument in relation to Surrey see Blair 1991, 161.

248 For a fuller discussion of this phenomenon in a different context see Blair 1991, 32–4.

249 S.902.

250 The leading writer on village formation is Christopher Taylor, whose views are conveniently summarised in Taylor 1983, chs. VII–X. For the relationship between settlement and lordship see (for a broad view) Chapelot & Fossier 1985.

251 *SMA* xviii (1988), 50–1, xix (1989), 34–5.

252 Cf. Bond 1985, 105, 109, 115–19.

253 As does Emery 1974, 69–82.

254 Good examples of such sites, and their limitations, are at Yarnton (E.M. Jope in *Oxo.* x (1945), 97–9) and 'Grimsbury', Banbury (T.G. Allen in *Oxo.* liv (1989), 25–44). The latest phase of the recently-excavated site at Worton Rectory Farm, Yarnton, may prove to be the best example so far of a late Anglo-Saxon rural settlement in Oxfordshire.

255 See *P-N Oxon.* for innumerable cases of this.

256 Taylor 1983, ch. VIII; Bond 1985, 115; surveys of Great Tew and Lewknor by C.J. Bond and J. Steane in *SMA* ix (1979), 98–101 and x (1980) 124–33.

257 *P-N Oxon.* i, xiv–xv.

258 S.678 (*P-N Oxon.* ii, 486).

259 S.883 (*P-N Oxon.* ii, 483).

260 Thus the remarks on floodplain grassland by Lambrick and Robinson (above, p. 130) are probably just as relevant to other kinds of resource.

CHAPTER FOUR

1 This chapter would have been impossible without their work, especially that of H.E. Salter, E.M. Jope, David Sturdy, Janet Cooper, Tom Hassall and Brian Durham; my debt to them is enormous.

2 See Biddle & Hill 1971, Biddle 1976a and Biddle 1976b for general context.

3 Hassall et al. 1989, 93.

4 Blair 1987, 89. Certain and likely 'altar-land' tenements are H.E. Salter, *Survey of Oxford*, i (O.H.S. n.s. xiv, 1960), Nos. SE 90–1, 235, 240–3, 245–7.

5 *VCH Oxon.* iv, 6–7.

6 Durham (forthcoming), section 5.

7 Salter 1936, 8–9.

8 The following is based on Durham (forthcoming), section 5, and Durham, Halpin & Palmer 1983, 14–18.

9 *VCH Oxon.* iv, 300–1; Hassall 1986, 118–20; reassessment of 1899 excavation by J.T. Munby in Durham (forthcoming).

10 Durham, Halpin & Palmer 1983, 19–23; Hassall et al. 1989, esp. 130–9.

11 *SMA* iv (1974), 23. The line shown on Fig. 86 is a compromise between the one suggested in Blair 1988b, Fig. 90, and the one which will be proposed in Durham

12　Blair 1988b, 236–7.

13　Hassall 1986, 120–1; Durham (forthcoming). For individual observations see Hassall et al. 1989, 121–8 (Church St. and Castle St.); *SMA* x (1980), 157–8 and xi (1981), 131–3 (New Inn Hall St.); PRN 6126 (St. Aldate's); *SMA* xii (1982), 158–61 (High St., Queen St. and Turl St.). The penny was found in New Inn Hall Street.

14　Jope 1958, 5–7; Sturdy & Munby 1985, 53.

15　Durham (forthcoming).

16　*VCH Oxon.* iv, 305. Cf. Biddle (ed.) 1976, 285: 'The streets of Winchester were its market-place'.

17　For the south intramural road see Blair 1988b, 236.

18　Good examples of this are Jope 1958, 7; Hassall et al. 1989, 93–7, 129. I differ here from Durham (forthcoming), who believes that the intramural area would have been divided into house-plots from the beginning. A general model of low-density occupation in the burghal towns until the late tenth century is proposed by Astill 1991, 103–9.

19　Biddle (ed.) 1976, 340–2, 453, 382–5.

20　Sturdy 1965, Appendix 6; *VCH Oxon.* iv, 8–9.

21　*Cart. Eynsham*, i. p. viii; DB 154a (B 8); Sturdy 1965, Appendix 6, pp. 51, 55.

22　S.964; *Chron. Abingdon*, i, 439–42; *VCH Oxon.* iv, 384; Sturdy & Munby 1985, 61. The suggested identification of Æthelwine is from Lawson 1993, 151–2.

23　Blair 1978, 54–64.

24　Blair 1978, 62; Clinton states that a grant of property *in magno vico Oxenefordie* (probably Cornmarket) by one of his tenants was ratified 'in my court in Oxford before my bailiff William de Rampenna and before the men of Oxford'.

25　See Hinton 1990, 82–94, and Astill 1991, 103–14, for the general context.

26　For lists of moneyers' names see North 1980.

27　Blunt 1974, 45, 66–9, for what follows.

28　Cf. Biddle (ed.) 1976, 454–63.

29　*VCH Oxon.* iv, 35–6.

30　Jope 1956, 244; Jope 1958, 72–3.

31　Jope 1952/3, 108–10; PRNs 6019, 6023–4, 3533; Hassall 1971, 30–3.

32　Cf. Reynolds 1987, 298, 307.

33　In DB 154d (I.12) the borough farm and proceeds of the mint are lumped in with shire revenues; cf. Reynolds 1987, 301 n. 10.

34　DB 154a (B 1); 154d (I.12).

35　*VCH Oxon.* iv, 6–7.

36　DB 154a (B 2).

37　It seems to me that Turner 1990 goes too far in this direction, though she proves conclusively that the system changed radically between 900 and 1066. See also *VCH Oxon.* iv, 302.

38　*P-N Oxon.* ii, 485, 486, 489; i, 2–3, 22; Cooper 1985, 16, 21; *P-N Berks.* iii, 786; DB 154b (B 11). For the usage see Reynolds 1987, 297.

39　*VCH Oxon.* iv, 336, 384.

40　See above, p. 195 note 83. Simon Keynes points out to me that a charter of 1050 (S.1022) is witnessed by Godwine *praepositus civitatis*, presumably the same man.

41　*VCH Oxon.* iv, 48 suggests that 'the lease was perhaps made before the borough court', but the general context of the document makes this unlikely.

42　M.M. Archibald in Vince (ed.) 1991, 334.

43　I am very grateful to Marion M. Archibald for her detailed advice on this point.

44　Cf. Biddle (ed.) 1976, 423–5, for the interlocking spheres of the portreeve of Winchester and the sheriff of Hampshire.

45　Cf. Biddle (ed.) 1976, 400–22; Campbell 1987, 209–10.

46　DB 154b (B 10); 56b (Berks. B 1).

47　DB 154a–b (B).

48　Reynolds 1987, 303–6, for the usefulness of the urban entries in Domesday Book. Earlier analyses of the Oxford entry are: Parker 1885, 221–304; Salter 1936, 20–39; Jope 1956; *VCH Oxon.* iv, passim.

49　DB 158b (XXVIII.8); these figures do not correspond with the stated totals of Robert's mural mansions.

50　Houses of Earl William, the bishops of Bayeux and Coutances, the count of Evreux, Ernulf of Hesdin, Berengar of Tosney, Miles Crispin, Richard of Courcy, Robert d'Oilly, Roger d'Ivry and Walter Giffard.

51　DB 57d (Berks. I.39); the jurors suspect that Robert d'Oilly now has them. I have assumed that these do not equate with Robert's twelve houses in the Oxford entry.

52　The king's house TRW; Risborough was the king's TRW and Harold's TRE, and the entry notes that 'in hoc manerio iacet et iacuit quidem burgensis de Oxeneford' (DB 143c

53 The king's houses TRW; Twyford was the king's TRW, Godgifu's TRE: DB 151c (Bucks. XXXVII.1).

54 Bishop of Lincoln's houses TRW.

55 Earl Hugh of Chester's houses TRW. For the identification and earlier history of this property see *Cartulary of Oseney Abbey*, ed. H.E.Salter, i (O.H.S. lxxxix, 1929), 13–14, and Sturdy and Munby 1985, 50.

56 The Bishop of Hereford's houses TRW, when 'Bishop Robert' (i.e. of Hereford) also held Bampton church manor of the Bishop of Exeter (DB 155a (V.1)). The claim in 1203 that the church of St.Peter-le-Bailey pertained to the *capellaria* of Bampton (*Curia Regis Rolls*, ii, 143) may provide a clue to the location of these houses.

57 *Chron. Ab.* ii, 133; i, 439–42 (S.964).

58 Above, p. 151.

59 The entry for Roger d'Ivry's Whitehill manor (DB 158d (XXIX.15)) includes a *burgensis*; presumably his house was one of Roger's fifteen *mansiones* in Oxford. Whitehill had belonged to St. Frideswide's minster in 1004.

60 The abbot of Bury's house TRW. Since the 'abbot of Bury' was Baldwin, former monk of Saint-Denis and physician of Edward the Confessor, it is clear that this house belonged to the manor of Taynton which Edward gave to Saint-Denis in 1059 (S.1028).

61 Manasseh's son's house TRW. Ælfwig still had Bletchingdon after the Conquest, and it is unclear whether he held it TRE.

62 Henry de Ferrers's houses TRW. Bondig was his main *antecessor* in Oxon. and elsewhere.

63 Earl Aubrey's houses TRW; the church of St. Mary the Virgin later belonged to Iffley (*VCH Oxon.* iv, 390), held by Earl Aubrey TRW and Azur TRE.

64 In the Berks. folios (DB 62a (Berks. XXXVIII.6)).

65 The Count of Mortain's houses TRW.

66 William Peverel's houses TRW.

67 Jernio's house TRW.

68 Earl Aubrey's house TRW.

69 Edward the Sheriff (i.e. of Salisbury)'s houses TRW.

70 Ranulf Flambard's house TRW.

71 Guy de Raimbeaucourt's houses TRW.

72 The so-called 'contributory burgesses': cf. Reynolds 1977, 94.

73 Turner 1990.

74 *ASC* 68.

75 *Henrici Archidiaconi Huntendunensis Historia Anglorum*, ed. T. Arnold (Rolls Ser. 74, 1879), 185–6.

76 *ASC* 105; S.1467.

77 *ASC* 94.

78 Below, pp. 174–5. Although it can never be proved, much of Robert d'Oilly's urban estate could have come from Wigod.

79 Cf. Reynolds 1987, 305–6.

80 Hill 1978, 214–17; Hill 1981, maps 222–3; Metcalf 1978, 159–60, 183–7; but note Metcalf's caveats about estimating town size from mint output.

81 Biddle (ed.) 1976, 468 (where Oxford is slightly under-counted).

82 Nightingale 1987.

83 *ASC*, 94, 97, 102–3, 138; Lawson 1993, 53, 61, 128.

84 *VCH Oxon.* iv, 9–10.

85 Keene 1976 for the general context.

86 Cf. Hinton 1990, 95.

87 DB 158c (XXVIII.28); cf. Dyer 1985, 95–6, on the manor of Walton and on gardens.

88 *VCH Oxon.* iv, 327–31.

89 *VCH Oxon.* iv, 310: although there are no pre-Conquest references to St. Frideswide's fair, it was old-established by the 1120s.

90 Durham 1977, 183–5 (structural phases 3 to 5); Durham (forthcoming), Trill Mill Stream section (Tr. TMS VII).

91 Jope 1952/3, 106–10; Jope 1956, 237–8; Rodwell (ed.) 1975, Oxford map 2.

92 Turner 1990; cf. Hassall 1986, 122, for the possibility that the extension was part of the rebuilding after the 1009 fire. A fuller discussion of the eastern extension by J.T. Munby will appear in Durham (forthcoming). In 1993 a section against the city wall behind New College Chapel revealed a well-constructed turf bank, presumably the eleventh-century one (Oxford Archaeological Unit).

93 *P-N Oxon.* ii, 485 (*of cere willa bricga*), i, 20.

94 *VCH Oxon.* iv, 265; PRN 6459.

95 Jope 1952/3; Hassall 1976, 248–54.

96 Sturdy 1965, i, 51f.

97 Bond 1979, 71–2.

98 The comments of Jope 1956, 238, scarcely need modification nearly forty years later.

99 Jope 1958; Sturdy & Munby 1985; Hassall 1971.

100 For details and references see Jope 1958, 9–10; J. Munby in Sturdy & Munby 1985, 92–4.

101 Sturdy & Munby 1985, 65–7, 80–2; Hassall 1976, 251–4.

102 Sturdy & Munby 1985, 67, 71–2 and Figs. 9–11. A fine example underlying All Saints church (Fig. 94) will be discussed in Durham (forthcoming).

103 For earlier discussions see Parker 1885, 283–97; Jope 1956, 239; Morris 1989, 201–4; Blair 1988b, 224–5, 233–5.

104 *Chron. Ab.* ii, 174–5; Blair 1988b, 233.

105 Above, note 56. The dedication of this church to St. Peter may result from the Exeter Cathedral connection.

106 One other possible case is St. George's in the Castle (Cooper 1976), but this remains unproven.

107 Durham (forthcoming).

108 Durham (forthcoming) for what follows.

109 Halpin & Palmer 1983, 16–18; Durham (forthcoming).

110 J. Blair in Durham (forthcoming) for a detailed discussion of the dating.

111 Blair 1985, 124, 132–5; Cooper 1976.

112 For the general context see Graham-Campbell 1980, 88–111. Reynolds 1977, 37–42, suggests qualifications.

113 The most up-to-date analysis will be M. Mellor's section in Durham (forthcoming); see also her contributions to Durham 1977 and Durham 1984.

114 S.909 (D. Whitelock's translation); *ASC* 86.

115 *ASC* 90. Evidence has been found for major burning in the early eleventh century at the junction of High Street with Turl Street (*SMA* xi (1981), 155–6; Durham (forthcoming)).

116 *ASC* 92.

117 Graham-Campbell 1988.

118 Lyon 1966.

119 Durham (forthcoming).

120 M. Mellor in Durham (forthcoming).

121 *VCH Oxon.* v, 264.

122 Crawford 1992 for this and what follows.

123 *Florentii Wigorniensis Monachi Chronicon ex Chronicis*, ed. B. Thorpe, i (1848), 194: the Danish soldiers buried King Harold I 'in the cemetery which they had in London'. Cf. Nightingale 1987, 567–8.

124 Seaby 1950. I am deeply grateful to Barbara Crawford for pointing out the implications of this find, which she and I will be discussing more fully in *Oxoniensia*, and to Arthur MacGregor and Blanche Ellis for their advice on the objects.

125 Hinton 1974, 48–51.

126 Brøndsted 1936, 219, 220, 222.

EPILOGUE

1 The one supposed piece of evidence that William visited Oxford is the writ calendared as *Regesta Regum Anglo-Normannorum, i* No. 9, where a marginal note states that it was issued at Oxford. Since the town is nowhere mentioned in the text this is mysterious, and must probably be dismissed as an editorial slip. I am grateful to David Bates for confirming this.

2 T.A.M. Bishop and P. Chaplais, *Facsimiles of English Royal Writs to AD 1100* (1957), No. 14.

3 *VCH Berks.* ii, 52; Hooper 1988.

4 *Chron. Ab.* i, 485; this translation is by Mrs M. Lockwood.

5 *Chron. Ab.* i, 484.

6 *Chron. Ab.* ii, 9.

7 *Chron. Ab.* ii, 13–15 (again Mrs Lockwood's translation).

8 For the tenurial composition of Norman Oxfordshire see the classic discussion in Lennard 1959, ch. III.

9 Ivens 1984.

10 Fleming 1991, 145–214.

11 DB 159c (XXXV.13, 24–5); cf. Fleming 1991, 202–4.

12 For the latest comments see Hooper 1988, 15, 18–19; Keats-Rohan 1989b. In a writ of 1065/6 (S.1148), Edward orders his kinsman 'Wigod on Wallingeforde' to effect the land transfer. Any estimate of Wigod's Oxfordshire holdings must depend on conjectures about what proportion of the TRW manors of Robert d'Oilly had been his; the land explicitly ascribed to him in Domesday Book totalled 41 hides at Goring, Chesterton, Cuxham and Gatehampton. Lawson 1993, 180, suggests that Wigod may have been a Dane who rose under Cnut and his sons.

13 This is the interpretation of Keats-Rohan 1989b. For earlier and sometimes different views, see *VCH Oxon.* i, 383; *VCH Bucks.* i, 214; *VCH Wilts.* ii, 102.

14 *ASC* 159.

15 DB 160a (XLIII); cf. Williams 1989, 289–90, for the holdings of Wigod's family.

16 *Regesta Regum Anglo-Normannorum*, i, No. 18. (The impossible form 'Swawold' is an error for 'Sawold'. I am grateful to David Bates for confirming this.)

17 DB 154b (B 10), 155c (VI.10, 16), 160d (LVIII.31–4). The assumption that there is only one Saewold could be wrong, but the

name is not a particularly common one, and it seems a reasonable inference that this substantial property-owner was the same man as the sheriff.

18 DB 160c (XLV. 3), 160d (LVIII.19).

19 DB 58a (Berks. I.40). Another possibility is the five-hide estate at Longney (Glos.) which was held by 'Elsi' both TRE and TRW (DB 170c (Glos. LXXVIII.12)), but this lies so far away from his other property that the identification seems relatively unlikely.

20 DB 154d (I.9), 160d (LVIII.28–9).

21 DB 63c (Berks. LXV.7), 57d (Berks. I.34).

22 DB 164b (Berks. I.2).

23 DB 165d (Glos. XI.14), 170c (Glos. LXXVIII.1), 63c (Berks. LXV.8).

24 DB 56b (Berks. B1), 161b (LIX.21).

25 *VCH Oxon.* i, 388.

26 DB 160c–161a (LVIII). It is unclear how many people the entries for Leofwine and Ælfwig refer to.

27 *VCH Oxon.* i, 387; Lennard 1959, 64. Cf. Campbell 1987, 210–12.

28 Campbell 1987, 210; Williams 1989, 290.

29 DB 154a–b (B); *VCH Oxon,* iv, 10, 23–4.

30 Jope 1952/3; Hassall 1976, 248–54.

31 *Chron. Ab.* ii, 15, 25, 284; Durham 1984, 82–95.

32 Sturdy 1965, 51f; Hassall 1986, 124.

33 Davis 1973, 266–7.

34 North 1980.

35 *Regesta Regum Anglo-Normannorum,* iii, No. 640.

36 Blair 1978, 60–4; Keats-Rohan 1989a. *Contra* Blair 1990, 18, I no longer find convincing Keats-Rohan's proposed descent from the family of Leofwine of Nuneham; cf. Williams 1989.

37 Blair 1978, 62–3.

38 Schumer 1984.

39 *VCH Oxon.* i, 384; Lennard 1959, 69, 210–12; S. Harvey in *Agrarian History of England and Wales,* ii (1988), 118–19.

40 A process which is exceptionally well-documented on the Abingdon estates: *Chron. Ab.* ii, 3–7.

41 *VCH Oxon.* ii, 65; *Cart. Eynsham,* i, 28–37; *SMA* xxii (1992), 46–7.

42 Blair 1988b, 227–8 for Oxford; *SMA* xviii (1988), 89–93 for Bampton; *SMA* xv (1985), 113–15 for Witney.

43 Blair (ed.) 1988, 9–10, 21–30.

44 Taylor & Taylor 1965–78, i, 367–72, 464–5, ii, 640–2; for Waterperry see also *Oxo.* xxxvii (1972), 245. Features suggesting Norman influence are the cushion capitals and bases of the belfry shafts at North Leigh, and the rectangular squared stones and the apse at Waterperry.

45 R. Gem in Blair & McKay 1985, 41–2.

46 Blair & Steane 1982, 43–7.

47 *VCH Oxon.* vii, 53; Blair 1988b, 227–8; *VCH Oxon.* ii, 93–4.

48 For a development of this argument see Blair 1985, 138.

49 For the general context see especially Campbell 1986, 209–10, 216–19, 224–6.

50 Blair 1987; Blair 1988b.

51 There is no evidence that the king entered the walls on any of the occasions listed in *VCH Oxon.* iv, 10, 304–5, if it can be assumed that the various of Henry I's *acta* issued at Oxford were in fact issued at Beaumont Palace; there seems no reason to assume that the foundation of Beaumont can be dated by the reference to a 'new hall' in 1133. The narrative of the translation of St. Frideswide in 1180 (Blair 1987, 118) carefully notes that Henry II was 'in palatio suo extra Oxoniam' and not present at the ceremony. The chronicler Wykes states that in 1263 Henry III 'intravit ecclesiam Sancte Fredeswythe cum magna devotione, quod nullus rex attemptavit a tempore regis Algari', and that in 1275 Edward I refused to enter the city for fear of the curse (*Annales Monastici,* ed. H.R. Luard, iv (Rolls Ser. 36d, 1869), 142–3, 264).

52 Blair 1987, 108–9 (Life B, sec. 13).

53 Ibid. 112–14 (Life B, sec. 18).

54 Mayr-Harting 1985; Blair 1987, 116–19.

55 Heslop 1988.

BIBLIOGRAPHY AND ABBREVIATIONS

Alcock 1973.　　　　　　L. Alcock, review of Brodribb et al. 1972, *Med. Arch.* xvii, 189–90.

Allen & Dalwood 1983.　D. Allen and C.H. Dalwood, 'Iron Age Occupation . . . Aylesbury, 1981', *Records of Bucks.* xxv, 1–60.

ASC.　　　　　　　　　*The Anglo-Saxon Chronicle*, trans. D.Whitelock (1961).

Astill 1984.　　　　　　G. Astill, 'The Towns of Berkshire', in J. Haslam (ed.), *Anglo-Saxon Towns in Southern England*, 53–86.

Astill 1991.　　　　　　G.G. Astill, 'Towns and Town Hierarchies in Saxon England', *Oxford Journal of Archaeology*, x, 95–117.

Bailey 1989.　　　　　　K. Bailey, 'The Madley Brook: Some Reflections on an Oxfordshire Stream Name', *Oxo.* liv, 403–5.

Baines 1981.　　　　　　A.H.J. Baines, 'Turville, Radenore and the Chiltern *Feld*', *Records of Bucks.* xxiii, 4–22.

Bassett 1985a.　　　　　S.R. Bassett, 'A Probable Mercian Royal Mausoleum at Winchcombe, Gloucestershire', *Antiq. Jnl.* lxv, 82–100.

Bassett 1985b.　　　　　S. Bassett, 'Beyond the Edge of Excavation: the Topographical Context of Goltho', in H. Mayr-Harting and R.I. Moore (eds.), *Studies in Medieval History Presented to R.H.C. Davis*, 21–39.

Bassett 1989.　　　　　　S. Bassett, 'In Search of the Origins of Anglo-Saxon Kingdoms', in S. Bassett (ed.), *The Origins of Anglo-Saxon Kingdoms*, 3–27.

Bassett 1992.　　　　　　S. Bassett, 'Church and Diocese in the West Midlands: the Transition from British to Anglo-Saxon Control', in J. Blair and R. Sharpe (eds.), *Pastoral Care before the Parish*, 13–40.

Bassett (forthcoming).　S. Bassett, 'The Administrative Landscape of the Diocese of Worcester in the Tenth Century', in N. Brooks (ed.), *St. Oswald of Worcester: Life and Influence* (forthcoming).

Bede, *HE.*　　　　　　　Bede, *Historia Ecclesiastica Gentis Anglorum,* ed. C. Plummer (1896).

Benson & Miles 1974a.　D. Benson and D. Miles, *The Upper Thames Valley: an Archaeological Survey of the River Gravels.*

Benson & Miles 1974b.　D. Benson and D. Miles, 'Cropmarks near the Sutton

Courtenay Saxon Site', *Antiquity*, xlviii (1974), 223–6.

Berisford 1973. — F. Berisford, *The Early Anglo-Saxon Settlement Sites in the Upper Thames Basin, with Special Reference to the Area around Cassington and Eynsham* (unpublished Oxford B.Litt. thesis).

Biddle 1976a. — M. Biddle, 'Towns', in D.M. Wilson (ed.), *The Archaeology of Anglo-Saxon England*, 99–150.

Biddle 1976b. — M. Biddle, 'The Evolution of Towns: Planned Towns before 1066', in M.W. Barley (ed.), *The Plans and Topography of Medieval Towns in England and Wales* (C.B.A. Research Rep. 14), 19–32.

Biddle (ed.), 1976. — M. Biddle (ed.), *Winchester in the Early Middle Ages: an Edition and Discussion of the Winton Domesday* (Winchester Studies I).

Biddle & Blair 1988. — M. Biddle and J. Blair, 'The Hook Norton Hoard of 1848: a Viking Burial from Oxfordshire?', *Oxo.* lii (1987), 186–95.

Biddle & Hill 1971. — M. Biddle and D. Hill, 'Late Saxon Planned Towns', *Antiq. Jnl.* li, 70–85.

Biddle & Kjølbye-Biddle 1988. — M. Biddle and B. Kjølbye-Biddle, 'An Early Medieval Floor-Tile from St. Frideswide's Minster', *Oxo.* liii, 259–63.

Biddle, Lambrick & Myres 1968 — M. Biddle, G. Lambrick and J.N.L. Myres, 'The Early History of Abingdon, Berkshire, and its Abbey', *Med. Arch.* xii, 26–69.

BL — British Library

Blair 1978. — J. Blair, 'Frewin Hall, Oxford: a Norman Mansion and a Monastic College', *Oxo.* xliii, 48–99.

Blair 1984. — J. Blair, 'Saint Beornwald of Bampton', *Oxo.* xlix, 47–55.

Blair 1985. — J. Blair, 'Secular Minster Churches in Domesday Book', in P.H. Sawyer (ed.), *Domesday Book: a Reassessment*, 104–42.

Blair 1986. — J. Blair, 'Hook Norton, *Regia Villa*', *Oxo.* li, 63–7.

Blair 1987. — J. Blair, 'Saint Frideswide Reconsidered', *Oxo.* lii, 71–127.

Blair 1988a. — J. Blair, *Saint Frideswide, Patron of Oxford*.

Blair 1988b. — J. Blair, 'St. Frideswide's Monastery: Problems and Possibilities', *Oxo.* liii, 221–58.

Blair 1988c. — J. Blair, 'Minster Churches in the Landscape', in D. Hooke (ed.), *Anglo-Saxon Settlements*, 35–58.

Blair 1988d. — J. Blair, 'Thornbury, Binsey: a Probable Defensive Enclosure Associated with St. Frideswide', *Oxo.* liii, 3–20.

Blair (ed.) 1988. — J. Blair (ed.), *Minsters and Parish Churches: the Local Church in Transition, 950–1200*.

Blair 1989. — J. Blair, 'Frithuwold's Kingdom and the Origins of Surrey', in S. Bassett (ed.), *The Origins of Anglo-Saxon Kingdoms*, 97–107.

Blair 1990. — J. Blair, 'An Introduction to the Oxfordshire Domesday', in R.W.H. Erskine and A. Williams (eds.), *The Oxfordshire Domesday*, 1–19.

Blair 1991. J. Blair, *Early Medieval Surrey: Landholding, Church and Settlement before 1300.*

Blair 1992a. J. Blair, 'Anglo-Saxon Minsters: a Topographical Review', in J. Blair and R. Sharpe (eds.), *Pastoral Care before the Parish*, 226-66.

Blair 1992b. J. Blair, 'The Origins of the Minster Church at Shipton-under-Wychwood: Human Burials from Prebendal House', *Wychwoods History*, vii, 4–9.

Blair (forthcoming) a. J. Blair, 'The Minsters of the Thames', in J. Blair and B. Golding (eds.), *The Cloister and the World: Essays in Honour of Barbara Harvey.*

Blair (forthcoming) b. J. Blair, 'A Saint for Every Minster? Local Cults in Anglo-Saxon England', in R. Sharpe and A. Thacker (eds.), *Local Saints and Local Churches.*

Blair & McKay 1985. J. Blair and B. McKay, 'Investigations at Tackley Church, Oxfordshire', *Oxo.* l, 25–45.

Blair & Millard 1992. J. Blair and A. Millard, 'An Anglo-Saxon Landmark Rediscovered: the *Stan ford/Stan bricge* of the Ducklington and Witney Charters', *Oxo.* lvii (1992), 342–8.

Blair & Steane 1982. J. Blair and J.M. Steane, 'Investigations at Cogges, Oxfordshire, 1978-81: the Priory and Parish Church', *Oxo.* xlvii, 37–125.

Blunt 1974. C.E. Blunt, *The Coinage of Æthelstan, 924–939: a Survey: British Numismatic Jnl.* xlii.

Boddington 1990. A. Boddington, 'Models of Burial, Settlement and Worship: the Final Phase Reviewed', in E. Southworth (ed.), *Anglo-Saxon Cemeteries: a Reappraisal*, 177–99.

Bond 1979. C.J. Bond, 'The Reconstruction of the Medieval Landscape: the Estates of Abingdon Abbey', *Landscape History*, i (1979), 59–75.

Bond 1981. C.J. Bond, 'Otmoor', in *The Evolution of Marshland Landscapes* [no editor: Oxford University Dept. for External Studies], 113–35.

Bond 1985. C.J. Bond, 'Medieval Oxfordshire Villages and their Topography: a Preliminary Discussion', in D. Hooke (ed.), *Medieval Villages* (O.U.C.A. Monograph 5), 101–23.

Boyle & Mudd (forthcoming). A. Boyle and A. Mudd, *An Anglo-Saxon Cemetery at Didcot Power Station, Oxon.*

Boyle et al (forthcoming). A. Boyle, D. Clarke, D. Miles and S. Palmer, *An Anglo-Saxon Cemetery at Lechlade, Glos.*

Bradley 1986. R. Bradley, 'The Bronze Age in the Oxford Area', in Briggs, Cook and Rowley (eds.) 1986, 38–48.

Bradley 1987. R. Bradley, 'Time Regained: the Creation of Continuity', *J.B.A.A.* cxl (1987), 1–17.

Briggs, Cook & Rowley (eds.) 1986. G. Briggs, J. Cook and T. Rowley (eds.), *The Archaeology of the Oxford Region.*

Brodribb et al. 1968. A.C.C. Brodribb, A.R. Hands and D.R. Walker, *Excavations at Shakenoak Farm, near Wilcote, Oxfordshire: Part I: sites A and D.*

Brodribb et al. 1972. Ibid. *Part III: Site F.*

Brodribb et al. 1973. Ibid. *Part IV: Site C.*

Brodribb et al. 1978. Ibid. *Part V: Sites K and E.*

Brøndsted 1936. J. Brøndsted, 'Danish Inhumation Graves of the Viking Age: a Survey', *Acta Archaeologica*, vii, 81–228.

Brooks 1984. N. Brooks, *The Early History of the Church of Canterbury.*

Brooks 1989. N. Brooks, 'The Formation of the Mercian Kingdom', in S. Bassett (ed.), *The Origins of Anglo-Saxon Kingdoms*, 159–70.

Brown 1972. P.D.C. Brown, review of Brodribb et al. 1972, *Britannia*, iii, 376–7.

Butterworth & Lobb 1992. C.A. Butterworth and S.J. Lobb, *Excavations in the Burghfield Area, Berkshire* (Wessex Archaeology Rep. No. 1).

Cam & Crawford 1935. H. Cam and O.G.S. Crawford, 'The *Hoga* of Cutteslowe', *Antiquity*, ix (1935), 96–8.

Campbell (ed.) 1982. J. Campbell (ed.), *The Anglo-Saxons.*

Campbell 1986. J. Campbell, *Essays in Anglo-Saxon History.*

Campbell 1987. J. Campbell, 'Some Agents and Agencies of the Late Anglo-Saxon State', in J.C. Holt (ed.), *Domesday Studies* (1987), 201–18.

Cart. Eynsham, i. *Eynsham Cartulary*, ed. H.E. Salter, i (O.H.S. xlix, 1906–7).

Chambers 1973. R.A. Chambers, 'A Cemetery Site at Beacon Hill, near Lewknor', *Oxo.* xxxviii, 138–45.

Chambers 1976. R.A. Chambers, 'The Cemetery Site at Beacon Hill, near Lewknor', *Oxo.* xli, 77–85.

Chambers 1979. R.A. Chambers, 'Excavations in Westcote Barton Parish Church, Oxon., 1977', *Oxo.* xliv, 99–101.

Chambers 1987. R.A. Chambers et al., 'The Late- and Sub-Roman Cemetery at Queenford Farm, Dorchester-on-Thames, Oxon.', *Oxo.* lii (1987), 35–69.

Chambers & McAdam (forthcoming). R.A. Chambers and E. McAdam, *Excavations at Barrow Hills, Oxfordshire, 1983–5: II.*

Chapelot & Fossier 1985. J. Chapelot and R. Fossier, *The Village and House in the Middle Ages* (trans. H. Cleere).

Charles-Edwards 1972. T.M. Charles-Edwards, 'Kinship, Status and the Origins of the Hide', *Past and Present*, lvi, 3–33.

Charles-Edwards 1989. T. Charles-Edwards, 'Early Medieval Kingships in the British Isles', in S. Bassett (ed.), *The Origins of Anglo-Saxon Kingdoms*, 28–39.

Chron. Ab. *Chronicon Monasterii de Abingdon*, ed. J. Stevenson, i–ii (Rolls Ser. 1–2, 1858).

Clayton 1973. N.B. Clayton, 'New Wintles, Eynsham, Oxon.', *Oxo.* xxxviii (1973), 382–4.

Coates 1989-90. R. Coates, 'On Some Controversy Surrounding *Gewissae/Gewissei, Cerdic* and *Ceawlin*', *Nomina*, xiii, 1–11.

Coatsworth 1988.   E. Coatsworth, 'Late Pre-Conquest Sculptures with the Crucifixion South of the Humber', in B. Yorke (ed.), *Bishop Æthelwold: his Career and Influence*, 161–93.

Cole 1982.   A. Cole, 'Topography, Hydrology and Place-Names in the Chalklands of Southern England', *Nomina*, vi, 73–87.

Cook & Rowley (eds.) 1985.   J. Cook and T. Rowley (eds.), *Dorchester through the Ages*.

Cooper 1976.   J. Cooper, 'The Church of St. George in the Castle', *Oxo.* xli, 306–8.

Cooper 1985.   J. Cooper, 'Four Oxfordshire Anglo-Saxon Charter-Boundaries', *Oxo.* l, 15–23.

Copeland 1988.   T. Copeland, 'The North Oxfordshire Grim's Ditch': a Fieldwork Survey', *Oxo.* liii, 277–92.

Crawford 1989.   S. Crawford, 'The Anglo-Saxon Cemetery at Chimney, Oxfordshire', *Oxo.* liv, 45–56.

Crawford 1992.   B. Crawford, 'The Cult of St. Clement of the Danes in England and Scotland', in *Medieval England 1992: Pre-Printed Papers Vol. 6: Religion and Belief* (Society for Medieval Archaeology etc., York), 1–3.

Davidson 1989.   H.E. Davidson, 'The Training of Warriors', in S.C. Hawkes (ed.), *Weapons and Warfare in Anglo-Saxon England* (O.U.C.A. Monograph 21), 11–23.

Davis 1973.   R.H.C. Davis, 'The Ford, the River and the City', *Oxo.* xxxviii (1973), 258–67.

Day 1989.   P. Day, 'Reconstructing the Environment of Shotover Forest, Oxfordshire', *Medieval Research Group Annual Report*, iv, 6.

Dickinson 1973.   T.M. Dickinson, 'Excavations at Standlake Down in 1954: the Anglo-Saxon Graves', *Oxo.* xxxviii, 239–57.

Dickinson 1974.   T.M. Dickinson, *Cuddesdon and Dorchester-on-Thames* (B.A.R. 1).

Dickinson 1976.   T.M. Dickinson, *The Anglo-Saxon Burial Sites of the Upper Thames Region, and their Bearing on the History of Wessex, circa AD 400-700* (unpublished Oxford D. Phil. thesis).

Dickinson & Speake 1992.   T.M. Dickinson and G. Speake, 'The Seventh-Century Cremation Burial at Asthall Barrow, Oxfordshire: a Reassessment', in M. Carver (ed.), *The Age of Sutton Hoo*, 95–130.

DB   Domesday Book. Citations are by folio and column number in Great Domesday, followed in brackets by the 'tenant-in-chief plus manor' system used by J. Morris (ed.), *Domesday Book: 14: Oxfordshire* (Phillimore, 1978). Thus the reference for Wigginton would be 'DB 160a (XLIV.1)'. For entries in other counties the Phillimore reference is prefixed by a county abbreviation.

Doggett 1986.   N. Doggett, 'The Anglo-Saxon See and Cathedral of

	Dorchester-on-Thames: the Evidence Reconsidered', *Oxo.* li, 49-61.
Dom. Geog. S.-E.	*The Domesday Geography of South-East England*, eds. H.C. Darby and E.M.J. Campbell (1962).
Dumville 1985.	D.N. Dumville, 'The West Saxon Genealogical Regnal List and the Chronology of Wessex', *Peritia,* iv, 21–66.
Dumville 1989	D. Dumville, 'Essex, Middle Anglia, and the Expansion of Mercia in the South-East Midlands', in S. Bassett (ed.), *The Origins of Anglo-Saxon Kingdoms,* 123–40.
Dumville 1992.	D. Dumville, 'The Treaty of Alfred and Guthrum', in idem, *Wessex and England from Alfred to Edgar,* 1–27.
Durham 1977.	B. Durham et al., 'Archaeological Investigations in St. Aldate's, Oxford', *Oxo.* xlii, 83–203.
Durham 1984.	B. Durham et al., 'The Thames Crossing at Oxford: Archaeological Studies 1979-82', *Oxo.* xlix, 57–100.
Durham (forthcoming).	B. Durham, *Oxford Before the University* (Oxbow Monograph).
Durham, Halpin & Palmer 1983.	B. Durham, C. Halpin and N. Palmer, 'Oxford's Northern Defences: Archaeological Studies 1971-1982', *Oxo.* xlviii, 13-40.
Dyer 1980.	C. Dyer, *Lords and Peasants in a Changing Society.*
Dyer 1985.	C. Dyer, 'Towns and Cottages in Eleventh-Century England', in H. Mayr-Harting and R.I. Moore (eds.), *Studies in Medieval History Presented to R.H.C. Davis,* 91–106.
Edwards 1988.	H. Edwards, *The Charters of the Early West Saxon Kingdom* (B.A.R. British Ser. 198).
Edwards & Lane (ed.) 1992.	N. Edwards and A. Lane, *the Early Church in Wales and the West.*
Emery 1974.	F. Emery, *The Oxfordshire Landscape.*
Esmonde Cleary 1989.	A.S. Esmonde Cleary, *The Ending of Roman Britain.*
Everitt 1974.	A. Everitt, 'The Banburys of England', *Urban History Yearbook,* 28–38.
Evison 1967.	V.I. Evison, 'A Sword from the Thames at Wallingford Bridge', *Archaeol. Jnl.* cxxiv, 160–89.
Evison 1969.	V.I. Evison, 'A Viking Grave at Sonning, Berks.', *Antiq. Jnl.* xlix, 330–45.
Faith (forthcoming).	R. Faith, *The English Peasantry and the Growth of Lordship.*
Fernie 1982.	E. Fernie, *The Architecture of the Anglo-Saxons.*
Fleming 1991.	R. Fleming, *Kings and Lords in Conquest England.*
Foard 1985.	G. Foard, 'The Administrative Organisation of Northamptonshire in the Saxon Period', in S.C. Hawkes, J. Campbell and D. Brown (eds.), *Anglo-Saxon Studies in Archaeology and History,* iv, 185–222.
Foot 1992.	S. Foot, 'Anglo-Saxon Minsters: a Review of Terminology', in J. Blair and R. Sharpe (eds.), *Pastoral Care before the Parish,* 212–25.

Frere 1962.   S.[S.] Frere, 'Excavations at Dorchester-on-Thames, 1962',
                     Arch. Jnl. cxix, 114–49.
Frere 1984.   S. S. Frere, 'Excavations at Dorchester-on-Thames, 1963',
                     Arch. Jnl. cxli, 91–174.
Gelling 1957.   M. Gelling, 'The Hill of Abingdon', *Oxo.* xxii, 54–62.
Gelling 1967.   M. Gelling, 'English Place-Names Derived from the
                     Compound *Wīchām*', *Med. Arch.* xi, 87–104.
Gelling 1978.   M. Gelling, *Signposts to the Past.*
Gelling 1984.   M. Gelling, *Place-Names in the Landscape.*
Gelling 1988.   M. Gelling, 'Towards a Chronology for English Place-
                     Names', in D. Hooke (ed.), *Anglo-Saxon Settlements*, 59–76.
Gelling 1992.   M. Gelling, *The West Midlands in the Early Middle Ages.*
Gem 1978.   R. Gem, 'Church Architecture in the Reign of King
                     Æthelred', in D. Hill (ed.), *Ethelred the Unready* (B.A.R.
                     Brit. Ser. 59), 105–14.
Graham-Campbell 1980. J. Graham-Campbell, *The Viking World.*
Graham-Campbell 1988. J. Graham-Campbell, 'The Gold Finger-Ring from a Burial
                     in St. Aldate's Street, Oxford', *Oxo.* liii, 263–6.
Green 1990.   J.A. Green, *English Sheriffs to 1154.*
Hamerow 1991.   H.F. Hamerow, 'Settlement Mobility and the "Middle
                     Saxon Shift": Rural Settlements and Settlement Patterns
                     in Anglo-Saxon England', *Anglo-Saxon England*, xx,
                     1–17.
Hamerow 1992.   H. Hamerow, 'Settlement on the Gravels in the Anglo-
                     Saxon Period', in M. Fulford and L. Nichols (eds.),
                     *Developing Landscapes of Lowland Britain: the Archaeology of the
                     British Gravels*, 39–46.
Hamshere 1987.   J.D. Hamshere, 'Domesday Book: Estate Structures in the
                     West Midlands', in J.C. Holt (ed.), *Domesday Studies*,
                     155–82.
Harden & Treweeks   D.B. Harden and R.C. Treweeks, 'Excavations at Stanton
    1945.   Harcourt, Oxon., 1940, II', *Oxo.* x, 16–41.
Harmer 1952.   F.E. Harmer, *Anglo-Saxon Writs.*
Hart 1973.   C. Hart, 'Athelstan 'Half-King' and his Family', *Anglo-
                     Saxon England*, ii, 115–44.
Haslam (ed.) 1984.   J. Haslam (ed.), *Anglo-Saxon Towns in Southern England.*
Haslam 1987.   J. Haslam, 'Market and Fortress in England in the Reign of
                     Offa', *World Archaeology*, xix.1, 76–93.
Hassall 1971.   T.G. Hassall, 'Excavations at 44-46 Cornmarket St.,
                     Oxford, 1970', *Oxo.* xxxvi (1971), 15–33.
Hassall 1973.   T.G. Hassall, 'Excavations at Oxford, 1972', *Oxo.* xxxviii,
                     268–98.
Hassall 1976.   T.G. Hassall, 'Excavations at Oxford Castle, 1965-1973',
                     Oxo. xli, 232–308.
Hassall 1986.   T.G. Hassall, 'Archaeology of Oxford City', in Briggs,
                     Cook and Rowley (eds.) 1986, 115–34.

Hassall et al. 1989.   T.G. Hassall, C.E. Halpin, M. Mellor et al., 'Excavations in St. Ebbe's, Oxford, 1967–76: Part I', *Oxo.* liv (1989), 71–277.

Hawkes 1986.   S.C. Hawkes, 'The Early Saxon Period', in Briggs, Cook and Rowley (eds.) 1986, 64–108.

Heslop 1988.   T.A. Heslop, 'The Late Twelfth-Century Seal of St. Frideswide's Priory', *Oxo.* liii, 271–4.

Heighway 1987.   C. Heighway, *Anglo-Saxon Gloucestershire.*

Heighway & Bryant 1986.   C. Heighway and R. Bryant, 'A Reconstruction of the Tenth-Century Church of St. Oswald, Gloucester', in L.A.S. Butler and R.K. Morris (eds.), *The Anglo-Saxon Church: Papers . . . in Honour of Dr H.M. Taylor* (C.B.A. Research Rep. 60), 188–95.

Higham 1992.   N. Higham, *Rome, Britain and the Anglo-Saxons.*

Hill 1969.   D. Hill, 'The Burghal Hidage: the Establishment of a Text', *Med. Arch.* xiii, 84–92.

Hill 1978.   D. Hill, 'Trends in the Development of Towns during the Reign of Æthelred II', in D. Hill (ed.), *Ethelred the Unready* (B.A.R. British Ser. 59), 213–26.

Hill 1981.   D. Hill, *An Atlas of Anglo-Saxon England.*

Hills 1979.   C. Hills, 'The Archaeology of Anglo-Saxon England in the Pagan Period: a Review', *Anglo-Saxon England*, viii, 297–329.

Hinchcliffe & Thomas 1980.   J. Hinchcliffe and R. Thomas, 'Archaeological Investigations at Appleford', *Oxo.* xlv, 9–111.

Hinton 1970.   D.A. Hinton, 'Two Late Saxon Swords', *Oxo.* xxxv, 1–4.

Hinton 1974.   D.A. Hinton, *A Catalogue of the Anglo-Saxon Ornamental Metalwork, 700–1100, in the Department of Antiquities, Ashmolean Museum.*

Hinton 1990.   D.A. Hinton, *Archaeology, Economy and Society: England from the Fifth to the Fifteenth Century.*

Hohler 1966.   C. Hohler, 'St. Osyth and Aylesbury', *Records of Bucks.* xviii (1966–70), 61–72.

Hood & Speake 1987.   N. Hood and G. Speake, 'An Anglo-Saxon Gilt-Bronze Lozenge-Shaped Mount from Culham', *Oxo.* lii, 184–5.

Hooke 1981.   D. Hooke, 'The Droitwich Salt Industry: an Examination of the West Midland Charter Evidence', in D. Brown, J. Campbell and S.C. Hawkes (eds.), *Anglo-Saxon Studies in Archaeology and History*, ii (B.A.R. British Ser. xcii), 123–69.

Hooke 1985.   D. Hooke, *The Anglo-Saxon Landscape: the Kingdom of the Hwicce.*

Hooke 1986.   D. Hooke, 'Territorial Organisation in the Anglo-Saxon West Midlands: Central Places, Central Areas', in E. Grant (ed.), *Central Places, Archaeology and History*, 79–93.

Hooke 1987.   D. Hooke, 'Anglo-Saxon Estates in the Vale of the White Horse', *Oxo.* lii, 129–43.

Hooke 1988.	D. Hooke, 'Regional Variation in Southern and Central England', in D. Hooke (ed.), *Anglo-Saxon Settlements*, 123–51.
Hooper 1988.	N.A. Hooper, 'An Introduction to the Berkshire Domesday', in R.W.H. Erskine and A. Williams (eds.), *The Berkshire Domesday*.
Hoskins & Jope 1954.	W.G. Hoskins and E.M. Jope, 'The Medieval Period', in A.F. Martin and R.W. Steel (eds.), *The Oxford Region*, 103–20.
Ivens 1984.	R.J. Ivens, 'Deddington Castle, Oxfordshire, and the English Honour of Odo of Bayeux', *Oxo.* xlix, 101–19.
James, Marshall & Millett 1984.	S. James, A. Marshall and M. Millett, 'An Early Medieval Building Tradition', *Arch. Jnl.* cxli, 182–215.
Jope 1952/3.	E.M. Jope, 'Late Saxon Pits under Oxford Castle Mound', *Oxo.* xvii/xviii, 77–111.
Jope 1956.	E.M. Jope, 'Saxon Oxford and its Region', in D.B. Harden (ed.), *Dark Age Britain: Studies Presented to E.T. Leeds*, 234–58.
Jope 1958.	E.M. Jope, 'The Clarendon Hotel, Oxford. Part I: the Site', *Oxo.* xxiii (1958), 1–83.
Jope 1964.	E.M. Jope, 'The Saxon Building-Stone Industry in Southern and Midland England', *Med. Arch.* viii (1964), 91–118.
Keats-Rohan 1989a.	K.S.B. Keats-Rohan, 'The Making of Henry of Oxford: Englishmen in a Norman World', *Oxo.* liv, 287–309.
Keats-Rohan 1989b.	K.S.B. Keats-Rohan, 'The Devolution of the Honour of Wallingford, 1066–1148', *Oxo.* liv, 311–18.
Keene 1976.	D.J. Keene, 'Suburban Growth', in M.W. Barley (ed.), *The Plans and Topography of Medieval Towns in England and Wales* (C.B.A. Research Rep. 14), 71–82.
Kelly (forthcoming).	S. Kelly, *Anglo-Saxon Charters: Abingdon* (British Academy Anglo-Saxon Charters Series).
Keynes & Lapidge 1983.	*Alfred the Great: Asser's 'Life of King Alfred' and Other Contemporary Sources*, trans. S. Keynes and M. Lapidge.
Kent 1972.	J.P.C. Kent, 'The Aston Rowant Treasure Trove', *Oxo.* xxxvii, 243–4.
Kirby 1991.	D.P. Kirby, *The Earliest English Kings*.
Kirk & Marshall 1956.	J.R. Kirk and K. Marshall, 'A Saxon Cemetery near the Village of Harwell, Berkshire', *Oxo.* xxi, 22–34.
Knowles, Brooke & London 1972.	D. Knowles, C.N.L. Brooke and V. London, *The Heads of Religious Houses: England and Wales, 940–1216*.
Lambrick & Robinson 1988.	G. Lambrick and M. Robinson, 'The Development of Floodplain Grassland in the Upper Thames Valley', in M. Jones (ed.), *Archaeology and the Flora of the British Isles* (O.U.C.A.), 55–75.
Lawson 1993.	M.K. Lawson, *Cnut: The Danes in England in the Early Eleventh Century*.

Leaver 1988.   R.A. Leaver, 'Five Hides in Ten Counties', *Econ. Hist. Rev.*
                        2nd ser. xli, 525–42.

Lennard 1959.   R. Lennard, *Rural England 1086–1135.*

Longworth & Cherry   I. Longworth and J. Cherry (eds.), *Archaeology in*
  (eds.) 1986.   *Britain since 1945.*

Loyn 1984.   H.R. Loyn, *The Governance of Anglo-Saxon England,*
                        500–1087.

Lyon 1966.   C.S.S. Lyon, 'The Significance of the Sack of Oxford in
                        1009/10 for the Chronology of the Coinage of Æthelred
                        II', *British Numismatic Jnl.* xxxv, 34–7.

Lyon 1970.   [C.S.] S. Lyon, 'Historical Problems of Anglo-Saxon
                        Coinage (4): the Viking Age', *British Numismatic Jnl.* xxxix,
                        193–204.

Lyon 1976.   [C.S.] S. Lyon, 'Some Problems in Interpreting Anglo-
                        Saxon Coinage', *Anglo-Saxon England*, v, 173–224.

Maddicott 1989.   J.R. Maddicott, 'Trade, Industry and the Wealth of King
                        Alfred', *Past and Present*, cxxiii, 3–51.

Marshall 1943.   M. Marshall, *The Land of Britain: Part 56: Oxfordshire.*

May 1977.   J. May, 'Romano-British and Saxon Sites near Dorchester-
                        on-Thames', *Oxo.* xlii, 42–79.

Mayr-Harting 1985.   H. Mayr-Harting, 'Functions of a Twelfth-Century Shrine:
                        the Miracles of St. Frideswide', in H. Mayr-Harting and
                        R.I. Moore (eds.), *Studies in Medieval History Presented to*
                        R.H.C. Davis, 193–206.

Meaney 1964.   A. Meaney, *A Gazetteer of Early Anglo-Saxon Burial Sites.*

Mellor 1980.   M. Mellor, 'Late Saxon Pottery from Oxfordshire: Evidence
                        and Speculation!', *Medieval Ceramics*, iv, 17–27.

Metcalf 1972.   D.M. Metcalf, 'The "Bird and Branch" Sceattas in the
                        Light of a Find from Abingdon', *Oxo.* xxxvii, 51–65.

Metcalf 1977.   D.M. Metcalf, 'Monetary Affairs in Mercia in the Time of
                        Æthelbald', in A. Dornier (ed.), *Mercian Studies*, 87–106.

Metcalf 1978.   D.M. Metcalf, 'The Ranking of Boroughs: Numismatic
                        Evidence for the Reign of Æthelred II', in D. Hill (ed.),
                        Ethelred the Unready (B.A.R. British Ser. 59), 159–212.

Metcalf 1984.   D.M. Metcalf, 'Monetary Circulation in Southern England
                        in the First Half of the Eighth Century', in D. Hill and
                        D.M. Metcalf (eds.), *Sceattas in England and on the Continent*
                        (B.A.R. British Ser. 128).

Metcalf 1993.   D.M. Metcalf, *Thrymsas and Sceattas in the Ashmolean*
                        Museum, Oxford: I [thrymsas and primary sceattas].

Metcalf (forthcoming). Ibid. *III* [secondary sceattas].

Miles 1974.   D. Miles, 'Abingdon and Region: Early Anglo-Saxon
                        Settlement Evidence', in T. Rowley (ed.), *Anglo-Saxon*
                        Settlement and Landscape (B.A.R. British Ser. 6), 36–41.

Miles 1986.   D. Miles, 'The Iron Age', in Briggs, Cook and Rowley
                        (eds.) 1986, 49–57.

Miles (ed.) 1986.   D. Miles (ed.), *Archaeology at Barton Court Farm, Abingdon, Oxon.* (C.B.A. Research Rep. 50).

Miles & Palmer n.d.   D. Miles and S. Palmer, *Invested in Mother Earth* (Oxford Archaeological Unit).

Milnes-Walker 1978.   H. Milnes-Walker, 'A Saxon Church at Cottisford?', *Oxo.* xliii, 255–6.

Moore 1989.   J.S. Moore, 'Domesday Slavery', *Anglo-Norman Studies*, xi, 191–220.

Morley Davies 1947–52a.   A. Morley Davies, 'Abefield and Ackhamstead: Two Lost Places', *Records of Bucks.* xv, 166–71.

Morley Davies 1947–52b.   A. Morley Davies, 'The Hundreds of Buckinghamshire and Oxfordshire', *Records of Bucks.* xv, 231–49.

Morris 1927.   W.A. Morris, *The Medieval English Sheriff to 1300.*

Morris 1989.   R. Morris, *Churches in the Landscape.*

Nightingale 1987.   P. Nightingale, 'The Origin of the Court of Husting and Danish Influence on London's Development into a Capital City', *Eng. Hist. Rev.* cii, 559–78.

North 1980.   J.J. North, *English Hammered Coinage*, i.

Oxo.   *Oxoniensia.*

Parker 1885.   J. Parker, *The Early History of Oxford, 727–1100* (O.H.S. iii).

Parsons 1991.   D. Parsons, 'Stone', in J. Blair and N. Ramsay (eds.), *English Medieval Industries*, 1–27.

Pearn 1988.   A.M. Pearn [Bennett], *The Origin and Development of Urban Churches and Parishes: a Comparative Study of Hereford, Shrewsbury and Chester* (unpublished Cambridge Ph.D. thesis).

Phythian-Adams 1975.   C. Phythian-Adams, *Local History and Folklore: a New Framework* (Standing Conference for Local History pamphlet).

P-N Berks.   M. Gelling, *The Place-Names of Berkshire* (i–iii, E.P.N.S. xlix–li, 1973–6).

P-N Glos.   A.H. Smith, *The Place-Names of Gloucestershire* (i–iv, E.P.N.S. xxxviii–xli, 1964–5).

P-N Oxon.   M. Gelling, *The Place-Names of Oxfordshire* (i–ii, E.P.N.S. xxiii–xxiv, 1953–4).

P-N Worcs.   A. Mawer and F.M. Stenton, *The Place-Names of Worcestershire* (E.P.N.S. iv, 1927).

Postles 1987.   D. Postles, 'Markets for Rural Produce in Oxfordshire, 1086-1350', *Midland History*, xii, 14–26.

PRN   Centre for Oxfordshire Studies, Westgate Centre, Oxford: County Sites and Monuments Record (items cited by Primary Record Number).

Pryce 1992.   H. Pryce, 'Pastoral Care in Early Medieval Wales', in J. Blair and R. Sharpe (eds.), *Pastoral Care before the Parish*, 41–62.

Rackham 1986.   O. Rackham, *The History of the Countryside.*

Rahtz & Rowley 1984.   S. Rahtz and R.T. Rowley, *Middleton Stoney: Excavation and Survey in a North Oxfordshire Parish, 1970–1982.*

Rattue 1990.   J. Rattue, 'An Inventory of Ancient and Holy Wells in
                        Oxfordshire', *Oxo.* lv, 172–6.
Reynolds 1977.   S. Reynolds, *An Introduction to the History of English Medieval
                        Towns.*
Reynolds 1987.   S. Reynolds, 'Towns in Domesday Book', in J.C. Holt (ed.),
                        Domesday Studies, 295–309.
Robinson 1981.   M. Robinson, 'The Iron Age to Early Saxon Environment
                        of the Upper Thames Terraces', in M. Jones and G.
                        Dimbleby (eds.), *The Environment of Man: the Iron Age to the
                        Anglo-Saxon Period* (B.A.R. British Ser. 87), 251–86.
Robinson 1992.   M. Robinson, 'Environment, Archaeology and Alluvium
                        on the River Gravels of the South Midlands', in S.
                        Needham and M.G. Macklin (eds.), *Alluvial Archaeology in
                        Britain* (Oxbow Monograph 47), 197–208.
Robinson & Lambrick   M.A. Robinson and G.H. Lambrick, 'Holocene
  1984.   Alluviation and Hydrology in the Upper Thames Basin',
                        Nature, cccviii, 809–14.
Roden 1973.   D. Roden, 'Field Systems in the Chiltern Hills and their
                        Environs', in A.R.H. Baker and R.A. Butlin (eds.), *Studies
                        of Field Systems in the British Isles*, 325–76.
Rodwell (ed.) 1975.   K. Rodwell (ed.), *Historic Towns in Oxfordshire: a Survey of
                        the New County.*
Roffe 1986.   D. Roffe, 'The Origins of Derbyshire', *Derbs. Arch. Jnl.*
                        cvi, 102–22.
Rollason 1978.   D.W. Rollason, 'Lists of Saints' Resting-Places in Anglo-
                        Saxon England', *Anglo-Saxon England*, vii, 61–93.
Rowley & Brown 1981.   T. Rowley and L. Brown, 'Excavations at Beech House
                        Hotel, Dorchester-on-Thames, 1972', *Oxo.* xlvi, 1–55.
Rutherford Davis   K. Rutherford Davis, *Britons and Saxons: the Chiltern
  1982.   Region 400–700.*
S.   Anglo-Saxon charters are cited by their 'S.-number' in
                        P.H. Sawyer, *Anglo-Saxon Charters: an Annotated List and
                        Bibliography* (1968).
Salisbury 1991.   C.R. Salisbury, 'Primitive British Fishweirs', in G.L. Good,
                        R.H. Jones and M.W. Ponsford (eds.), *Waterfront Archaeology*
                        (C.B.A. Research Rep. 74), 76–87.
Salter 1936.   H.E. Salter, *Medieval Oxford* (O.H.S. c).
Schumer 1984.   B. Schumer, *The Evolution of Wychwood to 1400: Pioneers,
                        Frontiers and Forests.*
Scull 1988.   C. Scull et al., 'Excavations in the Cloister of St.
                        Frideswide's Priory, 1985', *Oxo.* liii, 21–73.
Scull 1990.   C. Scull, 'Scales and Weights in Early Anglo-Saxon
                        England', *Arch. Jnl.* cxlvii, 183–215.
Scull 1992.   C. Scull, 'Before Sutton Hoo: Structures of Power and
                        Society in Early East Anglia', in M. Carver (ed.), *The Age of
                        Sutton Hoo*, 3–23.

Scull 1993.   C. Scull, 'Excavation and Survey at Watchfield, Oxfordshire, 1983–92', *Arch. Jnl.* cxlix, 124–281.

Seaby 1950.   W.A. Seaby, 'Late Dark Age Finds from the Cherwell and Ray, 1876-86', *Oxo.* xv 29–43.

Sellwood 1984.   L. Sellwood, 'Tribal Boundaries Viewed from the Perspective of Numismatic Evidence', in B. Cunliffe and D. Miles (eds.), *Aspects of the Iron Age in Central Southern Britain* (O.U.C.A. Monograph 2), 191–204.

Shoesmith 1982.   R. Shoesmith, *Hereford City Excavations: II: Excavations on and close to the Defences* (C.B.A. Research Rep. 46).

Sims-Williams 1975. P. Sims-Williams, 'Continental Influence at Bath Monastery in the Seventh Century', *Anglo-Saxon England*, iv, 1–10.

Sims-Williams 1983. P. Sims-Williams, 'The Settlement of England in Bede and the Chronicle', *Anglo-Saxon England*, xii, 1–41.

Sims-Williams 1990. P. Sims-Williams, *Religion and Literature in Western England, 600–800.*

SMA.   *South Midlands Archaeology* (the *Newsletter* of Council for British Archaeology Group 9).

Smith 1990.   J.M.H. Smith, 'Oral and Written: Saints, Miracles and Relics in Brittany, *c.* 850–1250', *Speculum*, lxv, 309–43.

Speake 1989.   G. Speake, *A Saxon Bed Burial on Swallowcliffe Down* (English Heritage).

Stafford 1978.   P. Stafford, 'The Reign of Æthelred II: a Study in the Limitations of Royal Policy and Action', in D. Hill (ed.), *Ethelred the Unready* (B.A.R. British Ser. 59), 15–46.

Stafford 1985.   P. Stafford, *The East Midlands in the Early Middle Ages.*

Stafford 1989.   P. Stafford, *Unification and Conquest.*

Stenton 1913.   F.M. Stenton, *The Early History of the Abbey of Abingdon.*

Stewart 1978.   I. Stewart, 'Anglo-Saxon Gold Coins', in R.A.G. Carson and C.M. Kraay (eds.), *Scripta Nummaria Romana: Essays Presented to Humphrey Sutherland*, 143–72.

Sturdy 1963.   D. Sturdy, 'Traces of Saxon Nomadic Life near Oxford', *Oxo.* xxviii, 95–8.

Sturdy 1965.   D. Sturdy, *Topography of Medieval Oxford* (unpublished Oxford B.Litt. thesis).

Sturdy & Munby 1985. D. Sturdy and J. Munby, 'Early Domestic Sites in Oxford: Excavations in Cornmarket and Queen Street, 1959–62', *Oxo.* l, 47–94.

Taylor 1957.   C.S. Taylor, 'The Origin of the Mercian Shires', in H.P.R. Finberg (ed.), *Gloucestershire Studies*, 17–51.

Taylor 1983.   C. Taylor, *Village and Farmstead: a History of Rural Settlement in England.*

Taylor & Taylor   H.M. and J. Taylor, *Anglo-Saxon Architecture* (3 vols.).
  1965–78.

Thacker 1982.   A. Thacker, 'Chester and Gloucester: Early Ecclesiastical

Organisation in Two Mercian Burhs', *Northern History*, xviii (1982), 199–211.

Thacker 1988.   A. Thacker, 'Æthelwold and Abingdon', in B. Yorke (ed.), *Bishop Æthelwold: his Career and Influence*, 43–64.

Thorn 1990.   F.R. Thorn, 'Hundreds and Wapentakes', in R.W.H. Erskine and A. Williams (eds.), *The Oxfordshire Domesday*, 20–9.

Turner 1990.   H.L. Turner, 'The Mural Mansions of Oxford: Attempted Identifications', *Oxo.* lv, 73–9.

VCH Berks.   *The Victoria History of the County of Berkshire*, eds. P.H. Ditchfield and W. Page, i–iv (1906–24).

VCH Oxon.   *The Victoria History of the County of Oxford*, eds. L.F. Salzman etc., i–xii (1939–1990), in progress.

Vince 1985.   A. Vince, 'The Saxon and Medieval Pottery of London: a Review', *Med. Arch.* xxix, 25–93.

Vince 1990.   A. Vince, *Saxon London: an Archaeological Investigation*.

Vince (ed.) 1991.   A. Vince (ed.), *Aspects of Saxo-Norman London: II: Finds and Environmental Evidence*.

Wainwright 1975.   F.T. Wainwright, 'Æthelflæd, Lady of the Mercians', in H.P.R. Finberg (ed.), *Scandinavian England*, 305–24.

Watts 1991.   D. Watts, *Christians and Pagans in Roman Britain*.

Webster & Backhouse L. Webster and J. Backhouse, *The Making of*
  (eds.) 1991.   *England: Anglo-Saxon Art and Culture AD 600–900* (Catalogue of British Museum Exhibition).

Welch 1992.   M. Welch, *Anglo-Saxon England* (English Heritage).

Whybra 1990.   J. Whybra, *A Lost English County: Winchcombeshire in the 10th and 11th Centuries*.

Williams 1982.   A. Williams, '*Princeps Merciorum Gentis*: the Family, Career and Connections of Ælfhere, Ealdorman of Mercia 956–83', *Anglo-Saxon England*, x, 143–72.

Williams 1986.   A. Williams, ' "Cockles Amongst the Wheat": Danes and English in the Western Midlands in the First Half of the Eleventh Century', *Midland History*, xi, 1–22.

Williams 1989.   A. Williams, 'A Vice-Comital Family in Pre-Conquest Warwickshire', *Anglo-Norman Studies*, xi, 279–95.

Wilson 1965.   D.M. Wilson, 'Some Neglected Late Anglo-Saxon Swords', *Med. Arch.* ix (1965), 32–54.

Wood 1983.   I.N. Wood, *The Merovingian North Sea* (Alingsås).

Wormald 1983.   P. Wormald, 'Bede, *Bretwaldas* and the Origins of the *Gens Anglorum*', in P. Wormald et al. (eds.), *Ideal and Reality in Frankish and Anglo-Saxon Society*, 99–129.

Yeoman 1986.   P.A. Yeoman, 'Excavations at the Prebendal Court, Aylesbury, 1985', *SMA* xvi, 37–8.

Yorke 1988.   B. Yorke, 'Æthelmær: the Foundation of the Abbey of Cerne and the Politics of the Tenth Century', in K. Barker (ed.), *The Cerne Abbey Millenium Lectures* (Cerne Abbey Millenium Committee), 15–26.

Yorke 1989.   B. Yorke, 'The Jutes of Hampshire and Wight and the
                     Origins of Wessex', in S. Bassett (ed.), *The Origins of Anglo-
                     Saxon Kingdoms*, 84–96.
Yorke 1990.   B. Yorke, *Kings and Kingdoms of Early Anglo-Saxon England*.
Young 1986.   C. Young, 'The Upper Thames Valley in the Roman
                     Period', in Briggs, Cook and Rowley (eds.) 1986, 58–63.

INDEX

Places are in Oxfordshire except where otherwise indicated. Anglo-Saxon personal names are given in their correct form, except for names of well-known people (e.g. Alfred, Edward) where modern forms are familiar. Page-numbers in **bold type** denote pages bearing illustrations.